Policy Debate

Policy Debate

A Guide for High School and College Debaters

Shawn F. Briscoe

Southern Illinois University Press / *Carbondale*

Southern Illinois University Press
www.siupress.com

20 19 18 17   4 3 2 1

Cover illustrations: photographs by author (*top left, top middle,
and bottom right*), by Shane Ohms (*top right and bottom
middle*), and from Adobe Stock (*bottom left, image 4919554*);
all images used with permission.

Library of Congress Cataloging-in-Publication Data

Names: Briscoe, Shawn F., author
Title: Policy debate : a guide for high school and college debaters /
    Shawn F. Briscoe.
Description: Carbondale : Southern Illinois University Press,
    [2017] | Includes bibliographical references and index.
Identifiers: LCCN 2016020132 | ISBN 9780809335589 (paperback)
    | ISBN 9780809335596 (e-book)
Subjects: LCSH: Debates and debating. | BISAC: LANGUAGE
    ARTS & DISCIPLINES / Public Speaking. | LANGUAGE ARTS
    & DISCIPLINES / Speech. | LANGUAGE ARTS & DISCIPLINES /
    Rhetoric. | LANGUAGE ARTS & DISCIPLINES / Study & Teaching.
Classification: LCC PN4181 .B74 2017 | DDC 808.53—dc23 LC
    record available at https://lccn.loc.gov/2016020132

To my wonderful family, Becky, Ben, and Hannah, for their unending love and support

In memory of Kelly Jean Horner (1989–2008), class of 2007, South Anchorage High School, and Corey Taylor Tindall (1993–2010), class of 2012, South Anchorage High School

Contents

Illustrations

Acknowledgments

There are so many people who deserve thanks that I can't possibly name them all. Nevertheless, I'll do my best. TG, you were quite possibly the best coach a student could ever hope for. You shaped my perception of the activity and of what the world could be. Marshall, ultimately, this book is the result of your initial prodding. Robert, Baldy, Ryan, Aaron, Marshall, and Luke: partners, friends, and so much more. Each of you uniquely contributed to my growth in the activity and understanding of debate. Steve, thanks for taking a chance on me. Katy, thanks for being the ultimate assistant coach. To my many teammates at Nevada High School (Missouri) and the U.S. Air Force Academy, thank you for joining me on the journey and opening my eyes: Dave, Dave, Davey J, Jeff, Sully, and more deserve special recognition. To all of my students at Ft. Walton Beach High School (Florida), at South Anchorage High School (Alaska), at the University of Alaska Anchorage, and in the St. Louis Urban Debate League: thank you for continually pushing me to be a better coach and mentor and to see the activity through other lenses. While I can't name all of you, some certainly left an imprint on my coaching style, methods, and perspectives: Sean, David, Stefanie, Matt, Austin, Jesse, Kenny, Bexley, Corey, Tavish, Nicole, Kari, Terek, Skyler, and many more. Amy and Maria, thank you for prodding me to complete this project. Denice, Janet, Cheryl, and Becky, thanks for reviewing the manuscript. Karl, thanks for working with me through the editorial process.

The ideas I bring to this work are a compilation of discussions and lectures I have participated in during my twenty-five-plus years of high school and college debate with coaches, teammates, opponents, friends, judges, and students. Many of you have fallen into several of these categories. I thank all of you for being part of my life and helping my debate experience be both rewarding and fun.

I hope that you find debate as enjoyable and beneficial as I did. Have fun and learn something!

Policy Debate

Introduction: Debate Is Life

Have you ever experienced the thrill of going head-to-head with an opponent, your only weapons being your speaking skills and logic? Have you ever felt so good about the arguments you chose, developed, and delivered to an audience that you just knew you were on top of the world and that everyone was seeing (and understanding) your point of view? For anyone who has been involved with competitive debate for any length of time, you know exactly what I am talking about. For those of you who are just getting involved with this activity, I am somewhat envious. You have a whole world that is beginning to open up to you. You will experience the joys directly associated with outwitting your opponent logically and travel the country with people who will become the greatest of friends.

Personally speaking, nothing is quite like the experience of standing in front of an audience and watching people's faces as they realize you have just taken control of the debate round. I am speaking of that moment when you realize that all the time and effort you put into this activity has made you one of the best.

Although I have experienced this feeling many times to greater and lesser degrees, there was one moment where I felt it more than any other. In 1996, at the Cross Examination Debate Association, or CEDA, National Tournament held in Long Beach, California, my partner and I were pitted against the defending national champion from Michigan State University in triple-octafinals. Before the round, I was a basket case because I (a sophomore) knew we were going up against one of the premier teams in the country. I thought we were doomed from the get-go, but Aaron Rhodes (a senior in his second year of debate) calmed me down by saying something along the lines of "Dude. It's just a debate round. Probably my last . . . let's just have fun." To make a long story short, I eventually stood up for my last speech—the second negative rebuttal—and was filled with confidence and excitement. While I was giving my speech, I knew I was winning. I knew that I was taking it to one of the top teams in the country. I could also read the astonishment in the faces of the audience members. They too knew what I knew, that at that moment I owned the debate round and a relatively young U.S. Air Force Academy team was going to upset one of the nation's top debate teams. That was one of the moments you live for in debate. The amazing thing about it, however, is that the game is always up for grabs. Michigan State's final speaker turned the tables back in his team's favor and won the round in the second affirmative rebuttal. Nevertheless, that round will forever be one of the best debate experiences of my life.

This is a triumphant feeling, whether you experience it in round two of a local tournament, in the final round of that same tournament, at a high school national qualifying tournament, or at college nationals. In all honesty, it doesn't really matter because the excitement and the emotions are still the same, regardless of the level of competition.

In order to reach that stage, however, you must have a basic understanding of debate. I will not tell you that if you read this book you will miraculously become the greatest debater ever. I do believe that the fundamentals laid down in this work can help you achieve your debate goals as well as enhance your understanding of other forms of argumentation and debates. Debate is a continuous process. You can never become too good or too polished or too well researched or too knowledgeable or too prepared. You must continuously try to absorb knowledge from all sources: your coaches, teammates, opponents, experienced judges, and lay judges. No one is above learning. Do not presume that because you know more than someone else, you cannot learn from them. Even the best debaters need to engage in discussions with others in order to become better and attain their highest potential. Hopefully, this book has something for everyone, from the novice debater to the reigning national champion to the coach who is looking for new perspectives on how to teach academic debate.

Before delving into this work, I wish to caution and offer advice to you beginners. All too often, beginning and potentially gifted debaters get discouraged when they are paired against a team that is much more advanced in skill, that is many levels more researched, and/or whose members speak at a rate of delivery that seems incomprehensible. I urge you to stick with the activity.[1] Try to absorb what you can from your opponents; try to learn something from them that will make you a better debater and thinker. As you learn and practice, I assure you that you, too, can reach a similar level.

I begin this work with the fundamentals, discussing basic strategies and theories I have on how to understand debate rounds, and then work my way through more developed concepts within debate. You will find the endnotes in this book unique. In some cases, I have provided anecdotes from my debate experiences to help illustrate a concept. Other endnotes explain the idea from a slightly (or drastically) different point of view. <u>In addition, I have underlined key terms throughout the text that correspond to the glossary at the end of the work.</u>[2]

The strategies and structures laid out in this book create the foundation for understanding arguments not just in policy debate but in all formats and in all of life. My high school coach, Tim Gore, ensured I had a firm grasp on the fundamentals of policy debate, and I am convinced that is what allowed me to have success on the collegiate level and as a coach today. Furthermore, the concepts explored here can help you become a better thinker, writer, and communicator as you transition into college and the workforce. As an officer in the air force, I realized that the skills I developed in debate—thinking quickly, identifying points of contention and agreement, structuring logical responses, adapting to a specific worldview or paradigm, taking notes,[3] and presentation—enabled me to successfully navigate counseling sessions with subordinates, discussions with peers and supervisors, and meetings with senior leadership. The skills and practices of this activity are transferable to any number of situations outside the world of debate.

1. The Playing Field

Before the first debate, debaters require an understanding of the fundamentals and structure of the activity. Generally, one would refer to the rules of a sport. For example, track runners must understand that the objective is to reach the finish line before the other competitors, that they must not begin until the starting gun is fired, and that while running they are not allowed to cross into another lane or make contact with another athlete. If a runner does not understand these concepts or does not abide by these simple rules, he or she would not be able to win the race and could be disqualified.

I intentionally chose a relatively straightforward sport for comparison. Quite simply, the *rules* of debate are extremely straightforward and simple to grasp. Do not confuse the complex issues that will be discussed later in this work with the rules of debate. Those concepts are not rules but tools that can make you a more successful debater. For example, the rules in track are simple, but track athletes utilize weight training, nutrition, varied workouts, and intensity to enhance their performance. Debate is slightly different in that its rules sometimes fluctuate depending on the level of competition, the opinions of the school hosting the tournament, and the attitudes, dispositions, and moods of the debaters and judges themselves.

One Rule of Debate

Keeping the above in mind, let me set forth what I believe to be the one and only rule of debate. *There are no rules.* Everything in debate can be questioned. Everything is debatable. You can do anything and go anywhere as long as you can logically and persuasively state and defend your position. It is all up to you, the competitor.

There are, of course, a number of norms and conventions that are generally accepted nationally, regionally, and/or locally. These norms and conventions are so well entrenched that most competitors, judges, and coaches accept them as rules. After all, they form the foundation of debate and make the activity accessible for beginning students.

While most judges expect you to follow those norms and conventions, many allow you to stretch them, bend them, contest them, or debate them. In addition, some tournaments have a few special rules outlined in their invitations or operating manuals. Some judges still allow you to contest those, but that can be a risky proposition for all parties in the debate.

As you progress in your debate career, you can stretch the basic concepts of the activity to the very limits if you know how to defend your arguments. You can defeat the most traditional and widely accepted theory if you can logically explain why it is flawed and do a better job arguing against it than your opponent can do arguing for it. Furthermore, you can even invent a new theory in the middle of a debate round if it suits your purposes. You just have to be sure you can defend your position.

Three Basic Guidelines

Even though debaters are not bound by steadfast rules, there are three basic guidelines that rarely get questioned. *First, the affirmative team must support the resolution.* At the beginning of every year, a resolution is either established by a committee or voted on by the members of the organization, such as the National Federation of High Schools or the Cross Examination Debate Association. Regardless of the method used for establishing a resolution, it is generally accepted that the affirmative team will provide support for the resolution—hence the root, *affirm.* By showing significant arguments in support of the resolution, the affirmative team hopes to convince the judge to cast an affirmative ballot upon completion of the round. How team members go about providing that justification can vary widely from team to team and debate to debate.

Second, the negative team must attack the affirmative position. Note that I did not say the negative team must attack or negate the resolution. Although it is customary for the negative team to argue against the resolution, it is fundamentally tasked with refuting the affirmative team. Somewhere within the confines of the affirmative case the negative team will find something to refute, and it must show the judge that those points provide ample reason to vote negative in the round. In one round a negative team might choose to argue that the resolution as a whole is flawed, but in the next it might decide to disagree only with the affirmative's methods of supporting the resolution. In either case, team members have fulfilled their end of the bargain by negating the affirmative position.

Finally, there are a set number of speeches with predetermined times and a set amount of prep time for the debaters to get organized. Different organizations of debate establish different time limits, but speaking orders are generally the same. The debate begins with the first affirmative speaker establishing a case in support of the resolution or debate topic. After a brief <u>cross-examination</u> period, the first negative speaker casts doubt upon the affirmative case. This is also followed by a cross-examination period. During the next two <u>constructive</u> speeches, the second affirmative and second negative speakers attack their opponents' arguments, rebuild their own, and add depth to the existing argumentation. Each constructive speech is followed by another cross-examination period.

As the debate transitions to <u>rebuttal</u> speeches, the debate begins to narrow and become more focused. Although the first negative rebuttal is generally seen as an extension of the second negative constructive, the speaker is constrained in his or her ability to present new material that would significantly alter the course of the debate, since new arguments are not allowed in rebuttals.[1] Next, the first affirmative rebuttalist narrows the debate on each major point of contention to the most significant elements. Finally, the

Speech	Abbreviation	Speaker	Time (minutes)*
1st Affirmative Constructive	1AC	1st Affirmative (1A)	8
Cross Examination	CX	1A by 2N	3
1st Negative Constructive	1NC	1st Negative (1N)	8
Cross Examination	CX	1N by 1A	3
2nd Affirmative Constructive	2AC	2nd Affirmative (2A)	8
Cross Examination	CX	2A by 1N	3
2nd Negative Constructive	2NC	2nd Negative (2N)	8
Cross Examination	CX	2N by 2A	3
1st Negative Rebuttal	1NR	1st Negative	5
1st Affirmative Rebuttal	1AR	1st Affirmative	5
2nd Negative Rebuttal	2NR	2nd Negative	5
2nd Affirmative Rebuttal	2AR	2nd Affirmative	5
* Time limits for National Speech & Debate Association events.			

Figure 1.1. Speech order

second negative and second affirmative rebuttalists provide context for the debate by looking back at all the issues and at the debate that transpired on those issues, by evaluating the relative efforts of both teams on them, and by reflecting on what was most and least significant.

In addition to speeches and cross-examination periods, each team is given a few minutes of preparation time, which may be used at its discretion prior to speaking. Preparation time, or prep time, is akin to calling a timeout in the world of sports. However, unlike in football, which typically has one sixty-second and two thirty-second timeouts, debaters may use as much or as little prep time as they desire at any given time.[2] Typical prep time allowances by tournaments or one of the various governing organizations of academic speech and debate are five, eight, or ten minutes.

Two Basic Questions of Policy

Once a debater understands the guidelines that define the game of debate, he or she can then look to two simple questions. These form the basis from which all other policy arguments arise.[3] *First, is the affirmative plan necessary?* This question can generally be broken down into two subquestions. Is there a problem? And, can we identify the cause of the problem? That is, is there a problem in the status quo (or present system) that is not being solved by the system now? If the affirmative can prove that some harm is caused by the present system's current inaction, then the plan is probably necessary.

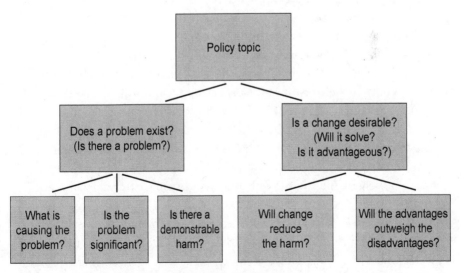

Figure 1.2. The two basic questions of policy discourse

Second, do the advantages of implementing the proposed solution (offered by the affirmative) outweigh its <u>disadvantages</u>? This is the most basic policy question in existence. If the affirmative debaters can show that their policy will lessen the harm or have additional advantages, then they have shown that their plan would be beneficial and, hence, warrants an affirmative ballot. However, the negative has the opportunity to explain why we would be better off without the affirmative plan.

The negative debaters can accomplish this in any number of ways. They might choose to show that the proposal makes the problem worse rather than better. They might show that there are unintended consequences or disadvantages of implementing the proposal. They might show that there are opportunity costs associated with that particular course of action. Finally, they may criticize the thought process used or advocated by their opponents. Ultimately, if the negative shows that the affirmative's advantages do not outweigh its disadvantages, then a negative ballot may be warranted. Keep in mind that these questions generally do not exist in a vacuum. Many times, it is a combination of arguments across the spectrum of these two questions that allows a team to win the debate round.

None of this should be new to any of us. The reality is that we have all worked in the world of policies throughout our lives. Any time we make a decision about what to do, we are—at some level—engaging in a policy debate internally about a potential course of action. Should I join the debate team? Should I skip class? Should I apply to college? Should I break curfew to go out with my friends? These are all policy questions, involving any number of hypothetical plans we might consider.

Take for example the very first question I just posited: Should I join the debate team? Any number of factors might lead students to the debate program. Their motivation might be that they really like to argue, that they wish to bolster their résumés for college applications, and that they are looking forward to the social environment found on their school's debate team. Then, they must consider whether joining the team will successfully help them fulfill those desires. Alternatively, students may also consider the time investment associated with joining the debate team. If the squad practices after school, they may lose the opportunity to participate in athletics, thereby trading off with the benefits they might gain from those sports. Many debaters spend countless hours practicing, conducting research, and revising strategies. That time engaged in debate trades off with time spent socializing with friends. However, much of the time spent getting prepared is done in the company of friends. In the end, students weigh the benefits and the costs to decide whether they will take the leap into the world of competitive, academic debate.

Even if we do not vocalize our thoughts on the questions listed above, we are probably thinking about the current choices or rules that brought us to this point, the needs or wants we hope to fulfill, whether the preferred course of action achieves those goals, what else might happen (good and bad) if we choose that path, and so forth. Debate simply addresses a real-world, current-events topic while explicitly vocalizing the answers to those questions.

Framing an Argument

From those questions, arguments unfold. To be clear, an argument is any idea designed to persuade another individual on a particular topic. In a debate round, arguments generally stem from one of the two questions mentioned earlier. As the debate progresses, the participants engage one another in a clash over those issues. By properly framing an argument, debaters convey their ideas in a way that makes sense to the judge and the other debaters, thus maximizing their chances of winning the round.

The first step in framing an argument is identifying the argument you are trying to make. Give the argument a name that relates to the subject matter of the argument.[4] In addition, the title should be very brief to ensure word economy. At the same time, the title must convey some sort of mental image in the judge's mind to ensure he or she has a basic idea of the issue being discussed, much like the title of a book or a chapter heading within that book. Later in the round, the title of the argument becomes a quick reference used by debaters to indicate what position they are talking about next or what position (that is, argument) is the most important issue in the round.

Next, break your argument into a few smaller parts and label those pieces of the argument. These smaller pieces are generally referred to by debaters as taglines or tags. A tag is similar to my use of subheadings within each of my chapters, as they give insight into the next thought within a bigger idea. Tags will also become an important part of the debate round as debaters use them as verbal shorthand when talking about an argument.

After labeling the pieces of the argument, the debater must provide the analysis of the subpoint.[5] This can be done in one of two ways. The first method involves the debater reading a piece of evidence (or quoting printed material) to support his or her assertion. This is the most common form of support a debater can provide to prove his or her claim because it shows that

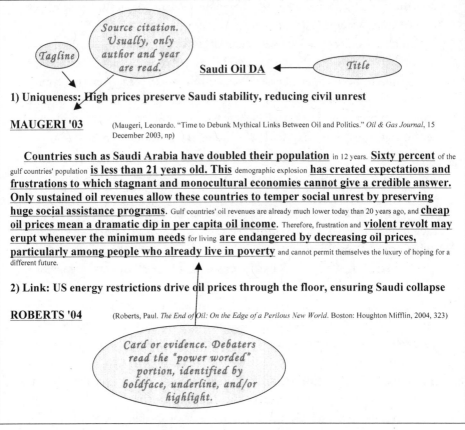

Figure 1.3. Blocking evidence

an expert agrees with the debater's point of view.[6] The alternative method is for the debater to provide his or her own analysis of the argument or point. This can be a very effective approach because debaters can utilize language that hits home with the judge, provides a more personal touch to the debate round, and shows that the debater is thinking critically.

The final step in framing your argument is to show its <u>impact</u> on the debate. The argument does you absolutely no good if you cannot explain to the judge why it is important. Therefore, you, as a debater, must be able to explain how your argument fits into the round. Explain to the judge why he or she should vote on this particular position. Why is your argument important? What does it mean to the judge? How does it interrelate with other arguments in the round? Is it more important than other issues being discussed, and if so, why? These are the types of questions you must answer when showing the impact of your argument. By using the approach described in this section of the chapter, you should be able create any argument in a debate round in a manner that allows you to effectively communicate with your judge and your audience.

Two Types of Arguments

After knowing how to set up an argument, a debater should know the two types of arguments discussed in policy debate rounds. The first type is known as a procedural argument. Procedural issues are ones that must be examined before you can look at the merits of a case. This is just like in a court of law. Do we, as participants in a debate round, have jurisdiction over the issue? Does the case meet the requirements to be in the debate round? In sports, this would be the playing field and rules governing the sport. Do we have the equipment and the facilities to accommodate the activity? If one team can prove to the judge that its opponents are not participating on an even playing field or are breaking the rules of debate, then it can win the judge's ballot and thus the round. As such, a procedural argument might indicate that a team is playing outside the rules of debate or that a traditionally accepted rule is flawed and should be rejected in this particular debate round.[7]

The second type is one that is substantive in nature. It deals with the issues a person generally imagines when he or she thinks of a congressional debate. Is the bill a good idea? What are the side effects of implementing it? In a debate round, the affirmative team makes substantive arguments in an effort to prove that its advantages outweigh the disadvantages of implementing its case.[8] Typically, this takes the form of cost-benefit analysis. The debaters weigh the advantages (or benefits) of implementing the affirmative plan against its disadvantages (or costs). In sports, this would be like judging the quality of play or comparing the scores of the two competing teams in order to determine the outcome of the game. In debate, the outcome is not quite as clear as in mainstream sports, since competitors are not shooting baskets or scoring touchdowns.

The team winning the most arguments is not necessarily the winner. Instead, substantive arguments are more like diving contests, since the judge examines the intricacies of the "play" in order to determine a winner. In addition, debaters have a direct influence on how the critic evaluates their arguments. In other words, debaters have the opportunity to tell the judge why their substantive arguments are more important than their opponents' arguments. By effectively using one or both of these types of arguments, debaters can show why they should win the debate and, thus, the judge's ballot.

Helpful Hints

Beyond arguments, tactics, and strategies, there a number of things you can do to become a more effective debater in every round.

1. *Take a stand.* Advocate something; do not waffle. On the affirmative, advocate for your affirmative case. On the negative, advocate the status quo, a <u>counterplan</u>, or some other development of your choosing. Nothing is worse than a team that dodges every issue, refusing to stand for anything. A team that continually changes its approach or does not have the guts to take a stand generally makes the round confusing for debaters and judges.

2. *Get organized before you speak.* Even if you do not have a clue about the subject matter being discussed, appearance goes a long way with judges. On the other hand, even if you are armed with the best arguments in the world and a great deal of knowledge about the material, a disorganized speech can destroy your ability to present a coherent case.

3. *Keep the big picture in sight.* Too many times I have seen people lose a debate because they cared so much about one point that they spent several minutes of their speech proving their opponents wrong on that one minor issue. Take a step back and evaluate how the arguments fit into the debate round and then allocate your speech time according to the importance of the issue. Some arguments warrant an entire speech while some require only fifteen or twenty seconds, and still others can be skipped entirely. Use your head and detach your personal feelings from the round when necessary, and you should be able to delegate your time appropriately.

4. *Stay on target.* Stay on a position, argument, or subpoint until you are finished with it. Do not skip around from point to point and back again. This becomes confusing to all participants and can cause the judge to overlook or miss the "killer" response that could have won you the round. Besides, skipping back and forth makes you look unorganized, eroding your credibility with the judge.

5. *Be your own expert.* Too many debaters, especially in high school, think they must have a quotation to back up everything said in the round. There is nothing magical about having words in print. Ideas must still be logically presented. Every debater has the ability to think critically and challenge the intellectual work of someone else. That is what debate is all about.

6. *Respect your partner.* You are a team; work with one another. Between tournaments and rounds, treat your partner the way you wish to be treated. Never talk behind his or her back. If you have a gripe, talk it out with one another. By all means, engage one another in discussions about strategies,

debate theory, and preparation. However, remember that you are working toward a common purpose. When in debate rounds, trust your partner to do his or her job. Do not second-guess everything your teammate says or does in the round. Even when your partner messes up royally, bring it to his or her attention and move on with life.[9] After all, it's only a debate round. Ultimately, you will both grow if you give each other space to learn from the debate experience.

Winning That *One* Round

In addition to the tips provided in the previous section, there are a few that can specifically help you win the "big one." This is the debate round you consider the most important. It could be a preliminary round that your friends or family are watching; one in which you are debating a district, state, or national champion; a break round; an out round at a local tournament[10]; or the round that determines who will be the national champion. Obviously, it refers to something different for everyone and can even change as you progress in your debate experience.

1. *Discover your greatest strength and exploit it.* If your greatest strength is your logical analysis, then you should focus on delivering that analysis. If your greatest strength is your ability to do research, then spend a lot of time outside of debate performing that research and cutting the best <u>cards</u> you can find. Let your judges see your strengths and be dazzled by them. I do not mean to imply that you should not try to improve upon the areas where you are weakest.[11] My point is to encourage you to know yourself. Be aware of your strengths so that you can show your best side to your critic and win that extra-important round.

2. *Think ahead.* Before attending the tournament, consider potential strategies that your opponents will use and prepare files in advance. While in the debate round, have a general plan of what positions you want to make into the winning arguments and how you want the round to unfold. By all means, remain flexible. However, a general plan of attack will improve your organization and ensure you are discussing the issues of which you have the most knowledge.

3. *Know and understand your positions.* Know all of your major arguments. Be intimately familiar with at least one or two negative positions and your affirmative case. You cannot be successful if you do not understand the arguments you are running. The key to winning most debates is knowing the material being discussed better than your opponents do.

4. *Be familiar with your files.* There is nothing worse than finding the evidence you need after you lost a round. If you know your files, you will minimize the time taken to pull the evidence you need. Thus, you can focus more time on developing a strategy, deciding which arguments are the most important, and organizing your speech.

5. *Find a partner with whom you "click."* You cannot win the important rounds if you do not work well as a team. In the world of partnerships, one plus one does not equal two. If the two best debaters do not get along, they will not be the best. Conversely, two average debaters who click together can have a remarkably successful season.

6. *Be wary of partnering with a best friend.* While debating with a close friend has potential benefits, it can also be a recipe for disaster. You may know each other so well that you develop synergy in debate rounds. On the other hand, you may find it difficult to separate the debate world from your personal relationship. I have had several good and bad experiences with this one, and I encourage you to seriously think it through before pairing up with a good friend.

The ideas in this chapter should benefit everyone, from the novice debater to someone with many years of debate experience. If only one thing sticks with you, it should be that there are no steadfast rules. As long as you can think it, deliver it, and defend it, it can be used to help win a debate round. Everything else is there to give you a starting point or perhaps a fresh perspective. The ideas and tips presented in this chapter and the ones that follow will help you enjoy and win debate rounds by improving your skills, organization, delivery, credibility, and ethos.

2. Stock Issues

Traditionally, debaters lived and died by the five <u>stock issues</u> of debate. Despite a transition to policy-oriented <u>frameworks</u> throughout the second half of the twentieth century and the incorporation of critical frameworks in recent years, the stock issues remain of utmost importance for all debaters. In addition, a number of people who hold a philosophy other than one focused on the stock issues still expect the affirmative team to meet the stock issues in the first affirmative <u>constructive</u> (1AC). Furthermore, the better a debater understands the stock issues and how they are applied in a debate round, the more effective that person will be at debating under other frameworks or philosophies. The reason is simple: *the stock issues create a foundation from which other arguments and philosophies can be built.* Simply, the concepts for examining the stock issues are the same ones that underpin virtually every form of argument used by debaters. A failure to understand them makes it exceedingly difficult to build on or deconstruct the ideas of other argument forms such as <u>disadvantages</u>, <u>counterplans</u>, and <u>kritiks</u>.

Prima Facie

Continuing the courtroom analogy in the previous chapter, the prosecution may present its evidence to a grand jury to demonstrate that it met the minimum burdens necessary to take the accused to court. Similarly, policy debaters on the affirmative team are tasked with presenting a <u>prima facie</u> (from a Latin phrase meaning "face first") <u>case</u>. Debaters usually refer to the "<u>a priori</u> prima facie burdens" of the affirmative team. Put simply, if the <u>status quo</u> is presumed innocent until proven guilty, then the affirmative has an obligation to prove certain elements if it hopes to convict the status quo. Thus, the affirmative team's first priority is to demonstrate the five stock issues in the 1AC. If at first glance the case does not present all these elements, the affirmative should lose the round for failing to meet the minimum requirements of a call to action. However, the negative must be prepared to make an a priori argument indicating such. This leads us to the stock issues: <u>significance</u>, <u>harms</u>, <u>inherency</u>, <u>topicality</u>, and <u>solvency</u>.

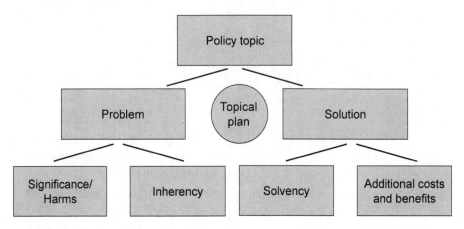

Figure 2.1. The stock issues

Significance and Harms

The first two stock issues are so intertwined they are somewhat interchangeable in contemporary debates: significance and harms. Clash over a significant harm is central to academic debate. The affirmative team must present a significant reason for change in the 1AC, and the negative team should attack that argument and/or present significant disadvantages to counter it. So, what is a significant harm? The short answer is that harms and significance refer to something bad that is happening in the status quo or is likely to happen in the near future. For example, possible harms cited by an affirmative team could include these: tuberculosis is spreading around the globe; global warming will cause severe droughts, which in turn will destroy our food supply and could potentially wipe out entire species; our present and ineffective foreign policies could allow a war to break out between India and Pakistan.

Essentially, there are two types of harms, quantitative and qualitative. A quantitative harm is embodied in the stock issue of significance and refers to a numerical amount of harm or advantage. For example, an affirmative team might point out that 1.5 billion people worldwide are infected with latent tuberculosis. A qualitative harm, on the other hand, refers to the effects of the problem—how people are hurt as opposed to how many are hurt.[1] The affirmative team could point out examples of this type of harm by noting that people with tuberculosis cough blood, have very large medical expenses, and could face an agonizing and early death.

Today, significance and harms are conceived as a single issue because some harms have been deemed to be so significant that the numbers may no longer be relevant. For example, the loss of one life may be deemed to be significant. Similarly, the dehumanization of a group of people may be deemed significant, regardless of how many people make up that group. Furthermore, in a purely utilitarian view, any problem—no matter how small—is worth fixing if there are no negative consequences of taking action.

On the negative team's side of the stock issue, there are three primary ways to attack significance. The first is to _turn the harms story against the affirmative team_. Rather than seeing the issue as a harm, the negative views it as beneficial. For example, an affirmative harms story might state that burning fossil fuels releases carbon dioxide into the atmosphere, causing global warming and a plethora of environmental impacts. The negative team could argue that while global warming is occurring, it is actually beneficial because a warming, CO_2-rich atmosphere promotes vegetation and agricultural growth. Obviously, turning an affirmative team's harms story against it yields huge strategic benefits, but it is also difficult to accomplish in most instances.

Negative teams may find it marginally easier to _deny the attack_ by maintaining that the harm stated by the affirmative team is simply not true. In this scenario, the negative simply provides evidence that the entire harms story is incorrect. In the global warming example, the negative team might deny the harms story by citing evidence that the global warming theory is untrue and that climate models do not demonstrate or predict a warming atmosphere. Obviously, this can be a strong tactic but can also be difficult for the negative to prove. Therefore, debaters must be prepared to show why their sources are more qualified than their opponents' sources, why their researcher's study was more accurate, or why their opponents' evidence is flawed. In other words, you must explain why your evidence and/or analysis is better than your opponents'.

The third method of refuting the affirmative team's harms is to _diminish the attack_. This is accomplished by simply reducing the amount of significance shown, by demonstrating that the harm is actually less severe than what the affirmative team would like the judge to believe, or by showing that fewer people are affected or that the degree of damage caused in the status quo is actually much lower than what the affirmative team claimed.

In the global warming example, the affirmative team might claim that the world faces a five-degree temperature increase over the next five years, causing millions of people to lose their homes as sea levels rise. The negative team could diminish the claim by showing that the temperature change will occur over a ten-year span, allowing people to adapt to the rising sea levels and causing only a few thousand people to be displaced.

By diminishing the affirmative harm, you give the judge less reason to vote for the affirmative team. This strategy, in conjunction with other types of arguments, can be a very effective means of winning the judge's ballot. For instance, as a negative you might show that only two hundred thousand of the 1.5 billion people infected by latent tuberculosis (as cited by the affirmative) will acquire active cases and that not all of those will die. Then, you might run a disadvantage showing how the affirmative policy will place a severe financial strain on medical institutions, causing several major cities to close their hospitals and emergency care facilities. This, in turn, means hundreds of thousands of people around the country will lose the care they need in the event of an emergency. Therefore, you have mitigated a virtually unbeatable harms story enough that you can now show how the affirmative will actually sentence more people to death than it will save, and the result is a negative ballot. That said, when attacking the affirmative harm, it is important to remember that the strongest defense of the status quo may be to use all three types of responses in conjunction with one another to make a stronger overall argument.

Inherency

The Affirmative Point of View

The next stock issue the affirmative team uses to present a prima facie case is inherency.[2] In general, the issue of inherency answers this question: If the status quo were left to its own devices, would it solve the problem cited in the affirmative case? In essence, the affirmative has four types of inherency it can use to show that the status quo is unwilling or incapable of solving the harm.

The first is *structural inherency*. With this form, the affirmative demonstrates that present law, administrative rules, or codified practices prevent the problem from being solved. For example, an affirmative team might argue that homelessness exists in America because the government has passed laws that make it nearly impossible for companies, cities, and institutions to build low-income housing. Maybe the government maintains zoning laws that severely inhibit this type of construction, or perhaps it passed a tax on construction materials that makes it too expensive for organizations and construction companies to build this type of housing. Since governmental policy prevents the solution (building more low-income housing), we have structural inherency.

The next type of inherency is known as *gap inherency*. With the gap motif, rather than show that an existing policy is the cause of the problem, the affirmative team proves that the lack of a law or rule causes the harm. For instance, the homeless have health problems because the government does not provide money to build and operate clinics for them. Essentially, the affirmative is saying that its policy is not being done now, and that alone is enough justification for inherency.

The third type is *attitudinal inherency*. Here the affirmative team demonstrates that a prevailing attitude or belief is so ingrained in the present system that a new plan is needed to get around the present attitudes and fight the problem. For instance, a Republican-controlled legislature may not pass legislation to support the homeless because lawmakers do not believe that is the appropriate role of government. Similarly, an affirmative team might argue that drunk driving persists in America because policy makers believe fines are a preferred method of addressing the problem rather than license revocation.

The fourth type of inherency is *existential inherency*. This form simply shows that the problem is ingrained in the system. For example, an affirmative team might offer a plan to clean up plastic debris floating in the ocean and may seek to bolster the case by showing that people are obsessed with plastic wrap. We use plastic bags to pack our lunches, we purchase water bottles rather than drink from the tap, consumer products are sealed in giant cartons of plastic, and retail outlets place our purchases in plastic grocery bags. Much of the waste works its way into waterways and oceans, poisoning the environment. Regardless of the cause, the result has created a need to solve the problem.

Many times, an affirmative team will use a combination of these types to demonstrate its inherent barrier. For example, an affirmative team might combine attitudinal and structural inherency by indicating that policy makers believe social programs for the homeless are an unwarranted drain on society and therefore refuse to pass legislation that would provide subsidies for housing. Thus, the inherent barrier has two parts. First, the status quo cannot solve the homelessness problem because of the prevailing attitude in

Washington. Second, there is a lack of laws in the status quo that could address the problem. Therefore, the affirmative policy is needed to get around the current political mindset and to establish new laws that promote the construction of low-income housing and/or provide subsidies for rent.

Refuting Inherency

Before I address the ways a negative team may answer inherency, let us dispel with a notion commonly passed on from one generation of debaters to the next: "Inherency is a stupid argument." Ninety-nine times out of a hundred it is not advisable for the negative team to attack the affirmative's inherency, for reasons that will be discussed in chapter 6. But for some reason, seasoned debaters have clung to the overly simplistic statement that inherency is a stupid argument. Unfortunately, they fail to recognize or articulate why it is not advisable to use inherency attacks in most instances. More important, the broad generalization fails to identify the rare example of when it actually makes sense to refute this particular stock issue.

When attacking the affirmative's inherency arguments, there are four primary methods at the negative team's disposal. First, the negative can *deny the barrier* by demonstrating that the specific actions of the affirmative plan have already been done. Such was the case my sophomore year in college. That season, there was a team running a case supporting a particular piece of legislation that pundits did not believe would successfully work its way through the legislature. The week of one particular tournament, the legislation actually cleared the U.S. Congress and was signed into law by the president while most of us were traveling to the tournament. The school running that case did not have time to research and write a new case before the competition. So, many of us carried the morning newspaper into rounds and read evidence that the specific plan found in the 1AC had, indeed, become law. Needless to say, that school did not win very many affirmative rounds that weekend. Of course, the chances of such a scenario playing out is quite rare.

Alternatively, the negative team can *demonstrate alternate solvency*. With this tactic, the negative agrees that the affirmative policy has not been implemented but shows that other programs within the status quo are currently solving the problem cited by the affirmative. For instance, the negative team might admit that the status quo is not building low-income housing but might also argue it uses vouchers as an income supplement to provide the poor with homes. In this way, the negative team shows that the problem is being solved in the status quo with income supplements.

Unfortunately, this type of response is not advisable with most judges because it makes your disadvantages <u>non-unique</u>. If the status quo is already taking measures to combat the affirmative harm but is not completely solving it, then the status quo should have already caused the disadvantage to occur. Therein lies the reason many debaters say inherency is a stupid argument. Simply, you run the risk of undermining all of your offensive argumentation while still allowing the affirmative to say, "We can still make things a little better."

The third method for refuting inherency identifies the affirmative plan as merely a *minor repair* of the present system. This argument says that if only minor adjustments, such as increased funding for a status quo program, are necessary to solve the problem, then the affirmative lacks true inherency. In essence, a policy offering a minor repair is not a departure from the perspective of the status quo. Rather, the affirmative is mirroring present policy. The status quo obviously thinks the policy is a worthwhile one. It has, after all, already implemented it; the appropriate level of resources devoted to the proposal simply has not been achieved. There is, in effect, no reason why the status quo cannot implement the affirmative case today.[3]

The fourth method of dealing with inherency is for the negative team to show how the *affirmative fails to overcome the barrier*. Once again, this type of argument has solvency implications but is directly related to inherency. With this argument, the negative uses the affirmative's inherency evidence against it by showing how its evidence cites a barrier that its plan does not overcome. This might work particularly well, for example, if the affirmative team cites an attitudinal barrier within society. In other words, just because the plan is implemented does not mean people will abide by it. For example, a case dealing with highway deaths might cite evidence indicating that under current law, the federal government allows states to establish their own speed limits. However, those speed limits are too high, leading to a large number of highway fatalities. Thus, the affirmative team wants to return to the old system of establishing national speed limits. Here is a hypothetical <u>card</u> the affirmative team might read in its inherency observation:

The current method for establishing speed limits contributes greatly to the large number of highway deaths that occur every year. High speed limits, coupled with the incessant desire of drivers to speed, have led to a national emergency of sorts. The federal government caused this "state of emergency" by letting states establish the speed limits on the nation's highways.

In this inherency evidence, the astute negative observer might key in on the phrase "coupled with the incessant desire of drivers to speed." With the following responses, the negative team could make a solvency argument on inherency by showing how the affirmative plan cannot overcome the inherent barrier:

1. The affirmative fails to overcome its own inherency. Its own evidence indicates that part of the problem is drivers' disregard for the law. The affirmative cannot change this attitude by lowering speed limits.
2. Post-plan, people still speed and accidents still occur.

Again, just like with significance and harms, the negative team could utilize several of these methods within one speech as independent arguments or in combination to form one cohesive inherency attack.

When refuting inherency, remember to look at the big picture and think about how your arguments interrelate with other arguments you might run. This will help you make stronger inherency attacks and avoid the pitfalls of running contradictory positions or running the weaker of two positions.[4] As the affirmative team, construct your inherency observations as straightforward as possible to show that your policy is not being done in the status quo. If you can demonstrate that the status quo lacks the propensity to implement your policy in the future, your case will be much stronger.

Topicality

Standard Topicality

THE NEGATIVE ATTACK. The fourth stock issue that the affirmative team must meet is topicality. As a general rule, the affirmative must provide a policy in support of the <u>resolution</u>. The first negative speaker presents a topicality argument when the negative team wants to show that the affirmative plan is not within the bounds of the topic. Keep in mind that while the actions of the plan are constrained by the resolution, the substance of the case may discuss harms and advantages that extend beyond the scope of the topic area.[5] However, if the plan violates even one word of the resolution, then the plan is not topical and the affirmative team has not upheld its burden to support the resolution.

Essentially, there are three basic models that define how a topicality argument is presented and why topicality matters to the judge. The first model on which topicality is based is *jurisdiction*. Simply, the resolution establishes the parameters of debate, similar to the rule that says a football field is exactly one hundred yards in length and fifty-three and one-third yards in width. As with any contest, the competitors must adhere to the rules governing the "sport," and debaters agree to abide by the rules and regulations governing it.

This construct has two primary schools of thought. First, traditionalists tied to the judicial model of debate believe the resolution establishes the judge's authority to hear debate on a particular case. Just as in a court of law, the judge can base his or her decision only on plans that fall within his or her jurisdiction—that is, within the bounds established by the resolution.

Second, as debate turned to legislative models, the view on jurisdiction shifted in that it served only to divide ground between affirmative and negative policy options. In other words, every policy that falls within the bounds of the resolution is fair game for the affirmative team's advocacy, while every policy option that falls outside the bounds of the resolution is fair game for the negative team's advocacy as a potential counterplan.

Regardless of the school of thought, the jurisdictional model establishes that every policy within the boundaries of the resolution is a viable option for an affirmative plan text. However, most contemporary judges do not find this line of reasoning very compelling. In short, they do not subscribe to the notion that we should always continue doing things the way they have always been done. Rather, they want to know why the rules should or should not exist. Thus, most debates on topicality—or any other debate over the rules of the game—now come down to one of two remaining justifications.

As such, the second model from which topicality stems is based upon *fairness*. In this form, the topicality argument contends that the resolution creates a stable playing field from which the debate can progress. In other words, as a competitive activity, both teams should have a reasonable chance of winning the judge's ballot. Thus, the resolution serves to prevent both the affirmative and the negative team from being abused by the other's interpretation of the topic.

Again, there are two schools of thought on the role of fairness in the debate. First, some argue that the resolution exists to ensure debaters on both sides of the topic have adequate cases and arguments at their disposal. There should be relatively equal amounts of potential material available on both sides of the issue. Second, some believe the resolution simply creates a predictable playing field so that both teams can reasonably prepare for the event. In this view, even a topic biased toward the affirmative or negative still ensures a fair debate since both sides knew the boundaries before the debate began. In either case, the fairness model prevents abusive interpretations of the topic and makes certain that both teams have a legitimate chance of winning in a competitive activity.

Finally, topicality arguments stem from the model of *education*. This is an educational event; thus, debaters may explain that the resolution exists to guarantee that all participants benefit from the educational value of the activity. At their most basic level, the rules of policy debate exist to ensure that students learn and grow from their participation in debate. Thus, the resolution limits discussion, focuses discourse, and promotes meaningful interaction.

In this view, there are three schools of thought. First, some strive for topic-specific education. The topic was carefully crafted to generate research and discourse on current controversies in our society. The specific resolution was then chosen using a democratic process. Thus, students are limited to discussions pertaining to those controversies. Second, some seek a breadth of knowledge. While the resolution points students toward certain themes, there is much to learn about the world. Thus, interpretations of the resolution that facilitate a broad understanding of the topic also create opportunities for students to explore some of the many issues at play. Third, some strive to achieve a depth of understanding. As such, narrowly defined topics and/or specifically interpreted meanings encourage deeper research and a more complete grasp of the most pertinent issues. This type of examination of the resolution leads to a meaningful understanding of the world around us. Regardless, this model of rules interpretations centers on knowledge production, the ability to make sense of the content being debated, and the capacity to apply that material in various settings.

While the models of jurisdiction, fairness, and education are where topicality begins, they are not necessarily incompatible ideas. Debaters may craft arguments using a combination of perspectives. Keeping these three models in the back of your mind should help you create any rules-based or procedural argument in debate and should help you respond to those types of arguments levied against you by other debaters. As we discuss the various elements of a topicality argument, reflect back on these models so that you can better utilize the information to construct topicality arguments, as well as articulate to the judge why he or she should vote (or not vote) on a topicality argument.

In fact, an increasing number of debate circuits or regions of the country are accepting the view of *competing interpretations* of topicality. Simply, critics do not think it is sufficient for both the affirmative and negative teams to offer legitimate or acceptable interpretations of the resolution. Rather, in their view, debaters should present competing interpretations and demonstrate why their understanding of the topic is superior to their opponents' view. Thus, establishing clear <u>standards</u> that create synergy with one or more of the models of topicality described above is incredibly important.

Put simply, a standard is a rule or method of assessing how good a definition or interpretation of the words within the resolution is. In other words, a standard explains the best way of determining how to define the resolution. For example, the negative team could utilize any number of standards, including (but not limited to) these:

> *Limits.* We should limit the resolution as much as possible to focus debate.
>
> *Fair burdens.* The resolution ensures that both teams have fair ground.
>
> *Legal definitions.* Legal definitions establish a clear framework using precedents found in the real world.
>
> *Field-specific definitions.* Experts in the topic area provide the most realistic definitions.
>
> *Each word.* Evaluate each word in the resolution independent of other words.
>
> *Resolutional context.* Uphold the meaning of the words as a complete sentence.
>
> *Precision.* Avoid ambiguity and use interpretations that are concrete and specific.
>
> *Grammar.* Use of words within the English language create a unique meaning.

Ultimately, the standards you select and their clear application to a model of fairness or education will go a long way in showing that your interpretation is the best in the round.

The next step is to present the <u>violation</u> or explain how the affirmative plan is nontopical. First, give a definition of the word or phrase in the resolution that you believe the affirmative team violates. Then, explain how the affirmative fails to meet that definition. These are the only two parts of the violation that must be present. However, you can provide additional information to further demonstrate how the affirmative exceeds the mandate of the resolution. In some instances, debaters may wish to further expound upon the interpretation by explaining why their interpretation should be preferred over a competing or alternate interpretation. Their reasons to prefer could include (but are not limited to) these:

Clear bright line. A bright line clearly separates what is topical from what is not. Imagine a solid yellow line down the center of a highway. On one side is topical ground, and on the other is nontopical ground.

Replacement test. If we could replace one word in the resolution with another word and the affirmative would be topical, then the affirmative team has supported an alternate resolution.

Additional standards. Support, for example, a fair burdens or precision standard by highlighting the importance of legal or field-specific definitions.

Finally, the negative team must provide an <u>impact</u> to the topicality argument by providing the <u>voters</u> (or explanation for why topicality is a voting issue). Ultimately, the voters stem from the models that frame our understanding of topicality arguments. At the most basic level, teams may simply provide a bullet statement about topicality being a voting issue for reasons of jurisdiction, fairness, or education.

Some negative teams may provide nuance to the voters through specific applications of those models. For instance, the negative could bolster the fairness model by arguing that topicality is necessary for the division of ground. Here, the negative indicates that the affirmative's broad interpretation of the resolution is bad because it decreases negative counterplan ground.

Similarly, a negative team could claim topicality as a voting issue for reasons of ensuring fair research burdens. In other words, allowing a broad interpretation of the resolution or nontopical cases skews research burdens and gives the affirmative an unfair advantage. Essentially, the negative states that there is already so much uncertainty about what the affirmative might run on any given topic that a broad interpretation would make it nearly impossible for negative teams to perform the research necessary to make them competitive.

Another possible voter is one of precedence. This says that allowing a fringe affirmative plan to be considered topical sets a bad precedent that in turn would allow many blatantly nontopical cases to soon be viewed as okay in future debates. Thus, even if the affirmative team proves that its plan does not create an unfair advantage in that particular round, the negative could still win on topicality due to the potential for abuse stemming from the precedent set by the judge in that round.

Again, several of these voters work very well with the standards given earlier in this section. When crafting a topicality argument, ensure the standards and voters work together to make the specific interpretation/violation more compelling to the judge. Ultimately, all topicality arguments should include a discussion of these core elements: standards, violation, and voters.[6]

TOPICALITY—WORD OR PHRASE (from the resolution)

A. Standards

    1. Provide the name of a standard you have chosen and a very brief explanation of it.

    2. Try to choose two or three standards that mesh well together and with your violation.

B. Violation

    1. Provide a definition with source citation.

    2. Explain the violation.

    3. Optional: Give a reason to prefer your definition or interpretation over any interpretation the affirmative might provide.

C. *Reason(s) to Prefer: Again this is optional. Use a R2P in sub-point B₃ or C, but not both. Make your decision based on where it fits best / makes the most sense.*

D. Voters

    1. Provide the name of the voter you have chosen and a very brief explanation of it.

    2. Use more than one voter if you like.

Figure 2.2. Example of the topicality argument or the 1NC shell

Be forewarned, however; topicality is frequently very difficult to win in the early stages of a debater's career. The reason is twofold. First, there is a lot of information to grasp when discussing topicality, and many novices simply go back and forth making statements like "Our opponents just aren't topical" and "Yes, we are." The ideas in this section should give you a fundamental understanding of how to conceptualize a topicality argument and a basic vocabulary to utilize when constructing your arguments. Second, many inexperienced judges do not want to sit through topicality discussions because the argumentation seems somewhat bland and often confusing; therefore, they tend to grant that the affirmative team is topical as long as the case seems reasonably topical to them. However, if you provide a judge with a well thought out and clearly explained topicality argument, I would not be surprised if you were able to convince him or her to vote negative.

Regardless, if you decide to go for topicality as the winning argument in the second negative <u>rebuttal</u>, be prepared to provide exceptional analysis.

THE AFFIRMATIVE RESPONSE. Once the negative team runs a topicality argument, the affirmative has five basic means of refutation. Although debaters may develop other responses to topicality, these are the most common. Furthermore, when responding to a topicality argument, debaters may use one, all, or a combination of these responses.

The first option is for the affirmative to offer *counterstandards*. Here, the affirmative provides better, alternative standards to the ones offered by the negative. Obviously, the affirmative may access any of the standards available to the negative: limits, fair burdens, legal definitions, field-specific definitions, each word, resolutional context, precision, grammar, and so on.[7] In addition, there are several others that are almost always associated with the affirmative side of topicality debates, such as these:

> *Reasonability.* The resolution merely establishes a guideline or starting point for debate.
> *Fairness.* As long as the case or plan provides fair ground to debate, the affirmative should not lose on topicality.
> *Expansive jurisdiction.* The benefits of the plan are so significant that the judge should hear the case, as long as it appears to be topic-related.
> *Affirmative's right to define.* Traditionally, the affirmative holds the right to define key terms.
> *100 percent.* Topicality is a no-risk argument for the negative. In order to justify a negative ballot, the negative team should have to win the argument 100 percent. If there is any doubt, the judge should give the affirmative team *leeway*.

The second option for the affirmative can be called *"we meet."* This strategy is very straightforward in that you simply show how the affirmative plan meets the negative's violation/interpretation. In this situation, the negative's topicality argument would be answered by showing how your plan meets all the criteria laid down in that argument.

The next strategy is to offer a *counterinterpretation*. Instead of demonstrating that the plan adheres to the negative interpretation, the affirmative provides an alternative understanding of the resolution, shows how it meets that interpretation, and explains why its interpretation is better than the negative's. Essentially, affirmative teams construct a new and different topicality argument but one that indicates their plan is topical.

The fourth strategy is for the affirmative to show that the *negative interpretation is flawed*. Here, you might show how its definition, its interpretation of the definition, or its interpretation of the resolution is skewed, thus making the team's topicality argument meaningless or even harmful to debate. An alternative is to show that the negative definition/interpretation violates the negative team's own standards, again indicating that its interpretation is flawed. In addition, you could argue that the negative interpretation overlimits the topic, meaning the negative team narrowed the topic so much that it fails to allow for any creativity, fair division of ground, or an educational exploration of the topic.

The final option is for the affirmative to *argue that topicality is not or should not be a voting issue*. Given that providing a topical plan has been a hallmark of the activity for decades, this is an extremely difficult argument to win with the majority of judges. Nevertheless, with well thought out analysis and the ability to outdebate opponents on the issue, it is a potential option for affirmative teams.

When answering a topicality argument, base which options you utilize on the judging philosophy of your critic (or judge), the experience level of your judge, and which types of arguments are strongest in relation to your case. In addition, keep in mind that some topicality violations can be more than adequately covered with only one or two responses, while others require a plethora of responses, depending on whether your case truly is nontopical and how well the negative's topicality argument is developed during the first negative constructive (1NC).

In addition to a standard topicality violation, there are two fundamental variants.

Variations on Topicality

THE FIRST IS <u>EFFECTS TOPICALITY</u>. In a nutshell, effects topicality says the affirmative policy falls outside the resolution but causes a chain reaction of events that eventually makes the affirmative appear topical. Once the affirmative plan is implemented, it would cause X to happen, which in turn leads to Y, which causes Z—a resolutional harm to be solved or a resolutional action to be implemented. However, the mere fact that a resolutional harm is solved has no bearing on whether or not the affirmative plan falls within the boundary established by the resolution. Allowing an affirmative to implement such a plan would place unfair research burdens upon negative debaters and would also destroy negative counterplan ground.[8]

THE SECOND VARIATION OF TOPICALITY IS <u>EXTRA-TOPICALITY</u>, which stems from a nontopical action in the plan from which the affirmative gains additional advantages or spikes disadvantages.[9] If the affirmative has even one action that falls outside the resolution, that team is taking away policy ground that actually belongs to the negative. Ultimately, the entirety of the plan must be topical, not just bits and pieces of it.

There are two ways to impact an extra-topicality argument. The first is to impact it just like any other topicality violation. If any part of the affirmative plan does not fall within the bounds of the resolution, the team has failed to meet the burden established by the resolution and should lose the round.

The second way to impact an extra-topicality violation is to allow the affirmative to sever the nontopical portions of the plan. Think of it as allowing your opponents and/or the judge to line-item veto the part or parts of the plan that are nontopical. The negative uses this strategy when it hopes to gain a strategic advantage on substantive issues by way of the extra-topicality argument. For instance, if the affirmative spiked your disadvantage, you might allow it to sever the spike so that your disadvantage now <u>links</u> to the case.[10]

By now you should have a basic understanding of what topicality is, how to present a topicality argument in the 1NC, and how to respond to it if someone runs topicality against you. Above all, ensure you adequately explain the violation to your critic. If he or she does not understand why the affirmative team's plan is nontopical or why it is important for the plan to be topical, you do not have a chance of winning topicality. For the affirmative, do not forget that topicality is a prima facie burden and a stock issue. Then, write your plan in a manner that minimizes the potential for a negative win on topicality.

Solvency

The last stock issue, solvency, examines whether the affirmative plan solves the harm(s) cited by the affirmative team. Obviously, the affirmative's solvency arguments indicate that its case will reduce, eliminate, or prevent the harms found in the status quo. The negative, on the other hand, attempts to show that the affirmative plan will be ineffective. As with significance, the negative is not required to completely disprove the plan's ability to solve. Rather, most negative teams seek to mitigate solvency to such an extent the disadvantages of implementing the affirmative's plan outweigh its benefits.

Solvency on the Affirmative

It is the affirmative's burden to demonstrate in the 1AC that its plan will effectively reduce or eliminate the harms it described in the status quo. After listening to debaters present an affirmative case, you should ask yourself the question, "Does the affirmative plan reduce, end, or prevent the harm(s) they cite from occurring?" If, at face value, the plan eliminates part of the problem, the burden of solvency has been met. That being said, it is not necessary for the affirmative to gain absolute solvency. To paraphrase the 1997 Cross Examination Debate Association national champions from Southern Illinois University, if they save one life (or gain 1 percent solvency), they have met their burden and their job has been done. However, do not confuse this with an affirmative ballot. If the affirmative saves only one life or merely improves the quality of life for a handful of people, it becomes a very simple task for the negative to demonstrate that some disadvantage of implementing the plan outweighs its benefits.

Solvency on the Negative

In reality, the affirmative will try to claim a much larger solvency impact than one life. To simplify the discussion, I break the negative's options into three types of attacks: offensive attacks, absolute solvency takeouts, and mitigators. The first is the most difficult to win but the most effective means of beating an affirmative case. Conversely, the last approach is easiest to do but cannot win the debate. Rather, it merely minimizes the benefit of the plan so that other arguments can win the debate.

OFFENSIVE ATTACKS OR CASE TURNS. The first category is generally referred to as a case turn. A case turn (or simply turn) seeks to *turn* the affirmative's solvency mechanism against it. To do this, the negative provides research or analysis that shows how the affirmative plan exacerbates the harms found in the case rather than solves them. Thus, a turn can be a single piece of evidence, a brief argument consisting of your own analysis, or a structured argument using two or more cards to demonstrate how the affirmative plan actually makes the harm worse.

For example, at the turn of the twenty-first century, the city of New Orleans sought to address the harms of poverty. The general belief was that a host of problems related to crime, malnutrition, economics, drugs, and so forth stemmed from the severe poverty suffered by those living in the city. A plan was hatched to tear down the high-rise housing units in the ghettos, replacing them with low-income housing in well-planned, idyllic neighborhoods.

Organizers intended to provide affordable housing and create a community that fostered pride among the residents. On the face of it, the program was a total success. Problem solved. However, many asked where all the people went. While the city built some extraordinarily nice housing in a wonderfully designed neighborhood, the problem was that hundreds of families were displaced in the process of destroying high-rise apartments that were replaced with condos and townhomes. Arguably, the plan made the problem of poverty worse by helping a fortunate few to the detriment of the many.

Technically, a turn refers to an argument that shows the affirmative team's plan exacerbates the harms story found in the 1AC. In recent years, however, judges and debaters began conceptualizing turns as any negative impact story that directly stemmed from the solvency mechanism of the affirmative. Thus, an affirmative plan might directly seek to reduce public health risks, but the actions taken in the plan might directly increase risks to public safety. Even though those are two distinct impact stories, some might classify the argument as a turn since they are both triggered by the solvency mechanism itself.

This may lead some experienced debaters to ask, "What's the difference between a case turn and a disadvantage?" To be frank, a case turn could be envisioned as a "mini-disadvantage." The overall goal of the two types of arguments is the same: to show the affirmative's plan causes more harm than good. Generally speaking, the difference is often found in the length of the story. Turns are usually directly tied to the initial action in the plan. Disadvantages often require more steps to reach the negative impact associated with passing the plan. The initial action of the plan sets in motion a cascading series of effects that eventually terminate in a harm the judge should seek to avoid. Regardless, a turn story can be a very effective means of winning a debate since the negative team demonstrates that the plan makes the problem cited in the 1AC worse or directly causes another harmful impact.

ABSOLUTE SOLVENCY TAKEOUTS. In addition to turns, the negative has the option to go on the defensive when addressing the affirmative's solvency story. The strongest defensive approach is to take out the affirmative's solvency completely. The first way to do this is to find a barrier to implementation. The negative could find something in the affirmative's inherency evidence that denies its ability to solve. Alternatively, the negative could demonstrate through evidence or analysis that something about the plan is not workable or feasible. Perhaps the technology required for the plan is not yet available. Perhaps the agency tasked with implementation of the plan is overburdened and cannot effectively administer the action. Regardless, the negative uses this approach to show that the plan will not work.

The second way to completely disprove the affirmative's solvency is through a time frame attack. Here, the negative considers when the affirmative harms will occur and when the solvency of the affirmative will kick in. For example, in global warming debates, oftentimes the harms evidence read in the 1AC indicates that present atmospheric CO_2 levels will cause a dramatic rise in temperature. Therefore, if the affirmative plan merely prevents additional carbon dioxide from being released, the team will not gain solvency because the plan prevents only future carbon dioxide from being released. Simply, the damage is already done. The only way to prevent global warming—according to the affirmative's own evidence—is to actually take CO_2 out of the air. Thus, the negative has completely taken out the affirmative's solvency in one fell swoop.

Obviously, there are ways for the affirmative to respond to such an attack. For example, it could turn these absolute solvency denials into mitigation attacks by arguing that the plan succeeds by slowing the rate of global warming so society can adapt to the rise in temperature. Additionally, the affirmative could discuss thresholds of change by arguing that current carbon dioxide levels will cause a temperature increase of x degrees. However, most harmful impacts of climate change will not be realized until we reach an increase of two times x degrees. Therein lies much of what debate is about. Recognizing that discussions on controversial issues are not black and white or right and wrong or absolute is important. The best debaters engage in give and take. Seeding some ground in order to gain a more stable footing from which to weigh the issues and frame the debate in their favor is an incredibly powerful tactic in debate and persuasion.

SOLVENCY MITIGATORS. The final way to attack the affirmative's solvency is through the use of mitigators. They include, but are not limited to, alternate causality, circumvention, workability, and necessary-versus-sufficient arguments. An alternate causality argument maintains there is some other cause of the affirmative harm that the plan will not solve. For example, on the 1995–96 Cross Examination Debate Association topic, some teams ran an affirmative that tried to stop lead poisoning by banning the import of lollipops with lead in the wrappers. Their argument was that x number of children were diagnosed with lead poisoning each year. Furthermore, they claimed that lollipop wrappers were the cause. We mitigated their solvency by reading a piece of evidence that said there were many sources of lead poisoning including, but not limited to, leaded gasoline, lead paint, and soil.[11] We also noted that their harms evidence referenced the incidents of lead poisoning globally, but the plan affected people residing only in the

United States. This strategy allowed the affirmative teams to still reduce lead poisoning but did not allow them to claim 100 percent solvency. In other words, the affirmative solved only for a fraction of the children who were poisoned by lead. This, in turn, allowed our disadvantages to outweigh the advantages of the case.

The second type of mitigator is circumvention. This solvency response argues that some people (policy administrators, businesspeople, the general public, and so on) will find ways around the affirmative policy. Here, the negative argues that someone in society will find loopholes in the policy so he or she will not have to comply with it. Take environmental policies, for example. Many times these policies are so costly for businesses that business owners find ways around them in order to maximize their profits.[12] These arguments generally require evidence to hold much weight in a round, but as with all other arguments, the negative could make such an argument through logical analysis and still convince the judge of the argument's merit.

Third, the negative could develop a workability argument to mitigate the affirmative's solvency. With this tactic, the negative argues that there are problems with the technology, administration, and the like required to implement the policy that will prevent the plan from successfully accomplishing its goals. For example, a policy mandating a transition to electric vehicles would face a workability solvency argument because electric engines and batteries cannot replace all transportation needs such as long distance travel; air travel; and land, sea, and air shipping. In other instances, the negative might argue that the agency in charge of administering the affirmative policy would not be able to carry it out because it falls outside the agency's area of expertise, or the agency is overworked now and could not possibly take on this additional tasking. The type of evidence supporting these statements would not deny solvency outright but would cast doubt on the plan's ability to solve the problems found in the status quo.

Finally, the negative could utilize the necessary-versus-sufficient standard to mitigate solvency. This type of attack says the affirmative may meet a necessary condition to solve but that the action is not sufficient. For instance, if there are five things that must be done to solve the problem and the affirmative does only one of those things, then its plan is not sufficient for solvency, even though that one thing is a necessary measure. This type of attack can be used frequently if you listen carefully to the affirmative's solvency evidence.[13] Generally, this is an effective argument the negative can make quickly without having to read a piece of evidence. Again, the end goal of using the necessary-versus-sufficient standard—as with all mitigators—is to cast enough doubt upon the affirmative's solvency mechanism that the negative can win the round with its disadvantages or with an alternate solvency mechanism.

In a nutshell, solvency is the stock issue that requires the affirmative to demonstrate that its plan will reduce, eliminate, or prevent certain harms found in the status quo. At the end of the 1AC, the judge should be fairly certain the affirmative plan will achieve that goal. The negative can then respond to the affirmative's evidence, turning the plan against the affirmative by showing how the plan will exacerbate the harm, by denying the solvency completely, or by mitigating the effectiveness of the plan's solvency. Keeping that in mind, remember the affirmative does not have to show 100 percent solvency.

The affirmative team's burden is to demonstrate that the plan's advantages outweigh its disadvantages. Thus, it is critical that teams focus on the big picture. Through a combination of mitigating the significance or harm in the status quo, minimizing the degree of solvency the plan achieves, and showing an unintended negative consequence or disadvantage of passing the plan, negative teams can easily win debate rounds.

Although fewer and fewer debaters and judges rely exclusively on the stock issues, they remain as the foundation of policy debate arguments. To build a compelling case for change, we must see the need for change, understand the cause of the problem in order to craft a viable solution, and then demonstrate that the proposal actually addresses the issue. Furthermore, almost all other arguments are spin-offs of the stock issues. So what are the affirmative's burdens? The affirmative must demonstrate a *significant harm* in the status quo. There must be something bad (that is, harmful, damaging) in the present system that the affirmative hopes to alleviate. The affirmative must show that the problem is either *inherent* to the status quo—that something about the status quo is causing the problem—or that the proposal is not being done now. Then, the affirmative is required to provide a *topical* plan—as defined by the resolution—in an attempt to overcome the inherent barrier and reduce the harm. Finally, the affirmative must show that its plan will *solve* the harms of the status quo. Traditionally, the affirmative had to meet all five stock issues, 100 percent. However, debaters and judges now evaluate the big picture and see whether, after the plan's implementation, we would be better off than we are now. In short, although most debate rounds do not come down to a single substantive stock issue, they do generally come down to a few arguments—stemming from the stock issues—used in conjunction with one another to tell a complete story.

3. Speaker Duties

After grasping the fundamentals, the next step is to understand the sequence of events during an actual debate round. Ultimately, debate is flexible. There are multiple ways of approaching the activity. However, the generally accepted approach is to establish a solid foundation for all the arguments during the first two speeches. Typically, this is accomplished with a heavy reliance on quoted evidence. The next three speeches see an expansion of the material as debaters build upon those foundations, deconstruct their opponents' arguments, and rebuild their own ideas. The first affirmative <u>rebuttal</u> (1AR) begins to shrink the debate, focusing on the most critical portions of each argument. The final two speeches primarily frame the debate by explaining what transpired in the discussion of each argument and comparing the various issues with one another. This chapter focuses on the general purpose of each speech, offers tips for preparing yourself for that speech, and provides an examination of what each speech should look like.

The First Affirmative Constructive

The first affirmative <u>constructive</u> (1AC) is the introduction to the debate. Therefore, you should ensure the 1AC is well polished before you go to the first tournament. There should be no mistakes, no oversights, and no confusion during or at the conclusion of the 1AC. Obviously, the purpose of the speech is to start the round in the affirmative team's favor. By the end of this speech, the judge should have absolutely no reason to vote against the affirmative team. In order to make certain this is the case, the 1AC must demonstrate all five of the <u>stock issues</u>. If you met that burden, you should be able to convince any judge—no matter what her judging philosophy—that your plan should be enacted.[1]

When constructing the 1AC, you should tailor the speech to your audience. Plan ahead. Perhaps you should write two or three versions of the same <u>case</u>. This allows you to meet the demands of your judge. For instance, if you have a judge with relatively no experience,[2] you might include an introduction that really grabs her attention. In addition, you may want to include more explanation in your <u>taglines</u> than you would in other rounds or include analytic arguments and summaries after you read evidence. If, on the other hand, your judge has more experience, you might want to shorten the introduction and taglines and focus on the arguments themselves. Furthermore, once you (and your judges) have more experience, you may want to put together a case that skips the introduction, is designed to be given at a high rate of delivery,[3] and focuses entirely on the meat of the arguments.

Once the 1AC is written, practice it several times before the first tournament. You should also discuss it with your teammates. Make sure you fully understand the purpose of the case, how it works, and why the judge should vote for it. This ensures you are familiar with the structure of the case, can pronounce all the words in it, know what those words mean, and give an overall positive impression to your judge.[4] In addition, this allows you to make eye contact with your judge. This is particularly important if your critic is a <u>lay judge</u> or anyone who feels debate is primarily based on communication skills. Finally, by knowing your case inside and out, you can prevent any surprise <u>cross-examination</u> questions from your opponents. Remember, the 1AC is your first chance to shine. Make sure you give the best first impression you can. If you fail to do this, you will face an uphill climb throughout the rest of the round.

The First Negative Constructive

The first negative constructive (1NC) is the negative team's opportunity to develop its own arguments and cast doubt upon the affirmative stance. The first negative speaker's job is to establish the negative strategy—to lay the foundation from which you and your partner will win the round. It is not your responsibility to win every argument or completely demolish the affirmative case. To successfully lay the foundation, there are several things you should keep in mind.

First, the 1NC should include all the negative positions you plan to run, or use, during the debate. Contrary to traditional conventions, I do not recommend saving big-picture arguments for the second negative constructive (2NC). The contemporary approach allows you to lay the foundation of the negative strategy while telling a cohesive story. Keep in mind that you do not have to fully develop all your arguments. Instead, <u>shell</u> out your major arguments in the 1NC. In other words, read the key ingredients that make up those arguments, ensuring that the judge understands the concept behind the argument, how the argument applies to the affirmative, and why she should want to vote on the argument. In addition, this approach gives you the flexibility to <u>kick</u> positions without wasting too much of your time, to develop your arguments from a slightly different perspective if need be (depending on the affirmative's answers), and to go into more depth on the arguments you are winning.

Think of it from this perspective. Some traditional coaches encourage debaters to save their <u>disadvantages</u> and plan attacks for the 2NC. The problem with this approach is threefold. First, if you spend two or three minutes developing the position in the 2NC and the affirmative's <u>front lines</u>, or first line of responses, are so good that you really have no chance of winning the argument, you have wasted a significant amount of your speech time and lack a fallback option. If, however, you spend one or two minutes in the 1NC painting broad brushstrokes on the position, the time lost is less severe because you still have the <u>negative block</u> to develop other positions.

Second, putting your offensive arguments in the 1NC allows you to hear the affirmative's initial round of responses early in the debate. In turn, this allows your team to spend three to eight minutes developing an offensive position in the negative block. Now you have an argument that has been fully developed, makes a lot of sense to the judge, and can be sold as the winning argument in the second negative rebuttal (2NR).

Third, the traditional approach leaves only two speeches for the negative team to develop its offensive, winning arguments. The negative is already at a disadvantage because the judge hears about the benefits of the affirmative case in every speech. If, however, you read your disadvantages, <u>counterplans</u>, <u>critiques/kritiks</u>, or other offensive weapons in the 1NC, you minimize that advantage. In this situation, the judge is immediately hearing why the plan is a bad idea and why it should, therefore, be rejected. While the emphasis is still slightly in the affirmative's favor, you are now on a much more level playing field. In addition, by running your <u>off-case</u> arguments in the 1NC, you can often cause the affirmative debaters to forget to place emphasis on their own case because they are so concerned with answering your offensive arguments. Thus, you have actually succeeded in placing the emphasis of the round on the arguments that explain why the plan should *not* be implemented, giving you a strategic advantage.

The second step in laying the foundation of the negative strategy is to mitigate harms and solvency as much as possible. This can be done by noting logical flaws in the case, making logical responses to the affirmative, and/ or reading evidence refuting the affirmative's case. This is where you focus on the negative strategies of answering harms and solvency as discussed in chapter 2.

In summary, by starting with your off-case arguments (topicality, disadvantages, counterplans, critiques/kritiks, and the like) and finishing up with on-case responses (harms, solvency, and so on) to the affirmative, you should effectively cast significant doubt upon the affirmative position and begin formulating a negative strategy.

Pre-round Preparation

1. *Create modular offensive arguments before the tournament.* Write topicality, disadvantage, counterplan, and kritik shells. Create shells that generically apply to the resolution. Generate topicality arguments on all or most of the words and phrases contained in the resolution. This allows you to pull the shells that apply to the particular affirmative case you are hitting.[5]

2. *Research between tournaments.* Conduct research against a variety of affirmative cases. Find specific disadvantage links to affirmative cases, harms and solvency mitigators/takeouts, topicality violations specific to a particular plan, and so forth.

3. *Engage in final steps preceding the round.* First, see if you can discover what the other team is running and prep answers to that case. Second, pull all of your major arguments before the round begins.[6] Third, pre-flow the shells you anticipate running.[7]

In-round Preparation

1. *Minimize prep time.* Pull the shells (or blocks) and case cards you want to read while the 1AC is speaking. Use your partner's three minutes of cross-examination as additional prep time.

2. *Take thirty seconds of prep time.* Scan the flow for hidden bombs, such as anything labeled an absolute voting issue or potential turns. Ensure your flows and evidence are in the order you need them for your speech.[8]

Organization

1. *Begin with procedural arguments.* You should almost always begin with topicality or any other argument you label an <u>a priori</u>—or rule of the game—issue.

2. *Proceed with substantive argument shells.* As a general rule of thumb you should spend 50–80 percent of the 1NC reading your off-case positions, since this is where the negative team usually generates its offensive arguments.

3. *Finish with on-case clash.* Always include some case debate, attacking the affirmative harms and solvency. Judges like clash. If you discuss only the negative's off-case positions, there is a tendency for it to look as though you are purposefully avoiding *debating* the affirmative. Furthermore, you end up resembling two ships passing in the night, completely unaware of each other.

Style and Delivery

1. *Diversity is key.* Maintain a cohesive story, but do not lock yourself into one line of reasoning. Your goal is to cast doubt upon the affirmative while giving yourself several options in the round.

2. *Fast or slow?* The 1NC should be as fast or as slow as both you and your critic can handle.

3. *Build a solid foundation.* Cast doubt upon the affirmative. Do not save anything new for the 2NC; shell out all of the negative positions. Save development of those positions for your partner's 2NC and your first negative rebuttal.

The Second Affirmative Constructive

The next speech, and perhaps the most pivotal for the affirmative, is the second affirmative constructive (2AC). The reasoning is simple. If the 2AC speaker answers a negative position incorrectly, the affirmative will most likely lose the round. If the 2AC undercovers a negative position, it will be very difficult to win the round. Therefore, the 2AC speaker must make the proper answers to each and every negative position while also leaving the 1AR multiple options. In the midst of all this, the 2AC speaker must also extend and enhance the judge's reasons to prefer the affirmative case so that by the end of the speech, the round is heavily in the affirmative's favor.[9] Finally, display a calm and confident attitude. If you show the judge that you are comfortable with your case and that you are confident it will outweigh the negative team's arguments, you may gain that extra advantage you need in order to win the ballot in a close round.

Pre-round Preparation

1. *Create front lines.* Brainstorm all the ways your case can be attacked, including topicality arguments, kritiks, counterplans, disadvantages, case side attacks, and so on. Then, make generic blocks for answering those arguments. Include a diversity of responses and approaches to answer variations of the same argument and have more responses than you have time to read in a single speech. This allows you to pick and choose the best responses for answering the specific position run by the negative, gives you the flexibility the first affirmative rebuttalist will need for her speech, and lets you spend as much or as little time as necessary to answer the argument at hand.[10]

2. *Organize your files.* Know them forward and backward so you can find the information you need when you need it.

3. *Power-word your evidence.* Underline the important portions of the card so that you do not read unnecessary or extraneous information.[11]

4. *Plan ahead.* Begin pulling files for the 2AC as soon as you learn the negative team's strategy. Discover their strategies by talking to these debaters or asking friends who debated them already, or simply pull the files responding to commonly run positions.

In-round Preparation

1. *Pull files immediately.* Pull front lines and write answers during the 1NC.

2. *Flow only the tags.* Do not waste your time flowing the body (or internal analysis)[12] of the 1NC's evidence. Listen to the evidence and write your corresponding answers on the flow.

3. *Prep during cross-examination.* Minimize the amount of formal prep before the 2AC.

4. *Look at the big picture.* Take a step back to examine all negative positions and determine which arguments are the most damaging to you. Focus your time and energy accordingly.

5. *Get organized.* Take thirty seconds of prep time to organize your thoughts; to get your flows, evidence, and front lines in order; and to make a final check to ensure you have not missed anything.[13]

Style and Delivery

1. *Be confident.* A winning 2AC speaker is persuasive yet avoids the tendency to orate. Sound confident and convincing (even when talking fast). A great 2AC speaker is intense, displays confidence, and loves what she does.

2. *Be fast.* Speak as quickly as both you and your judge can handle. Do not attempt to speak faster than you are capable or faster than your judge can flow. If your judge cannot keep up, your arguments—no matter how brilliant—are wasted. If you attempt to talk faster than either your mouth or your brain is able, you will only make it difficult for others to understand what you are saying. In many cases, attempting to speak faster than you are capable not only hinders your clarity but also slows you down as you begin to stammer, insert filler sounds, and double-suck for air.

3. *Be clear.* Everything should be clear: organization, signposting, delivery, and so on. As I have found in my experience in sitting behind judges in debates, many are often afraid to admit they cannot understand you. I have seen more than my fair share of judges with blank flows because the speaker slurred his or her words too much, yet the judge said nothing. When this happens, the decision is up for grabs regardless of how well either team debated.

4. *Be efficient.* If you are speaking at three hundred words a minute but one hundred of those words are extraneous, you have gained nothing.[14] Furthermore, if you are in a slow round talking at a conversational pace, you cannot afford to waste speech time. You must maximize word economy.

5. *Pause between positions.* When shifting from a topicality to a disadvantage or from Observation 1 to Observation 2, there should be a noticeable pause in your delivery (see the sample debate in chapter 14). Ensure the judge flips to the next flow sheet. Then dive into the meat of the next position.

6. *Turn, turn, turn.* Make responses that can win the round for you, not just mitigate the negative's positions. When dealing with disadvantages, attempt to turn the disadvantage into an affirmative advantage.[15] Even if your turn story is not a particularly strong argument, it is still in your interest to put it out there because it forces the negative on the defensive.

7. *Kick out of an advantage.* You give up a benefit of the plan, but free up time to answer more important arguments. If you are a slower team venturing onto the national circuit, creating an advantage that intentionally sucks 1NC speakers into a hefty case debate can be an incredible equalizer.[16]

Four Steps of Refutation

When responding to a specific negative position, there are four steps you can take to minimize confusion and ensure your arguments hold more weight in the judge's mind than your opponent's arguments do.[17]

1. *Identify where you are.* Repeat your opponent's tagline rather than just refer to the number assigned to that tag or to the author of the evidence. This is a precautionary measure that minimizes confusion in the event that you

accidentally numbered responses differently than the judge, the judge did not flow authors, or your opponents read multiple cards by the same author.[18]

2. *Signpost.* Always number and tag your responses. The number signals to the judge that you have something new to say. The tag serves as a one-sentence summary of the analysis that follows. It helps the judge understand where you are going. It also gives her a clear record of what you said as she jots it down on the flow.

3. *Identify weaknesses.* This creates a comparison between your analysis and your opponent's. Take it to the next level by explaining why your response is superior to your opponent's.

4. *Provide an <u>impact</u> to the argument.* Explain why the argument is important in the round or is not important in the round.

After the 2AC

1. *Compare flows.* Ensure you and your partner have all the 2AC speaker's responses on your flows.[19]

2. *Use the negative's prep.* Tell the first affirmative speaker which arguments are key in the round. For example, you should point out to your partner that "this disadvantage could kill us" or "this advantage is going to win the round for us." Identify one to three responses on each flow that are most important for the 1AR to extend.

The Negative Block: The Second Negative Constructive and the First Negative Rebuttal

Most people conceptualize the 2NC and the first negative rebuttal (1NR) as a single speech given by two speakers when they refer to it as the *negative block.* In fact, it is customary for the negative speakers to divide the material presented in the 1NC so that they do not overlap and needlessly repeat each other during this portion of the debate. The purpose of the negative block is simply to reestablish the negative team's strategic position in the round.

Your job is to remind the judge why she should reject the affirmative case; you do this by facilitating an in-depth discussion of the issues. The first portion of this step is simply answering the arguments made by the affirmative in response to each position. The second is to further develop the argument so that a complete story is told. The easiest way to accomplish this is to answer each of the 2AC's responses to the argument in order. Second affirmative speakers often include various responses on disadvantages such as, "No specific link," "No internal link," "No <u>brink</u>," "Show the <u>uniqueness</u>

on the internal link," "No scenario for the impact story," or "There is a leap of logic in the disadvantage's shell." These present great opportunities for you to demonstrate how good your argument actually is and that you are thinking critically. However, if you fail to answer any of these arguments in the negative block, they can become very persuasive rallying points for the affirmative later in the round.

When given these opportunities to develop the internal story of an argument, you can give two or three points for the answer and develop your argument more completely. For example, if the last 2AC response on a spending disadvantage was that there was no explanation of the scenario for war, I might respond with these tactics and points:

1. Extend the 1NC subpoint C: economic stagnation leads to war.
2. Economic stagnation causes turmoil within states.

(Read a piece of evidence stating such.)

3. As politicians seek to save their jobs, they begin looking for ways to either bolster their economy, protect their own economic resources, or divert public attention away from economic problems; this inevitably leads to interstate conflict.

(Read a piece of evidence stating such.)

Then depending on the speed of the round and the judging philosophy of my critic, I might read one final piece of evidence:

4. International conflict caused by economic turmoil leads to nuclear war.

In addition, each speaker in the negative block must ensure that the judge sees and understands each major argument before moving on to the next issue. Providing the internal analysis and further developing the argument will go a long way in accomplishing this step. Making these arguments in a logical manner helps you achieve that end.

After addressing the <u>line-by-line</u> debate on each major argument, take the time to summarize it. On topicality you might summarize your <u>standards</u>; on a disadvantage you might briefly reiterate the link story; on the affirmative case you might simply restate that the harms stated by the affirmative are minimal. Then, briefly explain some of the more important aspects of the argument.

Finally, make sure you explain why the issue is important. On a topicality argument, stress that topicality is a voting issue for reasons of fairness or education. On a disadvantage, reemphasize the impact of the disadvantage as compared with the advantages of the affirmative. <u>On case</u>, point out that since harms and/or solvency has been mitigated, the impact of the disadvantage outweighs the affirmative advantage. By taking ten to thirty seconds to summarize the argument in the negative block, you will make certain that the judge knows how the argument applies to the affirmative and why the argument is important.[20]

A brief impact comparison during the negative block will go far in helping the 2NR convince the judge to vote for the negative team. This gets the judge thinking along the same lines as you and shows her that you are thinking ahead. Working to incorporate these tactics into the negative block ensures that the negative accomplishes its goal of reestablishing the negative strategy and also gives the judge insight into where the debate round will end.

In-round Preparation

1. *Pull extension files early.* If you pre-flow your major negative positions before the tournament, the second negative speaker can retrieve the supporting evidence for those positions while the first negative speaker reads them.[21]

2. *Be ready to divide the block.* During the 2AC's prep time, decide who will take (or discuss) each of the major positions.

3. *Prepare during cross-examination of the 2AC.* Your partner's cross-examination of the second affirmative speaker provides three minutes of preparation time for the second negative speaker.

4. *Utilize hidden prep time.* Prepare responses for the 1NR while your partner takes prep time. As the 1NR speaker, you *do not need to listen to the 2NC*. Use the affirmative's cross-examination of the 2NC as prep. All told, the 1NR speaker has *at least* eleven minutes of prep time between the 2NC and cross-examination; therefore, the 1NR speaker should never need to take formal prep.

Organization and Delivery

1. *Be flexible.* Failure to adapt to the specific situation sets you up for failure. Debate the round that is happening, not the one you hoped would take place.

2. *Kick a position or two in the block.* Consolidate your strategy to the most important issues in the round.[22] Doing so frees up time for further developing the other positions in the round. Adding depth and clarity to your arguments is critical to making sure judges will vote on them. Just because you think you are winning everything does not mean you should try to win everything. The bottom line: do not let your ego interfere with your pursuit of better debating.

3. *Distribute the game winners between 2NC and 1NR.* Identify the two arguments that are most likely to win the round. Ensure the 2NC extends

one of those arguments and the 1NR extends the other. This increases your ability to double up on prep time to make certain that each speaker spends a significant amount of effort winning the most important issues. Better yet, identify the one argument that you believe will be *the game winner* and have the first negative speaker extend that issue. Why? The first negative speaker has lots of prep time to really think through the argument and ensure that all the 2AC's responses are answered and that the argument is further developed. It also gives the first affirmative speaker less time to prep responses to that position. Finally, it demonstrates teamwork for the judge when the second negative speaker collapses to the position run by his partner in the negative block.

4. *Give dynamic delivery.* Let everyone in the room know that you are in charge and that you are going to win the round. Let the judge see that you are not simply on the defensive. Show her that your arguments are important, that they have the ability to beat the affirmative, and that they will do so. Slow down when it matters most. Accelerate during the text of a card; slow down when you get to your own analysis or impact comparisons.

The First Affirmative Rebuttal

Now that the debaters of the negative block have successfully destroyed your case and made their off-case arguments into seemingly insurmountable obstacles between you and an affirmative ballot, it is up to the first affirmative speaker to rebuild the affirmative advocacy. The 1AR is quite possibly the most difficult speech to give in a debate round. Many debaters love it, hate it, look forward to it, and dread it simultaneously. The pressure is high partially because you are placed on the defensive and partially because you have only five minutes to respond to thirteen minutes of negative argumentation.

This requires the first affirmative rebuttalist to be incredibly smart and efficient. My high school long distance track coach, Larry Hurst, used to say, "Run smarter, not harder." In short, he cautioned us to be efficient, trust our training, and employ good strategy. The same applies to debaters, the first affirmative rebuttalist in particular. In short, *debate smarter, not faster; debate smarter, not harder.* If you debate intelligently, you can actually turn the tables rather quickly and leave the second negative rebuttalist scrambling to make up for lost ground. You may even spread the 2NR out of the round in the process, if you debate intelligently. Thus, your goal is to put the second negative rebuttalist back on the defensive. In order to do that, however, you must start preparing for the 1AR during (if not before) the 2AC.

In-round Preparation

1. *Choose which 2AC responses you want to extend.* You should mark the 2AC's best responses on your front lines. If you have done that before the tournament, you already know which arguments are the strongest and which ones you should pull through the 1AR.[23] You should never attempt to go point-for-point with the negative block; you will lose. There is simply too much information to cover in too little time. Prep responses for the most important items. Time permitting, make up additional responses on the fly during the 1AR.

2. *Be smart.* When you are in a time crunch, go only for the most important answers. This saves you time. And since you wrote them down during prep time, you should be able to rattle them off fairly quickly.[24]

3. *Prep when your opponents read new cards in the block.* If the second negative speaker during the 2NC or first negative rebuttalist during the 1NR reads a new impact story, don't bother flowing it; prep yourself to answer other parts of the argument.

4. *Do not plan to read evidence.* The last piece of evidence read in a round should be during the 1NR. It is extremely rare for the 1AR to need new evidence.

Style and Delivery

1. *Triage.* Put the most dangerous arguments at the beginning of the 1AR and the least dangerous at the end. This ensures that you have adequate coverage on the most important positions in the round. If you do happen to undercover the last position or two, it should have the least impact on the outcome of the round.

2. *Eliminate introductions.* You do not have the time, and it generally does not gain you that much ground with the judge.

3. *Use the 2AC structure.* Do not make up your own or try to follow a bad negative structure. Rather than deal with the issue holistically or follow the negative block's order, the 1AR should reference the 2AC #3 and the 2AC #5, for example. Identify those responses, highlight the negative's response, and then explain why the affirmative wins that part of the argument.

4. *Be fast and efficient.* The speed is relative to your judge and the round at hand and is only somewhat important. Efficiency is key. Minimize the use of extraneous words. This also refers back to making the arguments that count. Select the best 2AC responses and run with them.

5. *Know where to place new responses.* If you must make a new argument, put it near the 2AC response that justifies its existence. Try to limit yourself to extensions of the 2AC. This does not mean repeating the words of the 2AC. You have the flexibility in your speech to reword, rephrase, further develop, extrapolate analysis, and/or apply the original response to those made by the negative block.

6. *Avoid repetition.* You do not need to travel down an argument making the same no-link answer against every other negative response.

7. *Go for the jugular.* Do not allow the second negative rebuttalist the easy way out on arguments. Extending offensive responses puts him on the defensive. This minimizes his ability to tell a cohesive story in the final rebuttal.

The Second Negative Rebuttal

Finally, the last two speeches—the equivalent of football's game-winning drive in the fourth quarter. After more than an hour of debate, it comes down to two speeches to determine the outcome of the round. While no speaker can win the round alone, I believe it is the ability of the last two speakers to tell a cohesive story that determines how a judge will vote. This should not diminish the importance of the previous speeches. Without quality argumentation by both speakers early in the round, there would not be much hope of winning the judge's ballot. Nevertheless, the 2NR or second affirmative rebuttal (2AR) is your opportunity to make the final push and persuade the judge to vote for you and your partner. This is like having John Elway or Joe Montana on your football team in the final two minutes of the big game. It might have been a team effort to keep the game in close contention, but in the final two minutes, a coach wants one of them at the helm of the offense. In debate, you want a final rebuttalist who keeps calm, assesses the big picture, exploits the critical areas of arguments, and creates a persuasive picture of the round in the judge's mind.

Three Stages of the Second Negative Rebuttal

There are three parts to the 2NR: the overview, the line-by-line, and the underview. The best approach spends ten to fifteen seconds on the overview, close to four minutes on the line-by-line, and roughly forty-five seconds on the underview.[25] Ideally, the second negative rebuttalist spends those first few seconds simply explaining why the negative should win the debate, noting the one or two key negative positions. In doing so, he should attempt to make an "even if" comparison, meaning that "even if" the affirmative proved there was a harm and guaranteed solvency, the negative positions still hold enough weight to win the round. At its simplest, my 2NR overview sounded something like this:

> We win: two reasons. The Hegemony and Fiscal Tradeoff DAs outweigh the harms and potential solvency of the Aff. Even if they win case, the time frame and magnitude of the impacts on the DAs still justify a Neg ballot. Now, on the line-by-line . . . turn to the T flow.

The next step is to go through the line-by-line of the debate round. Kick positions first, and kick them as quickly as possible. Your aim as the second negative rebuttalist is to provide the judge with one or two major issues that beat the affirmative's case. Kick positions whose impacts will not outweigh case advantages, that were not clearly developed in the negative block, or do not seem to be persuading the judge to vote negative in the round. To a great extent, making this decision comes from experience—learning what works and what does not and gaining a feel for how the arguments in the round piece together to tell one overall story.

Once you have kicked positions that are not your game winners, the next step is to extend your responses to the affirmative case that will help you win the round. Ensure that you have a handful of persuasive case answers that question the harms story of the affirmative and/or the plan's ability to solve. Keep in mind that you can win a round completely on case argumentation if you have viable case turns against the affirmative's case/plan. If that occurs, then put those case flows in the third phase of the line-by-line debate.

Finally, finish strong with one or two negative positions that indicate that the affirmative represents a disadvantageous choice.[26] It is imperative that you respond to every answer the affirmative gave against your game-winning arguments. Ensure there is no way the affirmative can defeat your positions. Also, make sure you extend the key elements of the argument. Once you have responded to the affirmative answers, take a few seconds to summarize the position before moving on to your next argument.

To keep things simple, think of the line-by-line in this manner: first, eliminate the fluff in fifteen to thirty seconds. Then go defensive for thirty to sixty seconds, mitigating the affirmative case. Finally, go offensive for nearly three minutes. Finish strong with the argument or arguments that prove why voting for the affirmative or implementing the plan would be detrimental. It is important to conclude your line-by-line refutation with your strongest argument so as to leave its impression in the judge's mind at the end of your speech.

Once the overview and line-by-line are completed, you should have forty-five seconds of your speech remaining to devote to the underview. Use these last few seconds to write the judge's ballot for her. Explain the round in a nutshell. Point out the critical arguments and why they lead to a negative ballot. Impact comparisons are key in the 2NR. Make "even if" comparisons. Anticipate 2AR strategies and preempt them. Be a storyteller. In short, look at the big picture and talk to the judge, explaining that a negative ballot is the only possible ballot that can be cast in the round.

Style and Delivery

1. *Strategically vary the rate of delivery.* Savvy debaters, even on the national circuit, slow down as much as possible and focus on using persuasive speaking skills to drive points home to the judge. The overview should be moderately quick, giving a brief synopsis of the issues that matter most in the round. The meat of the speech—the line-by-line debate—should be as quick as it needs to be in order to thoroughly cover everything. At the end of each major argument, slow down slightly and give a five- to fifteen-second summary of the argument and why it is important. Then, pause slightly before moving on to the next major position. Finally, the conclusion should be clear, concise, persuasive, to the point, and relatively slow.

2. *Save time for the underview.* Use the last forty-five seconds to crystallize, to tell a story, and to win the round. At a minimum, with thirty seconds remaining in the speech, you should be finished debating the line-by-line. At that point, stop, take a breath, and explain why the negative won the debate. Use these final seconds to compare your offensive arguments with those of the affirmative and explain why yours are more relevant, realistic, and/or important. Above all, paint a clear picture of the round for the judge, a picture that consists of a negative ballot.

The Second Affirmative Rebuttal

This is it—the final speech of the round, the last chance to convince the judge to vote affirmative. Since the 2AR and 2NR have similar burdens, I will not expound too much on the 2AR. Just as with the 2NR, there are three parts to this speech. The overview should span ten to fifteen seconds, highlighting the major issues and setting the tone for an affirmative ballot. A typical 2AR overview might sound like this: "The DAs simply don't link.

The uniqueness and internal links are questionable. The clear-cut, concrete impacts on case and our solvency guarantee an Aff ballot."

The line-by-line should last nearly four minutes. It is imperative you answer every negative position and extend the most important portions of your own case. You do have the option to limit which of your own responses you extend. For example, the 1AR may have extended three major responses from the 2AC (with multiple subpoints to each response), but you need only one or two of those responses to win the argument.[27] In that case, you must answer every negative reply to the 1AR analysis on those one or two points. Make sure there is no doubt in the judge's mind that you win those two responses and that those responses defeat the negative position as a whole.

Finally, conclude with a forty-five-second wrap-up that focuses on the big picture and writes the ballot for your judge. This conclusion should be approached in the same way the second negative rebuttalist approached his final seconds. Make impact comparisons, summarize the key issues, and leave no doubt in the judge's mind that the only possible ballot is an affirmative one.

By now you should have a basic understanding of how the speeches fit together in a debate round. The first two speeches (1AC and 1NC) lay the foundation for each side's arguments and are heavily built upon quoted evidence. The next three speeches (2AC, 2NC, and 1NR) explode the discussion. They examine the intricacies of the arguments. In short, this is where the positions get developed with both quotations and analysis. Next, the 1AR starts to whittle the debate down by focusing only on the crucial portions of each argument. Finally, the last two speeches (2NR and 2AR) collapse the argumentation to only the key positions, focus on the most critical points within the arguments, and crystallize the round for the judge by comparing the relative importance of each argument. By following this format and using the tips mentioned in this chapter, you should be able to effectively debate your opponents and win your judge's ballot.

4. Judging Paradigms

There are three basic models that serve as <u>frameworks</u> for understanding academic debate. They determine how we, as debaters and judges, view the world through the <u>resolution</u>. Which model is used in a particular debate round is determined by the format, the era, the wording of the resolution, the competitive circuit, and the preferences of the debaters and judge. Within each model, there are multiple <u>paradigms</u>, each one providing a specific outlook of the world. The value model is predominantly associated with the Lincoln-Douglas format and turns our attention to the principles that drive our decision-making. The quasi–policy model is most closely tied to events like public forum and relies on broad generalizations of the topic. Finally, the policy model evaluates the resolution through a specific policy action established by the affirmative team. This plan becomes the driving force for evaluating the worth of the resolution. Within this model, judges hold unique perspectives, or paradigms, that color their understanding of the issues presented, the purpose of the activity, and the method of determining winners within a competitive framework.

The Stock Issues Paradigm

The <u>stock issues paradigm</u> is the oldest paradigm in competitive policy debate. It is the original. In this paradigm, the affirmative team must prove that its <u>case</u> meets all five of the <u>stock issues</u>: <u>significance</u>, <u>harms</u>, <u>inherency</u>, <u>topicality</u>, and <u>solvency</u>. Conversely, the negative team must prove only that the affirmative stance fails to meet any one of the stock issues. If the case fails to address a legitimate harm or a significant harm, the affirmative loses. If the case fails to demonstrate an inherent barrier, the affirmative loses. If the plan does not fall within the topical boundaries established by the resolution, the affirmative loses. If the plan fails to solve the problem, the affirmative loses. The catch for the negative in this paradigm is that mere mitigation often falls short of meeting the team's burden and that disadvantages, counterplans, and kritiks have no place in the debate round.

Mitigation fails because a critic utilizing this paradigm looks at each of the stock issues as separate and unrelated entities. Even if you mitigate solvency, the affirmative team has still shown that it helps alleviate a problem; never mind that you have also mitigated the harms story. Why? Because a harm still exists. Other arguments, such as disadvantages and counterplans, fail because they do not really fit into any of the five stock issues. That being said, you might convince your judge that one of those arguments does fall within the bounds of a stock issue. Perhaps you can persuade your judge that a disadvantage is actually an extension of harms or solvency.[1] Like everything else in debate, it boils down to your ability to believably and logically sell an argument to the judge.

The Policy Maker Paradigm

Next, the policy maker paradigm suggests that we view the debate round as policy makers might view a proposed bill. Simply, debaters use cost-benefit analysis to weigh the impacts, the pros and cons, or the good and bad of the particular case presented by the affirmative team. Depending on the arguments presented by the debaters, the analysis may center on how the policy will affect the judge, the people in the room, the United States, the world, the environment, or any number of different stakeholders. Which is more important depends on whether the competitors agree or on who can out-debate the other on that issue. Within this paradigm, there are two variations.

The Reasonable Policy Maker

The reasonable policy maker requires the affirmative case to meet all five stock issues out of the first affirmative constructive (1AC). If, by the end of the round, the negative team has shown that the plan does not solve the cited harm, the affirmative could still win the round if the plan is still deemed advantageous or there is no risk to voting affirmative. Therefore, if the negative debaters wants to win on stock issues, they must show that the affirmative did not adequately demonstrate one of the stock issues in the 1AC—for instance, he or she never explained what the <u>inherent barrier</u> was, or the plan did not meet the constraints established by the resolution (topicality).

Second, disadvantages and counterplans are acceptable to the reasonable policy maker as devices used in cost-benefit analysis. Absent a major oversight by the 1AC, the negative must use case <u>turns</u>, disadvantages, and/or counterplans in order to show a risk associated with the affirmative plan.

Finally, most reasonable policy makers listen only to real-world argumentation. In other words, <u>impacts</u> must be believable to the common layperson. For example, an affirmative plan that moves a significant number of U.S. military troops into Japan and South Korea may heighten tensions between the United States and China, leading to decreased economic engagement between the two nations, which in turn will hurt the long-term growth of the U.S. automobile industry. The impact is relatively small and believable. Depending on how developed this story is, how the affirmative attacks it, what the affirmative harms/solvency story is, and the negative attacks against the affirmative case itself, this may be enough for the negative to win the round with a reasonable policy maker.

In short, there are two ways for a negative team to win the round with a reasonable policy maker. First, show that the affirmative failed to uphold one of the stock issues in the 1AC. Second, show that we are better off under the <u>status quo</u> (because of the disadvantages associated with the plan) or a counterplan (because the plan prevents an alternate policy from being enacted that has more benefits than the affirmative plan).

The Modern Policy Maker

Although the modern policy maker still expects debaters to use cost-benefit analysis in determining the winner of a debate round, there are few similarities between the modern and reasonable policy maker. First, there are no supreme <u>voters</u> for the modern policy maker.[2] The debate comes down to cost-benefit analysis, pure and simple. Second, there are no constraints on the scale of the impacts. While the impacts must still be well thought out, logically explained, and supported by research, they do not have to be believable to the layperson. For example, an affirmative plan that moves a significant number of U.S. military troops into Japan and South Korea may scare China into thinking that we are beginning to act aggressively with respect to China's sovereignty claims over Taiwan and other areas under China's sphere of influence. Rather than wait for the inevitable confrontation, China launches a first-strike nuclear attack on the West Coast of the United States, wiping out Los Angeles, San Diego, San Francisco, and Seattle during the first attack.

As another example, an affirmative plan that mandates a complete U.S. conversion to renewable energy in five years results in two disadvantages. First, Middle East oil-producing nations immediately experience economic stagnation, since their economies are heavily reliant on the sale of oil. Oil prices plummet as supply severely overshadows demand. In an effort to gain a monopoly on this oil supply, those nations of the Middle East launch invasions against one another using chemical, biological, and nuclear weapons. Second, the United States is too heavily reliant on oil. Industries cannot make the change to renewable energy quickly, efficiently, or cheaply enough. As a result, the U.S. economy takes a nosedive into depression. The global economy is too interdependent and cannot handle the U.S. depression. The global economy, too, moves into depression. Nations eager to recover seek control over resources and markets; some even attempt to reinstate philosophies of expansionism, imperialism, and colonialism. Regional conflicts and wars ensue. As more nations are dragged into the fray, the global superpowers are forced into corners against one another, and World War III erupts.

As you can see, these impacts and impact stories are much larger than those used to persuade a reasonable policy maker to vote negative. As a result, they would also require much more in-depth development to explain how we get from point A (the affirmative plan) to point Z (nuclear war or World War III). The impact story is not necessarily as intuitive as those found under a reasonable policy maker mindset. Nevertheless, the game is the same for both reasonable and modern policy makers: prove that the benefits of the affirmative outweigh its disadvantages (or costs) and vice versa for the negative.

The Games Player Paradigm

The games player paradigm simply views debate as a game, one where the rules are established by the debaters and their judge. The possibilities are endless and allow you to evaluate the round from another perspective. You can change the speaker order, alter the speech times, limit the types of arguments that are permitted, work predetermined words into your speeches, challenge the traditional rules of debate, or make up some other rule. You can also make the debate itself a game. Whoever can read the most cards in the round wins. Whoever can do the most pushups wins. Play a game of chess. Play a game of poker. As long as you, your opponents, and your critic agree, you can establish the rules of the game however you wish.

Granted, this paradigm gets away from the traditional view and forms of debate, but it can definitely spice things up once in a while. It can allow you to do something new, particularly if you and your opponents have debated each other numerous times in the past and would just like to do something different for a change. Some judges may even let you incorporate some principles of the games paradigm into other, more traditional paradigms. For example, you may operate in the policy maker paradigm and agree that each debater must incorporate certain words into their speeches. If they do not, they lose.[3] If everyone succeeds, then the round is evaluated the same as any other policy maker round. In short, the games player perspective is very open-minded and allows the debaters to add some variety to their debate experience.

The Hypothesis Tester Paradigm

The hypothesis tester or hypo-tester paradigm views the resolution as a hypothesis that must be tested to determine its validity or truth. In this framework, the affirmative presents warrants (or examples) of the resolution and shows how they are true or beneficial. The negative, on the other hand, presents counterwarrants that show the resolutional statement to be false or detrimental.

The negative team should approach the resolution as a scientist approaches a hypothesis. A scientist has to show the hypothesis is false only once in order to disprove it. Much the same way, if the negative team can show that any one example of the resolution is false or harmful, then the resolution as a whole is flawed and should be discounted. In other words, if the affirmative team provides eight warrants for the resolution, the negative has two basic options. It can prove any one (or more) of those eight warrants harmful or false, or it can provide a counterwarrant to the resolution. Obviously, this places a tremendous burden on the affirmative.

Thus, the affirmative debaters should try to incorporate some games theory into the hypo-testing paradigm by arguing that they have to prove that only in most cases the resolution is true. Here, you start making a tally. For example, the affirmative provided six warrants for the resolution. In the end, four supported the resolution and two did not. The negative also provided three counterwarrants. One supported the resolution and two did not. Thus, the final tally is five support the resolution and four do not; the majority support the resolution and the affirmative wins.

This paradigm has numerous troubles. First, it can get rather messy. There can simply be too much on the table at any given time, preventing us from having a clear picture of the round. Second, how do you determine whether the negative has to prove the resolution false once or keep a tally? Do you view the resolution strictly the way a scientist views a hypothesis, or do you provide some fairness by incorporating "majority rules"? Third, the debate never develops. Debate rounds have precious little time to develop the arguments as it is. Under this paradigm, the debaters attempt to develop multiple plans, all with their own sets of costs and benefits. There is simply not enough time in a debate round to adequately address the issues intelligently under a hypo-tester paradigm.

The Tabula Rasa Paradigm

The last major paradigm is the tabula rasa paradigm (or simply "tab"). Literally, tabula rasa means "clean slate." It is defined as "a smoothed tablet; hence, figuratively, the mind in its earliest state, before receiving impressions from without."[4] A judge who presents himself or herself as a tab supposedly listens to anything and has no predisposed opinions. Thus, the debaters can run any type of argument or operate in any paradigm.

If the debaters do not agree on what paradigm to view the world through, then they must outdebate each other to establish the judge's paradigm. Furthermore, since the judge is a clean slate, even if the debaters choose to put the critic in a stock issues paradigm, they must tell the judge what the stock issues are and explain how they are used in the round. That being said, the debaters could even choose to create new stock issues or ignore the traditional ones such as topicality. With a tab, the boundaries of debate and the rules of the game are open to interpretation and argumentation. The direction, scope, and flow of the debate are entirely up to the four debaters competing in the round.

The Untrained or Lay Judge

Although the college circuit and the high school's national circuit utilize almost exclusively the types of judging paradigms described above, most debate at the high school level actually occurs in front of judges without any prior training in or experience with academic debate. They come from the ranks of parents, teachers, and community members recruited by the students of the host school. Although some of them may judge debates annually or have heard their children talk incessantly about the activity, they lack formal training or continued exposure to it.

Many debaters make the mistake of trying to force <u>lay judges</u> into a particular judging paradigm rather than simply communicating with them as they are when they enter the room. That is, national circuit debaters often attempt to run complex arguments such as topicality and kritiks in front of lay judges, then complain that they did not know how to evaluate the round. Many local circuit teams default to the stock issues with community members, then get upset that those judges did not understand the requirements of debate. In both scenarios, the debaters' inability to communicate effectively stems from the fact that they chose strategies that involved debating the rules of the game and usually included jargon-laced speech. Quite simply, coaches spend weeks, months, and years teaching debaters the intricacies of these strategies. Should we really expect a judge off the street to process the material and make a decision using those frameworks?

In the real world, we are all policy makers. Every day we are faced with any number of decisions. Should I stop for coffee on the way to school? Should I join the debate team? Should I blow off a quiz in order to spend time with friends? Should I get a haircut? Should I spend money to get organic products at the grocery store? Should I get an Apple or a PC? Should I plan to go to college or take a break from school? Our lives are full of policy decisions. Whether we think about them as policy debates or work through the decision-making process at the conscious level is irrelevant. Everyone is familiar with the idea of making a decision based on whether or not one will benefit from the action. Thus, debaters should treat lay judges as reasonable policy makers minus the stock issues burden placed on the 1AC.[5] The policy maker paradigm speaks directly to most people's instincts. As such, it is easy to explain the concept of voting for (or against) a plan based on whether it leads to more good than bad (or more bad than good).

Identifying Judges' Preferences

Understanding how judges view debates is only part of the equation. In addition, debaters need to know how to identify their likes and dislikes, preferences and tendencies, and outlook on debate. For those who compete nationally, there are multiple websites that host the paradigms uploaded by judges themselves.[6] Three of the most commonly used sites are the Judge-Philosophies wiki, Tabroom.com, and Planet Debate.[7]

There are three primary limitations to relying on these databases for background on your judges. First, you need to know who your judge is before the round and have access to the Internet in plenty of time to review his or her philosophy. Second, the lists are mostly limited to individuals who judge frequently at national-level competitions. Third, these sites require judges to know themselves well enough to self-reflect and articulate an accurate picture of how they view debates.

For example, at the 2014 high school national championship tournament, I sat on a panel with a judge who said, "I'm cool with anything. The debate is about you." That statement implied he was tabula rasa. However, at the end of the round, he gave an oral critique that told a very different story. He proceeded to tell the negative team—regarding almost every single argument—things like, "Kritiks really aren't very convincing arguments; you can't win that," "You won't get me to vote on that type of argument unless you . . . ," and so forth. In reality, he had a lot of preferences but did not communicate them clearly before the start of the round.

In the absence of an online judging philosophy, debaters can ask the judge for a paradigm, preferences, or likes and dislikes. As with the online examples, this requires the judge to know enough about himself or herself to give an accurate paradigm. In addition, you might not want to ask community members or lay judges what their judging philosophies are. In short, many of those judges are already apprehensive about judging. Asking them about their judging paradigm might trigger additional anxiety and probably will not help you adapt to them. As an alternative, you might try asking your friends and coach if they know who the judge is.

More importantly, observe your judge as he or she enters the room. Most judges will tell you a lot about themselves before they even sit down for the debate. Do they confidently walk to a desk and pull out <u>flow</u> paper and pens, or do they look tentatively into the room and ask if this is where the debate is supposed to be? Similarly, do they ask where they are supposed to sit? The judge who is confident probably attends tournaments frequently and can be approached about judging preferences. The one who seems unsure is likely attending his or her first tournament and should be treated as a lay judge. Once you receive that first impression, engage the judge in idle chitchat. You can learn significant information about judges in the minutes before a round starts simply by having a conversation with them. Lay judges will often share things like "My son has been debating for three years," "I judge this tournament every year," "My neighbor asked if I could help out this weekend," and the like. Every piece of information shared will give you some insight into how to communicate effectively with that particular judge.

Finally, keep notes on your judges if you expect to see them again in the future. Before and after the round, update your notes as you learn more about the judges. After the tournament, update them again as you read through the ballots. These records can enable you to adapt to judges at later tournaments. When I coached on the national circuit at Fort Walton Beach High School, I judged one particular team from Celebration High School four times between September and the state championship. Each time, both debaters grew, improved, and adapted. At the state championship, I listened to the second affirmative rebuttalist in the quarterfinal round and thought to myself, "I don't know how I would do that speech differently. He did exactly what I would have done if I were debating in this round." After it was over, I commented on how much I saw him and his teammate improve over the year and that I felt like he was speaking directly to me. He laughed and told me how his coach had him take pre-round and post-round notes on his judges. Before the round, he transcribed the judge's philosophy. After the round, he noted precise comments that reinforced or altered his understanding of the philosophy. In some cases, he said he found that judges' post-round critiques actually conflicted with their pre-round philosophies. After debating in front of me at three previous tournaments, his notes on me were pretty detailed. Thus, he was able to adapt his approach to me, even using language I had used during critiques at other tournaments. In essence, he *was* speaking directly to me.

Policy debates can be viewed through several paradigms, each offering a unique perspective on the activity. Nevertheless, most debates default to the policy maker framework and incorporate ideas from the other paradigms. Partially, the policy maker framework is generic enough to allow flexibility. Who is to say what goes on in a policy maker's head? The framework can always change and adapt. Perhaps traditional values have a role in a policy framework. Perhaps we need the education afforded by altering the rules slightly to account for the other paradigms. Whatever the case, a basic understanding of these models and paradigms should help you frame your arguments by providing a little direction or helping define the parameters of the round.

5. The Affirmative Case

Before the competitive season begins, you must write an affirmative case.[1] Begin the process by brainstorming the topic and discussing possible ideas with your debate partner, teammates, and coach. Those on high school teams that primarily compete in the local area should pick an affirmative you personally find interesting and can locate adequate research on and that would make sense to the majority of lay people in the surrounding area who will make up the preponderance of your judges throughout the year. Those in high school programs that regularly compete on the national circuit and college debaters should put together two or three affirmative cases the entire team can run. This allows squads to pool research efforts so you can provide much more in-depth analysis.[2] Once you have determined what your case will be and have conducted research, the next step is organizing the evidence into a coherent picture and writing your affirmative case, otherwise known as the first affirmative <u>constructive</u> (1AC). Various structures for crafting the affirmative case can aid your ability to use it as a persuasive storytelling device for the judge sitting at the back of the room.

General Themes

Before delving into the specifics of organizing the affirmative case, there are several terms debaters should know. The first is a theoretical viewpoint held by most debaters: *operationalization*. This term is generally used as a verb (operationalize) and is synonymous with parameterize, conceptualize, and contextualize. Essentially, all these terms refer to the idea that the affirmative team's plan becomes the sole example of the <u>resolution</u> after the

1AC. This provides the affirmative with one major advantage: the affirmative does not have to defend all <u>topical</u> cases. Instead, it has to support only its example of the resolution.[3]

Another term you may hear is that the affirmative has the *burden of proof*. This means the affirmative team must show that its case minimally meets all five of the <u>stock issues</u> during the 1AC. If its case and plan do not appear to meet all five stock issues out of the 1AC, the negative team has ample ground to argue that it should win the round automatically since the affirmative failed to meet its <u>prima facie</u> burdens.[4]

Finally, the game of policy debate hinges on the concept of <u>fiat</u>. Fiat gives the affirmative team the power to implement its plan.[5] In other words, we assume that upon completion of the round (assuming an affirmative ballot is awarded), the judge's signature acts as the passage of a bill into law. Since the resolution usually states that the U.S. federal government should do something, fiat allows us to debate why it should pass a plan rather than whether it would or could actually pass through the legislature. Thus, the affirmative can overcome political barriers and discuss the pros and cons of the plan by taking the debate beyond nitpicky arguments such as "Who will vote for the affirmative and who will not?" or "Prove that Congress will approve your plan."

There are limits to fiat, however. First, it encompasses only topical actions. Second, it does not remove the repercussions of passing the plan; thus, the affirmative team cannot wish away <u>disadvantages</u> that stem from the effects of the plan's passage. Finally, fiat does not cover individual members of government. Therefore, a disadvantage that says the proposed plan will cause a political backlash led by Senator X cannot be answered with "The affirmative fiats that Senator X will like our plan." Fiat ensures only that the plan will receive the necessary votes to be signed into law.

Assembling the First Affirmative Constructive

There are a number of ways the affirmative team can organize research in order to tell a compelling story to the critic, demonstrate the five stock issues, and tailor the round so as to encourage a particular <u>paradigm</u>. I will discuss the more common types of affirmative cases. Of those, the first two structures (need-plan and comparative advantage) are by far the most common. The third and fourth (goals and criteria) are generally combined (into a goals-criteria structure).

While there are additional structures, such as the alternate justification and the hypothetical, they are so rare that they are not worth exploring. I mention them because it is important for debaters to remember that the ways in which they construct their case are limited only by their imaginations and the content of their cases. When confronted with unusual case structures, negative teams should take a step back, look at the big picture, and see if there are any flaws in the case construction. In the development of the new case structure or use of a unique format, the affirmative debaters may have overlooked one of the stock issues or otherwise opened themselves to <u>theory</u>-based arguments.

The Need-Plan Case

The most useful type of case for novice debaters is the need-plan case since it offers the most straightforward case structure. This type of case has relatively few "moving parts," is designed by stepping the 1AC through each of the five stock issues, and attempts to minimize the introduction of more advanced debate theory.[6] In essence, the need-plan begins by showing there is an inherent problem in the <u>status quo</u>, offers a solution (or plan), and then concludes with analysis on how the plan will solve the problem.

Contention 1: Show there is an inherent harm in the status quo.

    A. Harms

    B. Inherency

Contention 2: State any additional harms or inherency. Alternately, Contention 1 could be harms and significance, while Contention 2 could be inherency.

Plan text

Contention 3: Solvency—the plan solves the cited harms.

Figure 5.1. Example of the need-plan affirmative case structure

The Comparative Advantage Case

The comparative advantage case structure is probably the most common in contemporary policy debate circles. This structure automatically caters to the <u>policy maker paradigm</u>, which, as discussed in chapter 4, is the most common judging paradigm. Much like the need-plan, the comparative advantage begins by noting an inherent <u>harm</u> in the status quo and then offers a plan to solve or at least minimize that harm. Next, the case must demonstrate that the plan reduces the harm found in the status quo. Unlike the need-plan, however, the comparative advantage case may demonstrate additional benefits, or advantages, that go beyond the scope of the resolution.[7]

Observation 1: Inherency

Plan text

Observation 2: The affirmative plan overcomes the inherent barrier.

Advantage 1: The affirmative plan solves a resolutional harm.

    A. Harm/Significance directly related to the resolution

    B. Solvency

Advantage 2: The affirmative plan offers additional advantages.

    A. Significance of the advantage (Demonstrate another resolutional

    or "nonresolutional" harm.)

    B. Uniqueness (Demonstrate why it is important to act now.)

    C. Solvency (Demonstrate how plan solves this additional harm.)

Advantage 3: Repeat the steps of advantage 1 and 2 as needed; you may

    have one or several additional advantages.

Figure 5.2. Example of the comparative advantage affirmative case structure

The Goals Case

As noted earlier, the need-plan and comparative advantage case structures are by far the most common in today's academic debate world. However, there are other ways of constructing the 1AC that may better suit your purposes in the debate round. The goals case identifies a goal that the United States (or other actor as identified by the resolution) should try to attain.

Generally, debaters select a preestablished goal the government has not been able to meet. Or you might identify a new goal of your own choosing and argue that the government should seek to attain that end. The next step is to identify why that goal is important through the use of harms and signif-icance. Then you should propose a plan that will either achieve or move us in the direction of the stated goal. Finally, the 1AC concludes with solvency evidence, proving the affirmative plan will meet the goal.

Observation 1: Identify the goal

Observation 2: Inherency (Show how the status quo fails to meet the goal.)

Observation 3: Harms/Significance (Demonstrate why that failure is detrimental.)

Plan text

Observation 4: Solvency (Prove the affirmative plan will meet the goal.)

Figure 5.3. Example of the goals affirmative case structure

The Criteria Case

The criteria case provides a list of standards for dealing with a particular problem identified in the status quo. In short, the affirmative team selects an issue within the resolution that should be dealt with and resolved. Then, the debaters provide a series of criteria, each of which must be met in order to adequately address the issue or harm in the status quo.[8] The affirmative then provides a plan to meet the criteria. In the solvency observations, the affirma-tive demonstrates how the plan meets the criteria and, thus, solves the harm.

Observation 1: Identify a problem in the status quo.

Observation 2: Establish criteria for judging the round.

Plan text

Observation 3: Show plan meets the criteria and solves the cited problem.

Figure 5.4. Example of the criteria affirmative case structure

The Goals-Criteria Case

In my opinion, a pure criteria case lacks development and is not very useful. An alternative is to combine the previous two structures through the use of a goals-criteria case. With this structure, the affirmative identifies a goal and then provides a set of criteria to determine whether or not that goal has been fulfilled.[9] The basic format of this case structure may be modified for value debates but can also be quite useful for teams wishing to uphold a value while still discussing actual policy options. In addition, my debaters have found this structure to be effective when running critical affirmatives on very traditional circuits.[10] In other words, by crafting progressive debate strategies around easily digested and familiar frameworks, debaters can sell their ideas to the most traditional of judges.

Observation 1: State the affirmative goal.

    A. Goal/principle/value to be upheld

    B. Criteria

Observation 2: The status quo fails to attain the goal.

    A. Inherency

    B. Harms/Significance

Plan text

Observation 3: Solvency (The affirmative plan meets the goal.)

Figure 5.5. Example of the goals-criteria affirmative case structure

Tips for Writing the First Affirmative Constructive

After determining the type of case to build and ensuring all five stock issues are met in the 1AC, there are several ideas affirmative debaters can utilize to strengthen their position out of the 1AC and foster a more effective second affirmative constructive (2AC). First, we must address how to construct the various observations and pieces within the 1AC. Earlier in this work, I discussed the basics of constructing harms/significance, <u>inherency</u>, and solvency stories for the 1AC. But, what should the plan text look like? In the plan, the 1AC lays out the affirmative's solution to the inherent harm of the status quo. The affirmative team generally wants to identify who will administer the plan, delineate the type of actions, and express some sort of enforcement mechanism. It is not necessary for the affirmative to spell out exactly how the plan will be implemented, who specifically will carry out the action, or any of the minute/specific actions that make up the theory behind the plan.

In short, academic policy debate is concerned with the discussion of concepts, ideas, and theories, not the field-level actions that will occur as a result of passing the plan. Teams debate the overarching ideas or concepts and determine the overall merit of those ideas but do not involve themselves with the specifics for a number of reasons. Primarily, there is no conceivable way the debate could clearly examine all facets of the action in less than two hours. Even in Congress, lawmakers do not consider that level of detail even when they have weeks or months or years to revisit the issue.

It would be unrealistic to expect debaters to answer every level of detail. To use a traditional debate term, such demands are *not real-world*. Just as legislators do not work out or answer every minute detail, neither do debaters. Everything is imperfect. No one can ever work through all the politics or all the potential problems. The important thing is that we have a good idea that can alleviate a problem. Over time, the wrinkles can be ironed out and the specifics can be addressed. Simply, the field experts can handle that during the implementation phase of the plan.[11]

Second, power-word the 1AC. Go through all the evidence and underline/boldface the portions you intend to read. Generally, there is a significant amount of information within the text of the evidence that is superfluous and can be left out of the speech. Power-wording your evidence allows you to accomplish two things: the elimination of extraneous information that could confuse the audience and the freeing up of speech time to present more evidence, more arguments, and/or more depth of analysis in favor of your case.

Third, think forward. Anticipate arguments your opponents may run against your case and include evidence to spike (or preempt) those arguments. Then, when your opponents run the argument, the 2AC can cross-apply the evidence from the 1AC as a response. This enables the 2AC either to read additional counterevidence, to spend extra time explaining the evidence and why it takes out the negative argument, or simply to provide another, different response.

Finally, revise your case as the season wears on. After a tournament or two, you may find weak areas of your case or disadvantages to which your plan is particularly susceptible. Treat your case as a living entity and allow it to grow throughout the season. If necessary, modify the plan text to avoid disadvantage <u>links</u> or topicality arguments. Insert <u>cards</u> to refute shortcomings in the case or to spike common arguments against it. Or, replace cards that you later realize have gaping holes or inconsistencies. You may even just come across better cards that you want to include in the 1AC. The overall point is to make the 1AC as strong as possible and set the stage for an affirmative ballot.

This chapter primarily examined ways to organize the 1AC. Each of the case structures presented is somewhat tailored for a particular model of the resolution or judging paradigm. For example, the need-plan sets the stage for a stock issues paradigm or possibly a policy maker. The comparative advantage screams policy maker, while the goals-criteria generally implies a value model of the resolution. In short, you should tailor your case construct to either the predominant judging philosophy in your area or the paradigm you want the judge to use.[12] Remember, it is also possible to combine many of these structures to fit your particular needs or those of the case you have chosen to run. In the end, as with most debate, you are limited only by your own creativity. As such, consider both new and old ideas when constructing the 1AC.

6. Disadvantages

The previous discussion of specific arguments (the <u>stock issues</u> and the affirmative <u>case</u>) predominantly dealt with the affirmative side of the <u>resolution</u>. In examining the fundamentals of the affirmative case, we explored possible negative responses to the affirmative. With the exception of <u>topicality</u> and case <u>turns</u>, however, those negative arguments have been defensive in nature, leaving the advantage to the affirmative. In the next three chapters we will discuss the major offensive weapons at the negative team's disposal. This chapter, in particular, deals with the tool that quite possibly forms the crux of the negative strategy within the context of a <u>policy maker paradigm</u>: <u>disadvantages</u> (or disads or DAs). Disads, as the name implies, attempt to show that the affirmative plan actually brings about more harm than good. Generally speaking, they explore the unintended consequences of implementing a particular course of action. In order to effectively run or defend against a disadvantage, debaters must be familiar with the types of disadvantages as well as have a working understanding of the many pieces that make up a well-developed DA.

Types of Disadvantages

Typical Disadvantage

Essentially, there are four types of disadvantages: typical disads, perception DAs, movements DAs, and complex DAs.[1] The first, your everyday, typical, garden-variety disadvantage, simply states that if the affirmative takes action X, it will cause impact Y. As with any disad, there are three parts to this type of disadvantage: <u>link</u>, <u>brink</u>, and <u>impact</u>. The link explains how the argument applies to the affirmative. The brink, or in some cases the <u>uniqueness</u>, indicates that the disadvantage is on the verge of happening in the <u>status quo</u>, but for the moment we are situated safely at the precipice. The impact identifies the specific harm associated with the disadvantage. Thus, the link-brink-impact chain explains how the affirmative case pushes us over the edge and causes the bad thing we wish to avoid. For example, a negative team might run a spending disadvantage against an affirmative that mandates a 100 percent switch to renewable energy to provide all our electrical needs. The link shows that the affirmative policy requires government spending to achieve the switch due to research and development as well as for implementation. The negative debaters could thus quantify the amount of spending required to implement the affirmative plan. Next, they might indicate the United States is currently in a steady state of spending. The budget is balanced. Finally, they could argue that spending is bad.[2] As you can see, this type of disadvantage is very simple and straightforward.

Perception Disadvantage

Ultimately all disadvantages follow the same pattern as the one described above. However, some disads incorporate other elements that may make them more complicated but also tell a more coherent or compelling story. In essence, the perception-based disad argues that an individual, group, or foreign government will perceive the action taken by the affirmative plan in a negative light and will therefore react in a negative way to the plan's passage. The group's response may be the impact of the disadvantage, or the response may trigger something else to happen that causes the impact. For example, a common perception disadvantage is the Business Confidence DA. This disadvantage says businesses perceive certain governmental regulations as detrimental to their future. Thus, they will become alarmed about the future of their industry and will decrease investment in the economy in order to protect themselves. This pullout creates a self-fulfilling prophecy, causing a downturn in the economy that leads to a depression in the United States, followed by global depression and (of course) global thermonuclear war.[3] The key to this disadvantage is the perceptions of the businesses. The affirmative debaters could argue until they are blue in the face that the regulations they are imposing are actually beneficial for businesses. The reality of the matter—according to the negative team—is that businesses will perceive the regulations as detrimental and will therefore react to protect themselves.

Movements Disadvantage

A movements disadvantage says that certain (usually social) movements are mobilizing around a particular issue. Incidentally, that issue is the one the affirmative team hopes to solve. When discussing the impact of the DA, the negative team must show that the movement would have solved the affirmative <u>harm</u> better than the affirmative plan or that the movement would have solved additional or alternative—more severe—problems than the affirmative plan would have.

For example, the Environmental Movements DA has been a recurring staple on the policy debate circuit. This disadvantage says that people are becoming increasingly aware of environmental problems and are taking action to address those harms, whether they be starting highway cleanup initiatives, purchasing fuel-efficient vehicles, recycling, or making energy-efficient upgrades to their homes. In short, an awareness is growing at the individual and local levels about the need for sustainability, and people are changing their behaviors accordingly. However, the affirmative plan represents a government action designed to solve one of the central issues of this movement: ratifying a treaty on climate change, instituting a cap-and-trade system for carbon dioxide emissions, cleaning up local waterways, or similar policy. The problem, according to the negative team, is that the plan is merely one solution for one problem imposed from the top down. Ultimately, it erodes the sense of urgency among individuals—who in the long term have a deeper impact on a wider range of environmental issues—at the grassroots and local levels to make everyday changes. The idea is simple. The affirmative solves only one aspect of the larger problem, which effectively shuts down (or slows) the movement that would have solved the problem in its entirety.

Complex Disadvantage

The final type of disadvantage incorporates elements of the disads discussed previously. For example, the negative may choose to run a perception-based movements disad where the perception of <u>solvency</u> effectively shuts down the movement. In the previous Environmental Movements DA example, the federal government stepped in to act on a specific environmental problem. As a perception-based movements disad, the negative team could argue that the affirmative plan fails to solve the problem because the government action achieves an insufficient amount of change to truly fix the problem; however, the action taken in the plan will convince many that the government is solving the problem, so they no longer need to focus on that issue.

Therefore, many people will abandon the movement. Again, the impact is that the stalled grassroots movement would have led to a more significant reduction in wasteful practices and long-term habitual changes that are more sustainable.

The four types of disadvantages described above (typical, perception, movements, and complex) should address 99 percent of the disadvantages you encounter during an entire debate career. The rest of this chapter focuses on the intricacies of the disadvantage by examining some of the key terms and elements as they are applied to the three parts of a disad: link, brink, and impact.

The Essential Elements of a Disadvantage

Link Analysis

The foundation of every disadvantage is the link. This portion of the disadvantage explains how the DA applies to the affirmative's case. In other words, the link explains what the affirmative does to trigger the chain of events leading to the negative impact of the disadvantage. In example, on the 1995–96 Cross Examination Debate Association topic,[4] the U.S. Air Force Academy ran a disadvantage titled the China South-South Strategy. We argued that if the affirmative plan improved relations between the United States and Mexico, it would disrupt China's development of a south-south strategy.[5] At the time, China was explicitly developing this strategy as a means to increase its own economic power, counter such regional agreements as NAFTA and the European Union, build political and military ties with other developing nations, and assert itself as a legitimate global power. If the affirmative plan was implemented and relations between the United States and Mexico were enhanced, China would feel threatened by U.S. influence in the "south," perceiving the United States' actions as intentionally disruptive to its strategic plan. This, in turn, would disrupt our growing cooperative stance with China on myriad international issues. Taken together, U.S.-China cooperation on global issues far outweighed the advantages from a single U.S. policy with Mexico. In this example, the initial link out of the first negative <u>constructive</u> (1NC) was "The affirmative policy increases relations with Mexico."

Typically, disad <u>shells</u> are constructed by reading a *generic link*, or one that applies to virtually any topical affirmative plan. For example, our DA shell on the China disadvantage indicated that "changing our foreign policy results in improved relations with Mexico." Obviously, this link could be utilized to show that virtually any affirmative plan on the topic would link to the disadvantage.

However, the disadvantage would be even stronger with a *specific link* to the affirmative. This version of the link illustrates how the particular plan chosen by the affirmative triggers the disadvantage. For example, if the affirmative ran a case to solve the multi-drug-resistant tuberculosis (MDRTB) problem along the U.S.-Mexico border, the negative might read specific link evidence during the <u>negative block</u> that "solving the MDRTB problem in Mexico improves political and social ties with Mexico." Obviously, this is a much stronger link as it both demonstrates that this affirmative plan causes the disad and explains how the case improves relations with Mexico. In some rounds, the affirmative solvency or advantage evidence may have even indicated that the plan results in increased relations between the two nations. In those instances, we cross-applied the specific <u>card</u> in the first affirmative constructive (1AC) to the disad as a specific link during the negative block.[6]

Once the negative debaters demonstrate the link, they may need to show an *internal link* or several internal links. Very rarely does the affirmative plan directly cause a negative consequence. Therefore, the internal link steps us logically from the initial link to the actual impact of the disad. In the China DA mentioned above, the specific link demonstrated that the plan increased U.S.-Mexico relations. An internal link explained that warming relations between the United States and Mexico disrupted China's developing south-south strategy. A second internal link showed that this disruption made China feel threatened that it would lose its growing status, authority, and power in world affairs. As a result, its leaders would take an adversarial rather than a cooperative approach with the United States.

It may be helpful to think of the link chain as an actual chain connecting the plan to the negative impact. Every link and internal link must be present to prove the argument. If any of those links are missing, broken, or questionable, then the entire chain is, in fact, broken.[7] As such, the negative team will want to research the argument fully to ensure that it can articulate with evidence and/or analysis every internal step in the disadvantage.

Brink Analysis

Next, the disadvantage must be unique to the affirmative plan in relation to the status quo. With uniqueness evidence, the negative shows that, but for the affirmative plan, the impacts of the DA would not come to fruition.[8] In other words, if we stick with the status quo, the disad will not occur. In the previous China DA, the negative team must show that relations between

Mexico and the United States are low, tenuous, sketchy, or nonexistent. In addition, it needs to show that China is developing its south-south strategy and that its focus is on enhancing relations with Mexico.

Closely related to uniqueness is the disad's brink. This portion of the DA says that now is the key time for the disadvantage to occur and so now is the key time to avoid or cause the disad. In other words, we are on the edge of the cliff, and with one misstep we will fall to our doom. Yesterday we may not have been at the edge. By tomorrow our path could move away from the precipice and we might be safe once again. But today our well-being is in jeopardy.

In the China example, the negative team may indicate that a combination of factors makes today a turning point in the south-south strategy. Previously, the strategy was in the theoretical stages of development, and China was building power and influence. Today, China is confident that its strategy can succeed and in its own power but is fearful that the United States will seek to tear down the strategy by moving into the key region: Mexico. In a few months, the south-south alliance will be so strong that our actions will not affect the Chinese strategy. By demonstrating this, the negative can argue that past actions in Mexico (or future predictions) are irrelevant to the disad, because now is the key time. We are currently on the brink. In addition, strong brink analysis can make the disadvantage's story more reasonable to the judge.

In some cases, however, disadvantages are linear and do not require uniqueness and brink analysis. This type of disad simply says the more you do something, the more influence you have and the more harm you can cause. For example, let us assume that you are on a strict diet calling for exactly two thousand calories per day. Once you have consumed two thousand calories, every additional calorie has negative consequences for your health. One additional calorie has minor consequences, fifty additional calories have more harm, one thousand extra calories make a significant impact, and so on.[9] Thus, the larger the affirmative case, the greater the negative consequence associated with the disadvantage. Obviously, the China example would not work as a linear disad. It is true that the more the plan increases relations between the United States and Mexico, the more displaced China feels as a result of the plan. However, the DA still requires that China does not feel too threatened in the status quo (uniqueness) and that as a result of plan action the Chinese government will reach a breaking point (brink) where it feels it necessary to cease cooperating with the United States on other issues.

Impact Analysis

The final piece of any disadvantage is the impact. The impact is the harm caused by the plan by way of the associated link and internal link(s). Put simply, the impact is the entire reason the disad should be avoided and a negative ballot should be awarded. As a result, the impact is probably the most important part of the DA because it allows the negative team to compare a negative consequence to the advantage of the affirmative plan. As for the China South-South Strategy DA, the initial impact in the 1NC shell was that China and the United States were beginning to cooperate on a number of environmental, economic, and social issues, each with their own unique consequences when ignored.

Often times, a 1NC disad shell uses a generic impact of war, disease, economic depression, racism, or any number of harms. Often, teams provide an *impact scenario*. Rather than discuss international cooperation, they might show that China would retaliate by asserting itself by way of invading Taiwan. In the negative block, this scenario could be further developed with additional internal links. Once China invaded Taiwan and established a military presence there, Japan would feel threatened by Chinese aggression and would take military action itself. Then, the United States—feeling concerned about losing two major economic partners and a major political ally—would enter the fray. As soon as this happened, China would seek to crush American resolve by launching one or two nuclear missiles toward America's West Coast. Rather than destroy U.S. morale, this would unite America behind a nuclear strike of its own; thus, the impact on the China DA by the end of the negative block could indicate that the affirmative plan would spark a global nuclear war.

Finally, the negative team should seek to make *time frame comparisons* between the impact of the disadvantage and the attainment of solvency by the affirmative. Let us compare the China South-South Strategy DA and the Taiwan impact scenario to a plan designed to prevent global warming. On the impact level, both stories can be apocalyptic, with global warming arguably holding the edge. According to the negative team, the affirmative's plan leads to a global nuclear war with China; according to the affirmative team, its plan avoids global extinction brought about by global warming. As temperatures rise, natural habitats change, weather patterns alter, and oceanic temperatures increase. These alterations increase in severity until species begin to disappear. Eventually, the food chain collapses and all life will perish.

Upon closer examination, however, the China DA poses a more immediate threat. With the appropriate evidence and analysis, the negative could demonstrate that the affirmative could spark war in Taiwan within weeks or months. Furthermore, the war would quickly escalate until millions, or even billions, of people were killed by a nuclear exchange between China and the United States, not to mention the long-term implications of nuclear fallout.

Conversely, it will take twenty to fifty years before we begin to witness dramatic climate change and its associated impacts. It would take many more years after that before the food chain actually collapsed. Meanwhile, our society continually evolves and new technology is constantly developed. These changes could potentially slow the warming process, enable adaptation, or solve the problem altogether. As a result, the negative could win a negative ballot by showing that the China South-South DA poses a more immediate threat than global warming.

Looking at the entire chain of events, notice the similarities between an affirmative case and a disadvantage. Both require a change (a link) based on the affirmative plan. Both require uniqueness. The plan is not being done now (inherency), and nothing else is triggering the disadvantage (uniqueness). Both rely on internal steps or internal links to reach the impact, benefit, and/or harm. In reality, constructing a disadvantage and developing an affirmative case are not all that different in their design.

Writing the Disadvantage

By now you should have a decent understanding of the disadvantage's elements, from the initial link to the impact analysis. But how do you actually construct the DA shell to be read in the 1NC? What must be included in the shell? To put it simply, the 1NC should tell a reasonable story without trying to address all the intricacies and particulars of the argument. Typically, this means reading three to five cards per disadvantage in the 1NC. Usually, the 1NC provides a generic link, brink or uniqueness evidence, and a generic (relatively small or extremely broad) impact. In some instances it may be necessary to provide an internal link, and very rarely the 1NC may choose to develop the impact story.

Essentially, the 1NC presents a coherent narrative that appears believable without investing so much time that the position becomes a liability. For instance, if the top story (including link, brink, uniqueness, and internal links) is developed over the course of several minutes in the 1NC, you may feel as though you cannot kick the argument in the negative block or second

Saudi Oil DA (1NC Shell)

1) High prices preserve Saudi stability, reducing civil unrest

MAUGERI '03   (Maugeri, Leonardo. "Time to Debunk Mythical Links Between Oil and Politics." Oil & Gas Journal, 15 December 2003, np)

Countries such as Saudi Arabia have doubled their population in 12 years. **Sixty percent** of the gulf countries' population **is less than 21 years old. This** demographic explosion **has created expectations and frustrations to which stagnant and monocultural economies cannot give a credible answer. Only sustained oil revenues allow these countries to temper social unrest by preserving huge social assistance programs**. Gulf countries' oil revenues are already much lower today than 20 years ago, and **cheap oil prices mean a dramatic dip in per capita oil income**. Therefore, frustration and **violent revolt may erupt whenever the minimum needs** for living **are endangered by decreasing oil prices, particularly among people who already live in poverty** and cannot permit themselves the luxury of hoping for a different future.

2) US energy restrictions drive oil prices through the floor, ensuring Saudi collapse

ROBERTS '04   (Roberts, Paul. *The End of Oil: On the Edge of a Perilous New World*. Boston: Houghton Mifflin, 2004, 323)

Because the United States **is so large a market for world energy** products, **a U.S. energy revolution would function as a catalyst** in the transformation of the global energy economy, initiating a "domino effect" in energy that could ultimately change everything from emissions and energy use in the developing world to our oil-dominated geopolitical order. **The last time the United States got** really **serious about** energy **efficiency** — after the 1974 oil price shocks — **U.S. oil use fell so low that OPEC was nearly wiped out. A more permanent reduction** — **even if** partly **offset by rising demand in** the fast-growing **Asian economie**s — **would completely change the global oil order. As oil prices fell** — to as low as fifteen dollars a barrel, some analysts say — **many big oil states would see their geopolitical status tumble. Some**, like Russia, Venezuela, Iran, and Qatar, which have enormous gas reserves, could compensate by stepping up efforts to sell gas, especially to gas-hungry markets like China, India, and the United States. Other petrostates — like Mexico and Algeria, for instance — **might be pushed into bankruptcy** and would then require a massive, and inevitably United States—led, bailout. **Falling oil prices would also splinter OPEC. As Saudi Arabia, Kuwait, the United Arab Emirates, and Nigeria** all **tried to compensate for lower prices by boosting oil production**, analysts say **the** inevitable **glut would drive prices down** further. Oil **revenues would fall so sharply that many OPEC countries would suffer profound civil unrest**. Some analysts believe **unstable countries like Saudi Arabia would collapse.**

3) Decline in oil revenue threatens strife, civil war, and ethnic conflict ← Impact

MCKILLOP '04   (McKillop, Andrew. "A Counterintuitive Notion: Economic Growth Bolstered by High Oil Prices, Strong Oil Demand." *Oil & Gas Journal*, 19 April 2004, np.)

Higher revenues for many low-income oil exporter countries—notably for the special cases of Nigeria, Saudi Arabia, and especially Iraq—**may be the only short-term way to stop these countries from falling into civil strife, insurrection, or ethnic war, let alone making vast investments to maintain or expand their current export capacity**.

Figure 6.1. Example of the disadvantage 1NC shell

negative <u>rebuttal</u> because of the amount of time you invested in the position. In other words, avoid putting all your eggs in one basket. Also, if you develop the impact story extremely well, the affirmative could put you in a bad place by proving the disadvantage <u>non-unique</u> and link turning the argument. Thus, the shell should be kept relatively short and tell a reasonable story.

When writing your own DAs, keep in mind that traditional and perception disadvantages generally provide the link evidence first, then the brink, and finally the impact, whereas movements DAs generally proceed with uniqueness, link, and impact. However, every disad is different and may require a modified structure in order to tell a logical story in the 1NC. As a result, you must sit back and analyze for yourself how to best organize the disadvantage so it makes the most sense to your audience. By logically presenting the disadvantage in the 1NC, you position yourself effectively for later speeches.

Affirmative Responses

As the affirmative team, you need to beat only one critical piece of the disadvantage to completely take the argument out of the decision-making calculus. For example, if the disad does not link, then it becomes irrelevant; if the impact is disproved, then it really does not matter whether you trigger the chain of events found in the DA's top story. If the status quo is triggering the DA, then it is non-unique, meaning the disadvantage will also be triggered by the status quo. Nevertheless, the second affirmative constructive (2AC) speaker should attack the position on multiple levels. Then, the first affirmative rebuttalist can narrow those down to the strongest arguments and/or the ones mishandled in the negative block. Finally, the second affirmative rebuttalist should devote time to the two to four most effective responses in that particular round.

Uniqueness Responses

Essentially, there are four types of responses to disadvantages: uniqueness answers, link responses, impact answers, and turns. The most intuitive uniqueness response is that the DA is non-unique. With this argument, the affirmative shows that the disad's story has already occurred or is going to occur in the status quo regardless of whether the plan is passed. This type of argument can serve one of two purposes for the affirmative.

First, a non-unique response can empirically deny the disadvantage. If the affirmative demonstrates that something in the status quo should have already caused the DA to occur, then the link story or impacts have been empirically denied, and there is no risk of the DA if we implement the affirmative policy. On the China South-South Strategy DA, for example, the affirmative team may show that the United States took action toward Mexico two weeks ago that improved relations between the two countries. Another response may be that U.S.-Mexico relations are at an all-time high. Either way, the DA should have already occurred. Since it did not, the DA is empirically denied.

Second, the affirmative could make the disadvantage irrelevant with a non-uniqueness answer. With this tactic, the affirmative proves the DA is going to happen due to a recent or future action in the status quo. Thus, no harm results from the passage of the plan. For example, the affirmative might read evidence indicating that the United States is already taking action to clean up hazardous waste spills in Mexico. If the premise of the disad is true, the status quo is actually going to disrupt China's south-south strategy, whether the 1AC's plan is implemented or not. In short, the DA cannot happen twice. If the disadvantage will occur regardless of whether or not the plan will be passed, policy makers might as well take this opportunity to do something beneficial.

When responding to the uniqueness of a disadvantage, keep in mind that all the individual pieces must be unique. That means the link, the internal link(s), and even the impact(s) must be unique. If the negative fails to demonstrate or defend uniqueness—at any level—you can use that to your advantage by mitigating or denying the disadvantage. If you can prove the DA is non-unique—at any level—you succeed in breaking a vital piece of the argument, and the position no longer holds any weight in the round.

The affirmative may also respond to the DA's brink analysis. The primary method of refuting the brink is to demonstrate that there is *no brink*. Here, the affirmative strategy simply disproves that *now* is the key time for the DA to occur. Essentially, affirmatives could tell one of two stories. On the one hand, they could argue that we are already *post-brink*. This means that the key time for the DA's story has come and gone. In other words, we were walking along the edge of a cliff, but we have now moved on to flat and stable ground. Returning to the China South-South Strategy DA, affirmative teams might show that China has already made so much progress on its strategy that there is nothing we could do to disrupt it. On the other hand, the affirmative team might simply argue that we are too far away from the edge of the cliff—or brink—to make any difference.

A second response to brink analysis is to argue that the *link outstrips the brink*. Here, the affirmative explains that the link provided by the negative is so great, or so all-encompassing, that any minor policy would trigger the DA. Then, the affirmative shows that some minor policy or policy similar to the affirmative plan that occurred in the status quo should have caused the DA. Since the DA has not already happened, the story told by the negative is empirically denied.

Third, the affirmative could argue that the disad lacks a *threshold*. In essence, a threshold describes how large the affirmative plan has to be before the chain of events described in the DA actually kicks in. In other words, it is a description of how much action must be taken to push us over the edge of the cliff. In a debate round, the negative might say something like, "*No threshold*: There is no indication that implementing a MDRTB control program along the U.S.-Mexico border would improve relations with Mexico enough to disrupt China's south-south strategy."

Out of the responses named above, only a pure non-uniqueness or post-brink evidence/analysis is likely to completely take out a negative team's disadvantage. However, a combination of the above responses, and others, can prove useful in convincing the judge that the benefits of the affirmative plan outweigh the potential risk of the mitigated disadvantage.

Link Responses

In any debate, one should remember there are multiple ways to beat an opponent's arguments. Eliminating the uniqueness of a disadvantage is just one way an affirmative team can beat a DA. A second option is to attack the link analysis. As with uniqueness, this can be accomplished in a number of ways.

The strongest responses are those completely taking out the link story of the disadvantage via a *no link* response. One way of doing this is to show that the DA's link does not apply to the affirmative case. Recalling the China South-South Strategy DA, we remember the link story is based upon the United States improving its relations with Mexico. That is, China is looking to extend its south-south vision into Mexico but will feel that strategy is in jeopardy if the United States increases its ties with Mexico. Thus, the affirmative might claim the link does not apply because it never increases political contact between the two nations. If relations are not improved between the United States and Mexico, then China's strategy will not be disrupted.

In addition, the affirmative could argue there is no link because the link story is simply untrue. For example, they might show that in the modern world, international politics is not viewed as a zero-sum game. An increase in political ties between two nations does not result in decreased relations between the other two. Thus, increased ties between the United States and Mexico do not necessarily lead to decreased relations between Mexico and China.

A variation on the concept of a no link response is that of *no specific link*. Here, the affirmative team explains that while the negative team provides a generic link on the DA, it fails to show how the specific action taken by the plan triggers the disadvantage. Thus, the affirmative debaters could claim that theirs may be the one example of a topical case that does not trigger the disad. In and of itself, this response will not beat a disadvantage. However, making it in conjunction with other responses may cast enough doubt upon the DA that the judge will not vote on it.

Another example of a link response is *no quantification of the link*. With this response, the affirmative highlights the fact that there is no explanation of how big the plan has to be in order to link to the disadvantage. In other words, there is no indication that the plan will increase relations with Mexico enough to cause China to feel its south-south strategy has been compromised. Astute observers will note that this response uses the same analysis as a no threshold response but comes at the issue from a slightly different angle.[10]

No perception of the link is yet another variation on link responses. This argument is useful against disads that require another agent to respond to the actions described in the plan text. For example, the China South-South Strategy DA is actually based on China's perception that the United States will crowd it out of Mexico by increasing diplomatic ties between the two North American nations via the plan. Assuming the affirmative ran the tuberculosis case described earlier, the affirmative might respond to the disad by saying there will be no perception of the link. Since the affirmative case deals with a health care problem along the U.S.-Mexico border, China will perceive the action to be a nonthreatening domestic policy.

Finally, the affirmative could take out the internal link(s) of a disadvantage. Most disadvantages have multiple steps to carry us from the link to the impact. For example, the Taiwan scenario on the China DA relies on multiple internal links: a Chinese takeover of Taiwan, a military buildup by Japan, and an increased U.S. military presence in the region, to name just a few internal steps. The affirmative might argue that there is *no internal link* for the takeover of Taiwan. They might argue that the annexation of Taiwan would occur peacefully or that Japanese militarization will not occur. If the affirmative can break the link chain at any point, the disadvantage no longer serves as a reason to reject the plan.

Impact Responses

In addition to attacking the uniqueness, brink, link, and internal links, the affirmative may attack the impact of the position. This is very similar to answering an affirmative team's harms story. Debaters might *diminish* or *deny* the impact of the DA. Typically, debaters diminish the importance of the DA with the use of *impact mitigators*. Simply, you point out that the impact of the DA is not as large as the negative team makes it out to be.

Often, this can be accomplished by merely listening to the evidence read by the negative team. For instance, many teams read evidence with <u>tags</u> along the lines of "Conflict in the Middle East leads to nuclear war." However, the actual evidence makes ill-defined, open-ended statements similar to this: "In a world with nuclear weapons this makes the stakes of such a proposition very high." Nowhere does the evidence say nuclear weapons will actually be used, nor does it give a scenario explaining who would use their weapons or on whom they would use them. In fact, it never even says a war will occur. Furthermore, many teams extrapolate from this evidence that nuclear war will cause human extinction or global destruction. I wonder, has anyone stopped and thought about the fact that the world has actually survived a nuclear war—World War II, anyone?[11] Granted, at that time the United States was the only nation with "the bomb," but it is the negative's burden to demonstrate the claim of its tag by indicating that the ensuing war would actually involve nuclear weapons and that the use of them would be global rather than localized in nature. Furthermore, a war impact does not necessarily end in millions, or even thousands, of lives lost. Since the disadvantage does not occur in a vacuum, you must necessarily compare the risk of those impacts against the benefits of implementing the affirmative plan.

Second, the affirmative could deny the impact of the disadvantage with an *impact takeout*. For example, it may claim that a war will never occur between China and the United States because the leaders of the two nations view each other's economic importance as too significant to sacrifice over other, *trivial* matters. Similarly, the affirmative could argue that a Chinese invasion of Taiwan does not necessarily mean that something bad would occur. Many invasions and transfers of government have taken place without bloodshed.

Third, the affirmative might point out that the negative team failed to quantify its impact. This response indicates that we have no idea how large the impact of the DA will be; therefore, the specificity of the affirmative harms story and solvency should be preferred. This line of thought can play out quantitatively or qualitatively. Referring back to the China disadvantage, the affirmative could note that there is *no quantification of the impact.* In other words, the negative failed to show what cooperative agreements would be reached in the status quo, what specific impacts would occur if those agreements were not reached, and so forth. All of these uncertainties put doubt into the theory of the disadvantage. With enough uncertainty, the judge may not be compelled to vote for the negative team.[12]

Finally, the affirmative could make a *time frame comparison* between the impacts of the disadvantage and those found in the 1AC. This concept should be self-explanatory at this point. Ultimately, this type of response is best if you can read specific evidence that highlights the potential time frames of the two impacts being compared. Nevertheless, you may be able to make logical time frame comparisons using your own knowledge of the subject matter.

Turns

The final and strongest affirmative responses to disadvantages are known as turns. Strategically, turns are significant because the affirmative has essentially turned the negative disadvantage into a new affirmative advantage. Tactically, turns are equally significant because they force the negative to spend time extending the disadvantage in the negative block. For example, if the 2AC speaker spends all of his or her speech time making uniqueness, link, and impact responses, the negative team could simply stand up, grant those responses, and spend the entire negative block discussing one of its better or stronger disadvantages. However, if the 2AC has turned that disadvantage into an affirmative advantage, then the negative team must spend time explaining how the affirmative plan fails to turn the disadvantage, how the turn has uniqueness problems, how there is no internal link getting from plan action to the turn, how the impact of the turned disadvantage is insignificant, and so on. In other words, a turn on a disadvantage puts the negative on the defensive, and the team must then respond to the argument as though there is a disadvantage being run on the status quo by the affirmative team.

LINK TURNS. How do turns work in a debate round? There are two basic ways the affirmative can turn a disadvantage: at the link level or at the impact level. As the name denotes, a link turn actually turns the link of the DA. In other words, rather than triggering the disadvantage, the affirmative plan prevents the disadvantage's impacts from occurring. Referring back to the previous MDRTB 1AC, the affirmative could show that China currently has advisers stationed in the Mexican government's health care agency. Those officials have jointly requested U.S. assistance in addressing MDRTB along the U.S.-Mexico border. Thus, the affirmative plan actually opens a conduit for dialogue with the Chinese government, improving our relations.

Similarly, the affirmative may argue that by solving a potentially disastrous health care problem, relations between the United States and China and between China and Mexico would actually improve. In other words, an MDRTB outbreak has the potential to disrupt China's economic plans in Central America. In the long run, such an outbreak would devastate the region, thus preventing any real benefits from increased relations with nations in the Americas. Thus, China will actually perceive the United States' actions as beneficial to its long-term gains and will be grateful for the policy's implementation.

There are two observations worth making at this point. First, this strategy is effective only if the affirmative has shown that the DA is non-unique. That is, you must demonstrate that the disadvantage was going to occur in the status quo in order for you to prevent it from happening. If you fail to achieve this critical piece, then your link turn will function only as a link takeout, since you cannot prevent something from happening that was not going to happen anyway. In other words, if war with China was not going to happen in the status quo, then you cannot prevent a war with China from happening.

Second, as the affirmative you do not have to limit your link turns to the direct link of the disadvantage. You may find that you can turn one of the internal links of the argument. In the south-south strategy example, one of the internal links of the disadvantage dealt with China's response to a lack of respect from international leaders. Given the current emphasis among world leaders on the importance of cooperation, the affirmative could demonstrate that improving relations with Mexico actually improves China's legitimacy in the world by enabling world leaders to see China and the United States working effectively alongside one another in Mexico. Therefore, the plan prevents an invasion of Taiwan that was going to occur in the status quo because China was at a point where it believed the only way to gain international legitimacy was to assert its authority over Taiwan. Thankfully, the plan offered China an alternative route to gaining international legitimacy.

IMPACT TURNS. Instead of pursuing link turns, however, the affirmative might argue that the impact of the disadvantage is actually a good thing by making an impact turn. This is accomplished in the exact same manner as turning an affirmative's harms story. Refer to chapter 2 to see an example of an impact turn related to a global warming harms story.

While impact turns can be an extremely useful tool for affirmative teams, they are generally harder to come by than link turns. That is, teams generally choose their DA impacts for a reason—they usually describe things that most people typically consider to be bad (war, loss of life, and so forth). As such, finding either the evidence that indicates the impact is a good thing or the judge who will buy into it can be difficult.

Despite these obstacles, link and impact turns provide affirmative teams with huge strategic and tactical advantages in debate rounds. Nevertheless, I give you one word of caution: beware of the double turn!

DOUBLE TURNS. A double turn occurs when the affirmative both link-turns and impact-turns the same disadvantage. Doing so results in a negative win on the DA. Again, let us consider the China South-South Strategy DA. First, the affirmative link turns China by saying, "We actually decrease relations with Mexico; therefore, we prevent any disruption of the south-south strategy and a subsequent invasion of Taiwan." Later, the team goes on to explain that a Chinese invasion of Taiwan would be bloodless and would actually be a good thing because it would lead to the rise of another global superpower. In turn, we would be faced with the international stability of a bipolar world, which is far superior to the anarchic world of today. The second story functions as an impact turn to the disadvantage.

In this situation, the negative simply grants both turns. Such a story in the negative block might look something like this:

Go to the 2AC #2 where they argue they decrease U.S.-Mexico relations. Grant the link turn; the plan severely disrupts relations between our two countries. Now, go to the 2AC #6 and #7 where they take out the immediate impact by showing that a Chinese invasion would be bloodless, then prove that a Chinese takeover of Taiwan sets up a bipolar world. Grant this analysis as well as the evidence indicating that a bipolar world has an inherent stabilizing effect, thus preventing the escalation of minor conflicts into bigger wars. We concede both turns, making the DA an undeniable reason to vote negative, especially since the stabilizing effect of the bipolar world also solves the war scenario found in the affirmative harms story. Last, do not allow the 1AR to contest the turns or any internal links on the DA; these would be new arguments in rebuttals and are not allowed.[13]

In a nutshell, a disadvantage is the unintended consequence of passing the affirmative plan. Although the affirmative debaters may seek a positive advantage, they will actually trigger a harmful sequence of events. Constructing a disadvantage is really not that much different than writing an affirmative case. Likewise, the same types of answers a debater uses to answer harms, inherency, and solvency can be used to answer the impacts, uniqueness/brink, and link/internal link. Although there is the risk of an affirmative turn on this type of argument, disadvantages generally provide the judge a reason to reject the affirmative's policy proposal. The stronger the disadvantage—with a clear link to the affirmative case, demonstration of a brink and/or uniqueness, and a concrete impact scenario—the more likely it is that a negative team can persuade the judge that the preservation of the status quo is desirable to the course of action outlined in the affirmative plan.

7. Counterplans

While <u>disadvantages</u> serve as the bread and butter for most negative teams operating within a <u>policy maker paradigm</u>, debaters on the negative may hope to show the judge there is an alternative policy option that is superior to the one put forth by the affirmative team. That alternative policy option is known as the <u>counterplan</u> (or CP). Typically, they agree that the <u>status quo</u> is flawed, and therefore refuse to support it. Instead, they offer the counterplan as an alternative policy advocacy to both the plan and the status quo.

The Role of the Counterplan

The role of the CP has changed over time and varies from judge to judge and debater to debater. As originally conceived, the CP presented an opportunity cost of voting for the affirmative.[1] In other words, the negative argued that by choosing to implement the affirmative plan, policy makers lose the opportunity to embrace a different solution to the affirmative's <u>harms</u> story. In time, debaters began thinking of the CP simply as a competing policy option for the judge to choose at the end of the round. Thus, they started to see the argument as a forced choice between the plan proposed by the affirmative and the plan proposed by the negative. Regardless of whether the CP is viewed as an opportunity cost or a competing policy option, debaters may choose to run one in debate rounds for any number of reasons. Six of the most common purposes or types of counterplans are advantage-reducing CPs (ARCs), uniqueness-generating CPs, alternative agent CPs, ban CPs, exclusionary CPs, and test of the topic CPs.[2]

Advantage-Reducing Counterplans

The ARC attempts to reduce the relative benefit gained by the affirmative so that the <u>impacts</u> of the negative team's disadvantages outweigh the benefits of the plan. The counterplan does this by solving part or all of the harms cited by the affirmative. It may also engage in time frame comparisons, showing that while the CP does not completely solve the affirmative harms, it solves much of the harm more quickly than the plan. In and of itself, this would not win the debate since the plan would still be the superior option. However, if the negative team wins one of its disadvantages, then it might outweigh the benefits of the affirmative case.

When is this strategy effective? One of the most likely instances occurs when the impacts of the affirmative <u>case</u> are simply bigger than the impact scenarios of the disadvantages. Perhaps the generic disadvantages, or DAs, on the current topic are relatively weak. Perhaps the negative team primarily competes on a small local circuit where the disadvantages must be closely tied to the plan text or <u>resolution</u>, whereas the affirmative competes on the national circuit, where large impacts rule the day. In either case, the negative may need an ARC to level the playing field with the affirmative.

Uniqueness-Generating Counterplans

Another counterplan specifically designed to aid the negative's persuasiveness with disadvantages is the uniqueness-generating counterplan. Here, the negative debaters run the CP because they know one or more of their disadvantages have <u>uniqueness</u> problems.[3] In other words, the negative believes the status quo is likely triggering the disadvantage, will trigger the disadvantage sometime in the future, or is simply too tenuous to predict at the moment. Thus, the negative runs a counterplan, which does not <u>link</u> to the DA, to make the uniqueness debate irrelevant. Since the negative team no longer advocates for or defends the status quo, it does not matter whether the present system triggers the disadvantage. The negative has shifted advocacy to the counterplan; thus, the judge evaluates only a world in which the plan exists versus a world in which the counterplan exists. As such, the affirmative plan uniquely links to the disadvantage.

For example, the negative debaters may run a Federalism Disadvantage on a resolution dealing with domestic policy. They argue that it is important to maintain a clear division between the states and the federal or national government. At the link level, they attempt to show that the action proposed by the plan is something generally reserved for the states.

They may enter the debate knowing that current events bring into question whether or not we truly protect state powers. Thus, they may choose to run a counterplan that implements the affirmative plan through state governments rather than through the U.S. federal government.[4] Or, they may have the Supreme Court rule that state powers should be upheld on a variety of cases. In either situation, they generate uniqueness for the DA by moving us away from national action toward actions taken by the states, thus making the disadvantage more relevant to the debate and, consequently, the judge's ballot.

Alternative Agent Counterplans

Some teams use an alternate agent of action[5] in their counterplan as a way of getting the benefits of the affirmative while avoiding the link to a disadvantage or to get around a solvency takeout. Typically, one of two scenarios leads to this strategy. Either the negative team has a disadvantage link to the specific actor identified in the plan text, or it has some pretty solid evidence indicating that the actor identified in the plan cannot effectively administer the action. In either case, the negative uses that evidence in the disadvantage or in the case (solvency) debate. Then, it identifies an alternate actor that either avoids the link or gets around the solvency deficit.

The alternate actor can take many forms, including other domestic agencies, state governments, other national governments, intergovernmental organizations, and nongovernmental organizations. The possible agents of action are as limitless as your imagination. Some of the most common alternate agent counterplans include these:

Executive Order CPs. When the affirmative uses the legislative process to implement a plan, the negative responds with a Politics Disadvantage, which indicates that presidential lobbying of Congress or even the legislative process alone will derail some other important piece of legislation. Finally, the negative runs an Executive Order CP to capture the affirmative's advantages but avoids linking to the Politics Disadvantage.[6]

States CPs. The negative argues that states are more effective at solving the problems identified by the resolution and/or the affirmative case. Typically, it attempts to win by showing that states have superior solvency and by running a Federalism Disadvantage.

Supra-agent CPs. If the resolution deals with a specific region of the world such as Africa, then the African Union might be a preferred agent of action. If the resolution deals with the security of one or more nations in the West, perhaps the North Atlantic Treaty Organization is a superior actor. Similarly, counterplans could implement the plan through the United Nations, the World Health Organization, the World Trade Organization, the Association of Southeast Asian Nations, and so on.

STATES CP

1. THE NEGATIVE OFFERS THE FOLLOWING COUNTERPLAN:
Each of the 50 states, the District of Columbia, and all relevant territories will adopt the affirmative proposal in cooperation with one another.

2. Federal government rolling back authority to states now; transportation dollars are crucial to federalism and better spent by states. The plan undermines ingenuity found at the local level.

MCGUIGAN '11   (Patrick B., Capitol Editor, "Transportation Federalism – and flexibility – proposed in new bill from Coburn, Lankford," Tulsa Today, July 29, http://www.tulsatoday.com/2011/07/29/joomla-2768/)

Joel Kintsel, executive vice president at OCPA, told CapitolBeatOK, "I am so proud of the leadership shown by Senator Coburn and Congressman Lankford. Hopefully, **this is the beginning of a broader effort by Congress to return to federalism and withdraw from areas of activity rightfully belonging to the States."**

Sen. McCain, the 2008 Republican nominee for president, said, "As a Federalist, I have long advocated that **states should retain the right to keep the revenue from gas taxes paid by drivers** in their own state. This bill would allow for this to happen and prevent Arizonans from returning their hard earned money to Washington. Arizonans have always received 95 cents or less for every dollar they pay federal gas taxes. This continues to be unacceptable, and for that reason I am a proud supporter of the State Highway Flexibility Act."

Sen. Vitter asserted, "**It's very apparent how badly Congress can mismanage tax dollars, especially the Highway Trust fund which has needed to be bailed out three times since 2008. The states know their transportation needs better than Congress, so let's put them in the driver's seat to manage their own gas tax."**

Hatch contended, "**The federal government's one-size-fits all transportation policies and mandates are wasting billions of taxpayer dollars and causing inexcusable delays** in the construction of highways, bridges and roads in Utah and across the nation.

Sen. Cornyn said the Lone Star State can manage public transportation spending just fine, and the bill, "will **provide** Texas **more flexibility to make transportation decisions locally and encourage innovative solutions to addressing our transportation infrastructure needs.**

Kintsel, whose areas of focus for OCPA include constitutional and other legal policy issues, said, "**Federalism is an indispensable check and balance between the States and the federal government and remains an important feature of our constitutional system. Unless it is a power expressly reserved by the Constitution to the federal government, Congress should not attempt to control the decisions of individual states. The more local decision making is eroded by an overbearing national government, the less freedom and ingenuity survives in states and local communities.** In this instance, Oklahoma leaders will know how to use these transportation dollars far more efficiently than anyone outside of Oklahoma.

Figure 7.1. Example of the counterplan 1NC shell

Replacement nation CPs. The negative identifies another nation to
carry out the affirmative plan. Perhaps China or Australia is better
positioned to carry out the plan than the United States. Like supra-
agent CPs, these counterplans tend to arise on international topics.

Ultimately, the decision to run an alternate agent counterplan is a strategic choice designed to achieve better solvency than the affirmative plan
or to avoid a disadvantage while still solving a portion or all of the affirmative harm.

Ban Counterplans

While an alternate agent CP tests the value of the actor identified by the
affirmative team, the ban counterplan tests the specific solvency mechanism it selected. In this instance, the negative questions the choices made
by the affirmative when determining what to implement. For example, if
the affirmative harnessed tidal power and ocean thermal energy conversion
on an oceans topics, the negative might choose to advocate a counterplan
that bans the use of ocean-based energy systems while simultaneously
promoting the use of solar, wind, and geothermal power to meet our energy demands.

Negative debaters most likely opt for this sort of counterplan when they
are concerned that the affirmative's advantages are too large to outweigh
(global climate change, low-level air pollution, peak oil crisis, national security entanglements, and so on). Thus, like the affirmative, they want to
transition away from an oil-based economy. In addition, they likely have
case evidence providing links to disadvantages or case turns. In this scenario, they might have links to disadvantages stemming from ocean energy
production, solvency mitigators regarding the effectiveness of harnessing or
transmitting energy from ocean sources, or environmental turns on tidal
power and ocean thermal energy conversion.

The biggest problem with this sort of counterplan is that it generally fails
to demonstrate that it is an opportunity cost of passing the affirmative plan.
Further, it is not really a competing policy option. Case in point: land-based
and ocean-based energy plants can coexist; there is nothing inherent in
the counterplan that makes it competitive with the affirmative. Rather, it
is merely *artificially competitive* because of the inclusion of the portion of
the counterplan text that bans the affirmative. Nevertheless, teams often
use ban counterplans effectively with policy maker judges to show that the
affirmative failed to craft the best policy option.

Exclusionary Counterplans

Like the ban counterplan, the exclusionary CP can resolve a problem found in the affirmative's plan text, but it can also test the plan for <u>extra-topical violations</u>. With this CP, the negative simply leaves out a portion of the affirmative plan, advocating for something only slightly different from what its opponents advocated. As stated, this likely plays out in one of two ways: to offer a plan that is actually better than the affirmative's or to test for abuse on a <u>topicality</u> argument.

In the first scenario, the negative team identifies an action in the plan that it deems harmful or bad. On an energy related topic, for example, the affirmative may choose to propose a plan using a wide array of renewable energy resources: wind power, solar power, hydroelectric power, geothermal power, tidal power, and ocean thermal energy conversion. The negative may have excellent disadvantage links, environmental turns, and social dislocation turns on hydroelectric power. Thus, it offers a counterplan that proposes using wind, solar, geothermal, tidal, and ocean thermal power. Therefore, it claims all of the affirmative's advantages minus the turns and disadvantage related to hydroelectric power. Ultimately, this counterplan shows that the affirmative choices were flawed rather than disproves the resolution statement.[7]

In the second scenario, the negative identifies a portion of the plan that is extra-topical, meaning a portion of the plan goes beyond the scope of the resolution. Perhaps the affirmative spiked a spending disadvantage by including a funding plank in the plan. Or it included an action beyond the resolution that provides the main advantage to the affirmative case. In other words, the harms solved by the affirmative are relatively small; however, the team included an extra-topical action that averts a war, promotes U.S. hegemony, or something similar. For instance, I have seen a number of plans on domestic topics where the affirmative team included a plank about sharing the new technology developed by the plan with the world in order to achieve global solvency and an American hegemony or leadership advantage. Then, it focused most of its efforts on developing that advantage.

When faced with this situation, the negative runs its extra-topicality violation. Then it runs a very short CP that is the plan text minus the extra-topical portion. The affirmative likely provides two kinds of responses to the counterplan: (1) "That's not fair," "They can't do that," or "That's topical," and (2) "The plan is the superior policy because it gains the additional advantage of X because of the plank left out of the CP text." The negative never really intends to go for the counterplan in this scenario. Instead, it seeks to use the CP to demonstrate the inclusion of the extra-topical plank and the abuse associated with allowing the affirmative team to include the extra-topical portion of its plan.

Test of the Topic Counterplans

Finally, a test of the topic counterplan seeks to polarize the debate (in a good way) so there is a clear division between the affirmative and negative advocacy while attempting to explore the truth of the resolution or examine the broader principles or approaches proscribed by the resolution. For instance, if the resolution calls for incentives to promote economic development, the affirmative may choose to offer subsidies for a particular industry. The counterplan, therefore, bans subsidies. This strategy enhances clash by getting at the core principle behind the affirmative case. To put it simply, the negative listens to the affirmative plan and proposes a counterplan that does the exact opposite.

In 2003–4, my top team at Fort Walton Beach High School, Matt Keith and David Williams, took this idea to one of its most extreme examples by running an inaction counterplan. The topic that year stated, "The United States federal government should establish an ocean policy substantially increasing protection of marine natural resources." As could be expected, the majority of affirmative cases that year dealt with some sort of environmental protection. Matt and David decided to craft a counterplan around the following text: "The United States government will suspend the right to create environmental policies. Over the next ten years, all federal environmental policies will be phased out." This enabled them to truly engage their opponents in debate about whether the federal government ought to be in the business of protecting the environment, the effectiveness of federal environmental regulation, the ability of corporations to police themselves, and the strength of social movements surrounding environmental issues.

While counterplans like these are extreme in nature, my debaters found them to be remarkably effective with diverse judging pools. With judges using the tabula rasa and modern policy maker paradigms, my teams have had success gaining access to big impacts via a hands-off approach like the inaction counterplan or even the Anarchism Counterplan.[8] On the lay judge circuits of Anchorage, Alaska, my debaters found inaction counterplans quite effective because they created a clear division between the affirmative and negative advocacies in the minds of judges who were not that familiar with the intricacies and technicalities of policy debate. It also allowed them to identify the crux of the affirmative strategy and really explore its ability to effect positive change.

Limits of the Counterplan

Obviously, the policy alternative of a counterplan can provide a tremendous strategic advantage for the negative debaters. However, it is insufficient for them simply to have a great idea and introduce it to the debate as a counterplan. Doing so would create a scenario in which the two teams present dueling oratories about two great ideas with little or no clash or *debate*. As with all arguments, there are structures that help us understand how the counterplan works and use it effectively in a debate. Counterplans are bound by certain stock issues, which the negative team must uphold if it wants to win the round with a counterplan.[9]

The Traditional View

When counterplans first came into play, they were viewed as opportunity costs associated with implementing the affirmative plan. This had a significant impact on the stock elements of the argument. Furthermore, the hard-and-fast interpretation of the stock issues helped ensure that CPs created clash in the debate round, provided a clear division between the affirmative and negative worldviews, and led to better debate in general. Thus, the debate community believed counterplans had four stock issue requirements: non-topicality, competitiveness, solvency, and net benefit. These stock issues helped focus debates and kept the number of counterplans being run relatively small but also made them an extremely effective negative strategy.

NON-TOPICALITY. The first requirement of counterplans held that the policy proposed by the negative must be non-topical.[10] This stemmed, in part, from the idea that the resolution served to divide ground between the affirmative and the negative teams. Any policy inside the resolution was deemed to be fair ground for the affirmative. Any policy outside the resolution—to include the status quo—was a potential option for the negative team's advocacy. Furthermore, it made sense that a negative counterplan must fall outside the bounds of the resolution, since the negative team was tasked with negating the topic. As such, if the negative debaters proposed a topical counterplan, they would give an additional warrant for the resolution (otherwise known as affirming the resolution).

This had the added benefit of preventing teams from simply running their affirmative case as a counterplan. Allowing them to do so would have multiple effects on the quality of debate. On a small scale, it could make rounds messy since the affirmative and negative both present cases in favor of the resolution. Essentially, the judge would be left with proposals that do not really clash with one another. On a larger scale, allowing negative teams to run their affirmative cases as counterplans hinders in-depth research on the topic, since they would really need to go into significant depth only on a single case for the entire year.

Furthermore, requiring counterplans to fall outside the resolution encourages debaters to consider the topic from both perspectives. One of the beauties of academic debate is that debaters must argue in favor of the topic and against the topic from one round to the next. This gives them the ability to see arguments from both sides, to see merit in opposing viewpoints, and to find connections with those with whom they may disagree. Allowing debaters to run topical counterplans erodes that unique opportunity for growth. For those reasons, and many more, counterplans traditionally must fall outside the topic area.

COMPETITIVENESS. Second, counterplans must be competitive with the affirmative policy. In other words, the counterplan must be an opportunity cost of choosing to pursue the affirmative plan; they cannot be done at the same time. If both plans can be implemented together, then the negative has not given the judge a reason to reject the plan. Ultimately, there are several ways the negative may demonstrate competitiveness on a counterplan.

The strongest method demonstrates that the two policies are truly <u>mutually exclusive</u>. Quite simply, you cannot do both policies at the same time. There is something inherent in one (or both) of them that will not allow the two to coexist. For example, you cannot both provide subsidies to developers of alternate energy sources and ban them. This is the strongest, best, and most difficult <u>standard</u> of competition to establish. Some traditional judges accept only this standard in competition, since it is (arguably) the only way to confirm that the two policies cannot coexist.

In some rounds, the negative may show that the two policies are *resource competitive*. In other words, both plans use the same resources for implementation of the policy.[11] This type of competition arises when the affirmative uses a finite resource that the counterplan also requires. Conceivably, there are a limited number of scientists with the expertise to plan interstellar space travel. If the counterplan uses those same scientists, and the negative demonstrates that we have only enough scientists to act on the affirmative plan, then the two policies would compete over resources. Debaters may find similar examples based on rare earth metals, technology development, fuel resources, and so forth.

Next, debaters might demonstrate *philosophical competition* between the policies. This standard arises when the counterplan challenges the philosophical underpinnings of the affirmative plan. Perhaps the plan works from the top down, while the counterplan approaches problem solving from the bottom up. Perhaps the plan relies on a paternalistic government to protect the people, while the counterplan pursues self-reliance. Perhaps the plan uses Western thinking, while the counterplan uses Eastern approaches. In some instances, this standard approaches the concept of mutual exclusivity, while in others the affirmative may be able to show that while they come at the problem from different directions, it is still possible for the approaches to exist side by side. In the latter instance, it would be up to the debaters to establish whether or not this is a sufficient test of competition.

The final common standard of competition is that of *redundancy*. Here, the negative argues that since the affirmative and negative solve the same advantages, there is no need to do both and that it would be wasteful to pursue both simultaneously. The affirmative, on the other hand, contends that the negative fails to answer the fundamental question of whether you can do both at the same time. Furthermore, governments often pass redundant laws.

Although these are the four main standards of competition, there are others.[12] As with anything in debate, you are limited only by your own creativity and persuasive logic. For example, some debaters have claimed *resolutional integrity* as a standard of competition. In this scenario, the negative argues that the resolution is a statement to be proven true or false by the two teams. The affirmative offers one proposal for the resolution, while the negative offers the antithesis of it.[13] Even if both plans could conceivably be enacted at the same time, the counterplan still disproves the resolution statement. In other words, since the counterplan directly refutes the resolution, it demonstrates the flaw of the statement, resulting in the judge rejecting the resolution and voting negative.

Another less frequently utilized standard is *functional mutual exclusivity*. With the truest form of mutual exclusivity, the negative shows that the two plans cannot coexist. With functional mutual exclusivity, it shows that while they may be able to coexist on paper (or textually), they will not work properly in the real world.

For example, the 2010–11 high school topic called for a U.S. withdrawal of military and/or police forces from one or more countries. South Anchorage High School ran a counterplan calling for increased interaction and cooperation between leaders in the target countries of the resolution and the United States using the International Military and Education Training program. This program brought military personnel and politicians to the United States for various types of technical training, education programs, and the like. Technically, we could have withdrawn troops from the countries in question and brought their personnel and leaders to our country for training. Functionally, however, this was problematic because the solvency mechanisms could not coexist effectively. The entire thesis of the counterplans's solvency stemmed from strengthened, long-term ties between political and military leaders in the United States and the target nation(s). If we decreased our presence—per the affirmative plan—the counterplan itself would be rendered meaningless. Thus, the two proposals were functionally mutually exclusive.

Another potential example of functional mutual exclusivity applies to States Counterplans. The thesis of most States CPs is that the fifty states are more effective than the federal government at implementing policy on domestic issues because they are closer to the problem, are more aware of the needs of the local area, and are far more flexible in their action. Affirmatives might argue that the states and the federal government could both pass similar or identical policies and that this sort of thing happens all the time in the real world. However, the negative could argue that the plan and the counterplan are functionally mutually exclusive because joint implementation is illusory. Introductory government classes teach us that the central government takes precedence when there is a conflict between the national and state governments. Therefore, the only policy really in consideration would be that implemented by the national government, making state action irrelevant. In short, the benefits of local eyes for local problems and state flexibility erode when the national government passes an overarching piece of legislation.

In the end, there are multiple ways of demonstrating a forced choice between the affirmative's plan and the negative's counterplan. Some are very persuasive with judges, such as the mutual exclusivity standard. Others, like redundancy, require more work to convince judges that the policies actually compete. Regardless, competition is a required element of the negative counterplan because it helps ensure clarity of the debate. Functionally, competitiveness serves the same purpose as a link on a disadvantage. Without proving competition, the negative fails to show that the affirmative plan prevents something even better from going into effect at the end of the round.

SOLVENCY. Traditionally, counterplans must also meet the solvency positions of the affirmative team. In other words, the same harms must be eliminated and the same advantages created as by the counterplan. Just as the affirmative plan must demonstrate solvency for its harms, so too does the negative's counterplan. This requirement focuses counterplans on reasonable alternatives to the problem identified by the affirmative and helps ensure that clash occurs between the two teams. It also narrows the scope of potential counterplans, helping balance the research burdens so that affirmative teams do not have to prepare to answer counterplans that do not relate to the topic matter at hand.

NET BENEFIT. Finally, counterplans must claim unique solvency in the round. There must be some good created by the counterplan that can never be established by the affirmative plan. Thus, the counterplan provides a net benefit over the affirmative plan. In short, the judge must have a reason to prefer the counterplan over the plan. The negative establishes this net benefit in one of three ways: achieve better solvency than the plan, gain an additional advantage that the plan does not, or avoid a disadvantage that links to the plan.

Changing Perspectives

Over time, the four stock issues of the counterplan became less paramount in debate rounds. In fact, we have seen four separate phases in the perspectives of judges. However, debaters should not presume that the traditional view vanished as the new forms took hold. Rather, different judges hold different views on the role of the counterplan and the requirements it must meet. Thus, debaters should be aware of the history of the counterplan so they can either speak directly to their assigned judge or know why the various views have existed so they can engage in a knowledgeable debate about what the rules of the game ought to be.

STAGE 1. The traditional view of counterplans is described above.

STAGE 2. The first change regarding the counterplan's stock issues simply eliminated the need to solve the affirmative's harm story. As the policy maker paradigm took hold in the debate community, replacing the stock issues paradigm, debaters no longer felt constrained by some of the stock issues. Most important for the counterplan, debaters felt that a reasonable policy maker—or a rational person—should simply choose the most advantageous course of action without an artificial constraint requiring the negative team to solve the initial harm cited in the round. As long as the counterplan is non-topical, is competitive, and offers a net benefit, the counterplan should be preferred.

STAGE 3. Next, the debate on counterplans narrowed itself down to two stock issues: non-topicality and competitiveness. Obviously, in a policy maker paradigm the negative must still demonstrate that the counterplan offers a better world than the one provided by the plan. However, debaters narrowed their conception of what a policy maker should do in the round.

That is, the ballot requires the judge to determine a winner and a loser. As such, the ballot establishes a forced choice for the critic. Debaters reasoned that as long as there was a net benefit to the counterplan, then it was competitive or better than the plan. For example, a reasonable policy maker would choose to prefer an action that avoided a disadvantage, even if both policies could be enacted simultaneously. As such, the counterplan was determined to be competitive because a rational person would avoid the damage of the disadvantage, choosing the counterplan as a competing policy option.

STAGE 4. In recent years, debaters started testing the affirmative plan text as written in the first affirmative <u>constructive</u> (1AC). They believed that rather than be forced to negate the resolution, they were required only to negate the affirmative's choices in the round. Thus, the non-topical requirement of the counterplan lost primacy in their minds. They reasoned that affirmative teams had unlimited prep time to prepare for the round, find supporting research, and craft the best possible plan text. Thus, if they could show the judge a superior way of doing things—even if it was topical—the affirmative should lose for failing to identify the superior policy option. As a result, everything fell back on the idea that the counterplan must only be the net beneficial policy in the round.[14]

While debate has clearly shifted and grown on the counterplan, there are very good justifications for any one of the views on a counterplan's requirements. As an affirmative, you can very easily use the analysis—or derivations of it—found in the traditional view of counterplans to answer a team crafting a CP in one of the latter phases. Likewise, negative teams can use the history of change to develop justifications answering those potential affirmative attacks.

Affirmative Responses

A carefully crafted counterplan can be the difference between an affirmative and a negative ballot. This is especially true if the negative writes a CP that meets all four of its traditional stock issues, as that creates a compelling advocacy and story for just about any judging paradigm. How, then, does the affirmative respond to the counterplan?

Shifting Presumption?

In the back of every affirmative debater's mind should be the thought about how the negative's introduction of a counterplan affects presumption in the debate. In a traditional <u>stock issues paradigm</u>, presumption resides with the status quo because it is deemed "innocent until proven guilty" by the affirmative case. With a counterplan, the negative agrees that the status quo is inadequate; however, it disagrees with the choices made by the affirmative when constructing the plan. Those with a sense of tradition believe the introduction of a counterplan shifts presumption to the affirmative because the negative has introduced the most recent change. As such, affirmative teams may be able to capitalize on that shift.

However, most modern judges subscribe to the legislative model of debate, meaning that presumption tends to rest with the affirmative in any given round. I do not believe that the counterplan changes that mentality. Since most policy makers view the negative as testing the affirmative case to determine whether it leads to more good than harm or more harm than good, the counterplan should be viewed as just another test of the plan. As such, the affirmative probably maintains its hold on presumption. If there is any question as to the validity of the CP or whether it will achieve a net benefit, affirmative teams should capitalize on the fact that they gain or retain their hold on presumption regardless of whether the judge is extremely traditional or on the cutting edge of contemporary debate practices.

Identifying Fiat Limitations

One of the first questions affirmative teams should ask themselves pertains to the scope of the negative's counterplan. Who is the agent of action identified in the counterplan? The fifty states acting independently, the fifty states acting in cooperation, the U.S. Centers for Disease Control, the World Health Organization, the North Atlantic Treaty Organization, the African Union, China, or Canada? Most resolutions limit the affirmative to the U.S. federal government. By extension, virtually any branch of government or any agency within the government can be tasked by the affirmative to carry out the plan. On the face of it, the negative can choose any agency in the world to implement any conceivable plan. In addition, the negative may use the U.S. federal government as long as the action itself is non-topical.

That said, there are two schools of thought regarding the limits of what the negative can do. One says the resolution serves to divide ground—the affirmative gets everything inside the resolution and the negative gets everything outside the resolution. Therefore, there are no limits to the fiat powers the negative can claim. The negative can claim fiat regarding any agency or government in the world to carry out any action it can imagine.[15]

The other school of thought believes the negative should be held to a relatively equivalent level of fiat as the affirmative. If the affirmative is limited to the unilateral actions of a national actor, then the negative should be limited to a single national actor or smaller entity.[16] This standard of fiat limitations ensures the affirmative and negative have an equal opportunity to win the round and prevents the negative from having an unfair advantage in the debate.

In the event the negative runs a counterplan that the affirmative believes has exceeded its fiat powers, it can run an argument on fiat abuse against the counterplan. The process resembles running a topicality argument against an affirmative. The affirmative debaters should offer an explanation of the limits of fiat powers. Then they should explain the violation found in the counterplan. Finally, they should provide an impact for the argument with <u>voters</u>, detailing why the judge should vote against the negative team or not include the counterplan in his or her decision-making calculus.[17] Keep in mind that voters usually come down to one of three explanations: the violation of a rule, the impact on education, or the effects on fairness in competition. If you believe the negative counterplan benefits from excessive fiat powers, explain why those powers should be limited and how the negative has gone too far. In fact, that is the process you should use against any affirmative or negative strategy that violates one of the rules of the game.

Establishing Resolutional Parameters

Next, determine whether the negative's action supports the resolution. If it does, refer back to the section on why non-topicality was a traditional requirement. Then craft an explanation as to why the negative counterplan or even the negative team should be rejected. Remember, the negative will likely argue that in a policy maker paradigm, the rational person simply chooses the best course of action; that the ballot provides for a forced choice over who has done the better debating, not over whether the resolution is proven true or false; or that operationalization allows for topical counterplans because the affirmative has to defend only itself, not the entire resolution. Therefore, when you craft your topicality attack against the counterplan, think ahead so you can counter these responses.

Denying Competitiveness

One of the most critical responses to counterplans is to show that they are not competitive—that they are not an opportunity cost to voting affirmative. If the negative fails to demonstrate competitiveness, then the counterplan is not a reason to reject the affirmative plan.[18]

ANALYTICAL RESPONSES TO COMPETITION. First and foremost, the affirmative can explain how the plan and counterplan are *not mutually exclusive*. This can be done with direct analysis: prove the negative's reasons for competition are false. Explain to the judge exactly why the plans can coexist. Use logic to demonstrate how and why they can be done at the same time. Alternatively, read evidence that explains how they can coexist or provides historical examples of similar policies being enacted at the same time. In addition, if the counterplan <u>shell</u> offered explanations of competition, be sure to answer them directly in the second affirmative constructive.

Furthermore, the affirmative could show that the plan somehow leads to the counterplan. In other words, the affirmative could concede that the two plans cannot coexist. However, the team could explain that implementing the plan now paves the way for the counterplan to be done later. This strategy succeeds by *capturing* the counterplan and demonstrating that the best policy option involves solving the immediate harm found in the case and still getting the additional benefits of the counterplan at a later time.

Finally, the affirmative could explain that something in the counterplan is an artificial construct designed to make the CP competitive. Any plan that bans the affirmative most likely suffers from *artificial competition*. This happens when the counterplan deals with a completely different harm/advantage but tacks on a plank that bans the affirmative solvency mechanism.[19] Doing so would be abusive to the affirmative because the options for counterplan ground become nearly infinite simply by including a "ban the affirmative" statement in the counterplan.

TESTING COMPETITION WITH <u>PERMS</u>. In addition to explaining why the counterplan fails to meet its burden of competitiveness, the affirmative can provide a perm—short for permutation—of the plan text, demonstrating an example of how the two plans can coexist. It should be noted, and stressed, that a perm is a *test* of competition, *not advocacy*. In other words, the affirmative does not support the counterplan or a revised version of the plan text but simply offers the perm as an example of how the plans are not mutually exclusive.[20] In fact, the affirmative can offer multiple perms to test the possibility of combining the affirmative case with the negative counterplan in multiple ways.

Since some affirmative teams may advocate the perm and some negative teams may argue that perms are abusive since they represent a shift in advocacy, we should examine the traditional view of perms. A perm is merely a test to see if the counterplan meets the stock issue of competition. If the two plans can be combined, then the judge has not been presented a forced choice or an opportunity cost. If the debate were truly taking place in Congress, the perm represents a possible amendment that could be made to the bill. In fact, the affirmative could present multiple perms to demonstrate multiple amendments that would all demonstrate that the counterplan is not prevented from going into effect simply because the judge votes to adopt the plan. Alternatively, the perms could simply demonstrate two policies that could coexist in the real world.

That said, there are multiple ways the affirmative can perm the counterplan. The most compelling of all perms is "Perm—do both." With this option, the affirmative simply combines the entire affirmative plan with the entire counterplan, showing that the two ideas can be done simultaneously. For example, on an oceans topic, the affirmative may develop offshore wind power facilities. The negative may argue that offshore wind is an inadequate source of energy and offer a counterplan with solar, land-based wind, and geothermal power. The obvious perm simply states, "Perm—do both. Develop offshore wind, solar, land-based wind, and geothermal power."[21] This subsumes all other standards of competition by proving that both plans can coexist.

Affirmative teams could also test competition through a *partial perm*. In other words, the affirmative chooses to offer a perm that incorporates the plan and part of the counterplan.[22] The most likely use of the partial perm arises during one of two scenarios. First, the counterplan is artificially competitive, meaning that it banned the affirmative. In the previous example, the counterplan may have stated something along the lines of "Develop solar, land-based wind, and geothermal power while banning offshore wind production." When I was in college, it was not unusual to hear negative teams present completely unrelated counterplans while banning the affirmative. For example, the affirmative may have dealt with drunk driving through license revocation. The negative's counterplan may have banned the affirmative policy while fully funding a mission to Mars. The partial perm could simply state, "Perm—do the affirmative's license revocation and begin an expedition to Mars." The partial perm, leaving out the part that bans the affirmative policy, demonstrates that the core idea of both policies could actually be done at the same time.

In the second scenario, the counterplan offers an action that has impacts so far beyond the reach of the affirmative that it would be nearly impossible for any affirmative to win through cost-benefit analysis. This usually happens when the counterplan is a pseudo-utopian counterplan such as the Anarchism CP, the Democratic Socialism CP, and so forth. These counterplans completely reform the U.S. federal government in an effort to solve impacts of the affirmative.

Again, let us assume the affirmative ran the drunk driving license revocation plan. The negative presents the Anarchism CP, arguing that we should dismantle top-down governmental structures and replace them with a bottom-up form of government. The counterplan's net benefits stem from analysis showing that much of the violence in the world results from the methods of control used by top-down mechanisms of authority. In addition, developing government from the bottom-up generates a spirit of community, achieves buy-in from the populace, creates policies more receptive to local needs, and generally makes the world a better place. At the impact level, the counterplan will win every time, unless the affirmative can win solvency takeouts and turns. However, the affirmative could circumvent that discussion through a partial perm, such as "Perm—have bottom-up governing institutions implement mandatory license revocation for drunk drivers." Ultimately, this partial perm can be summarized as implementing the affirmative solvency mechanism under the replacement government. This allows the affirmative to show that we can achieve most or all of the benefits of the counterplan while also gaining the specific benefits found in the 1AC.

Next, the affirmative might make use of the *third option perm*, in which it offers a third alternative that is not competitive with the affirmative plan but still gains all of the benefits of the counterplan. Like the partial perm, this can be effective against a utopian-style counterplan. Referring back to the previous example of license revocation, we can craft a third option: "Perm—implement mandatory license revocation for drunk drivers under a democratic socialist society, thereby gaining the same utopian advantages of the Anarchism Counterplan while still accessing the benefits of the case through top-down enforcement." In the truest sense, this does not prove the counterplan fails to meet its burden of competition; however, it does show that the CP lacks a unique reason to reject the affirmative. We can access the counterplan's utopian benefits in a different way while still benefiting from the affirmative.

Some more realistic scenarios involving the third option perm can be seen with alternate agent counterplans. On a domestic issue, the negative could offer a counterplan that all fifty states will implement the affirmative policy, gaining the unique advantages of flexibility and federalism. The third option perm: "Have the states implement the affirmative plan with federal oversight and funding." This keeps the federal government involved, gains the benefits of the counterplan, and avoids the budget shortfalls that could hamper negative solvency. On a foreign policy issue in which the United States engages in bilateral action with Mexico, the counterplan might opt for bilateral engagement between China and Mexico. Presumably, the negative would argue that China could solve the problem just as easily as the United States, but the plan would trigger a China Crowd Out Disadvantage in which tensions escalate between the United States and China or simply Chinese-U.S. cooperation on a number of international issues would be stymied by unilateral U.S. engagement. The third option perm argues that since there is nothing inherent in the affirmative policy that upsets China, we could engage in trilateral cooperation between the U.S.-China-Mexico on the issue identified in the plan text. Again, the perm shows there is an alternative to the counterplan that still accesses the impacts of both cases.

Finally, the affirmative could offer a *time frame perm*. Do the affirmative and then the counterplan, or do the counterplan and then the plan. This demonstrates the ability to solve the immediate harm cited by one and then solve the larger problem identified by the other. Obviously, this type of perm fails to truly demonstrate a lack of competitiveness, since the policies would not be implemented simultaneously. However, it can be used to either answer the net benefit or answer competition when the only standard for competition offered by the negative is that of the net benefit, as happens in many contemporary rounds. In other words, if the only justification given by the negative is that the counterplan is a superior policy option, the time frame perm—along with several examples of the third option perm—shows that the counterplan does not fulfill its burdens of being the only way to achieve the net benefit.

In a nutshell, affirmatives should be creative when crafting perms. There are multiple ways to combine the affirmative plan and the negative counterplan. Some of them clearly demonstrate that the counterplan fails as a competing policy option. Others undermine the CP by demonstrating that it is not the only way to achieve the net benefit. Regardless, perms can be an effective way to undermine the persuasiveness of the counterplan in the judge's mind.

Undermining Solvency

In addition to showing that the counterplan is topical and that it is not competitive, the affirmative can also attack the CP's ability to solve. Keep in mind that traditionally, counterplans were required to solve the affirmative harm. Thus, the affirmative should attack the CP's ability to address the harms story of the affirmative; refer back to the section discussing why this burden originally existed so that you can craft voters in the round. If nothing else, refuting solvency helps undercut the net benefit of the counterplan, opening the door for you to win on cost-benefit analysis.

Furthermore, many negative teams assume, rather than prove, solvency. They craft a counterplan using the affirmative's solvency mechanism (or similar mechanism) and implement it with a different agent of action (or even the same agent). In other cases, they provide extremely generic solvency. For example, a States Counterplan may simply have evidence saying the states are better suited for dealing with issues because they are closer to the problem and more responsive to unique circumstances. Similarly, a China counterplan may provide evidence that China's recent transformation economically gives it unique insight into working with countries in the developing world. Frequently, they never actually read evidence indicating the counterplan can actually be done, work, or meet the goals of the case. As such, affirmative teams may find it possible to create an a priori, prima facie voter against the counterplan on solvency. At the very least, affirmatives should question the solvency of the counterplan and compare that to the specificity of the evidence in the 1AC, paving the way for excellent policy maker paradigm analysis in later speeches.

Attacking the Net Benefit(s)

Finally, the affirmative should attack the counterplan's net benefit. Given that the net benefit hinges on solvency or on avoiding a DA (or kritik) link, it should be fairly obvious how to counter the net benefit. Attack the counterplan's ability to solve, or disprove the story of the disadvantage using the tactics discussed in the previous chapter. When the negative runs a counterplan, affirmative teams have the added option of showing that the counterplan links to the disadvantage or—even better—that it links to the disadvantage more than the plan does. No matter what, attacking the net benefit involves comparing the world of the plan to the world of the counterplan to see which one achieves the better results.

Ultimately, counterplans can be a very effective, but not essential, device when developing a negative strategy.[23] When constructing a counterplan, you are limited only by your own creativity.[24] Although the requirements or stock issues of counterplans have changed in the minds of some judges over the years, negative teams should attempt to demonstrate all four stock issues in the first negative constructive. While some claim this is unnecessary, negative teams have a higher likelihood of winning with the counterplan if they begin by showing them all because it ensures a solid foundation for the argument. As the affirmative, think about whether all the stock issues have been met by the counterplan. For the ones that are not met or are questionable, think about why those requirements originally existed and present <u>theory</u> arguments (or arguments about the rules of the game) using those ideas. Finally, be sure to address the substantive aspects (solvency and net benefits) of the counterplan just as you would if you were attacking an affirmative case.

8. Critical Argumentation

Up to this point, we have explored three negative offensive tools: <u>top-icality</u> arguments, <u>disadvantages</u>, and <u>counterplans</u>. We have also examined the argumentative structures that help the affirmative team explore whether or not a substantive change is needed. But what if the debaters wish to do more than simply explore whether the affirmative team violated a rule of the game like topicality or what the substantive policy implications of voting for the plan or for a different counterplan are? What if the debaters wish to examine the thought processes that are behind what we say, that form the assumptions behind the topic, or that drive how we construct our ideas? To grapple with these complex notions, debaters turn to the <u>kritik</u>. In this chapter, I unpack the kritik in order to understand what it was intended to do, how it is constructed, and the ways in which it can be used in the round.

The Role of the Kritik

Kritiks originated as a way to challenge the assumptions of the affirmative team. Some of the earliest examples of kritiks focused on sexist or racist language used in rounds. For example, on a health care topic, the affirmative debaters may have regularly used the pronoun "he" when referring to doctors and "she" when referring to nurses. The negative debaters would have then called them out on the use of sexist language and demanded the judge reject their opponents for contributing to antiquated and harmful gender stereotypes. Ultimately, the kritik is simple; it questions the assumptions, logic, or thought processes of the people involved in the debate. The best critical debaters are those who think rationally and use their own words to apply both the evidence and the argument in the round.

Simple Argumentative Structures

Furthermore, kritiks are actually built on basic structures that are not foreign to those who have spent time debating in the policy maker framework. They utilize the ideas and concepts found in other types of arguments. Simply, kritiks incorporate basic elements of disadvantages and counterplans to identify a flawed way of thinking and offer an alternative way of doing things. They begin by showing how the argument applies to the affirmative. Then, they explain why that way of thinking is bad. Finally, they offer an alternative viewpoint to the one used by the affirmative.

The Link

Like disadvantages, kritiks require a link to the affirmative. However, there are four distinct ways negative teams often link the kritik to their opponents: through rhetoric, through structure, through assumptions, and through structural assumptions. The first link stems from the rhetoric used by their opponents. As described above, the affirmative team may have used gendered or sexist language. Often, teams listen to the rhetoric used by opponents in their speeches—including the language of the authors they quote when reading evidence—or during cross-examination periods to establish this link. Conceivably, debaters could even link the kritik off the way they debate (using highly technical and fast language to exclude nonnative English speakers) or carry themselves in the round (using body language or loaded words to intimidate their opponents).

In time, debaters found they could easily incorporate kritiks as a primary negative strategy if they found structural links. That is, they found generic links for critical argumentation off the structures mandated by the resolution. Thus, it became easy to run Statism Kritiks (top-down governance is bad) off resolutions that identified the U.S. federal government as the agent of action. Likewise, teams could run Feminism Kritiks (patriarchal thinking is dangerous) off the mandate of top-down structures (again, the U.S. federal government is the actor) or off topics that blatantly incorporated patriarchal thinking as the solution to the problem. Similarly, teams could run Anthropocentrism or Deep Ecology Kritiks on topics that mandated exploration or control over environmental resources. In recent years, some debaters have even argued that the very activity of debate and the structures of policy debate entrench dominant white norms and disenfranchise minority students.

Next, debaters began finding links to critical argumentation based on the assumptions used to create the <u>harms</u> stories or <u>solvency</u> chains in the affirmative <u>case</u>.[1] Perhaps the affirmative treated a public health crisis such as drug abuse as a national security threat. The negative might then run a Securitization Kritik, discussing the harms of treating health issues as security threats. It would argue that addressing the problem in such terms eventually leads to the militarization of police forces through the "war on drugs" and poses a very real danger to society. One need look no further than the crisis in Ferguson, Missouri, in 2014 to see this story played out in the real world. Or perhaps the affirmative advocated a solvency mechanism, which used people as a means to an end or manipulated people to gain what it deemed beneficial. In that instance, the negative might run a kritik rooted in Kantian ethics such as the Biopower Kritik, which explores the ways institutions use methods of control to prop up their own power to the detriment of people.

Finally, some links combine the last two categories by identifying structural assumptions in the resolution that link to the argument. Thus, economic engagement topics may naturally support capitalist structures. Similarly, foreign aid topics may inherently propagate Western notions of development, imperialism, or colonialism. Regardless of the form, it is imperative that negative teams provide a link to the affirmative, whether it be something the debaters said overtly, the fact that they affirmed a flawed structure in the resolution, or the methods of thought they used to analyze or structure their case.

The Impact

The <u>impact</u> of a kritik is rather straightforward. Like a disadvantage, debaters must articulate why this thinking is bad. Specifically, they explain why the language or assumptions used by their opponents is harmful. Perhaps it fosters inequality in society, justifies conflict, or erodes an individual's or society's humanity. Ultimately, debaters must give the judge a reason to want to avoid the patterns of thought used by the affirmative.

The Alternative

Since kritiks deal with flawed thought processes, which are most likely prevalent in the <u>status quo</u>, the negative must give the judge an <u>alternative</u>. This is not unlike a counterplan, where the negative acknowledges that the status quo is flawed and proposes an alternative policy option. With kritiks, however, the negative often notes that both the status quo and the affirmative use flawed ways of thinking; thus, it endorses an alternative perspective. Rather than top-down governance, it advocates systems of bottom-up governance or grassroots movements; rather than patriarchal patterns of thought, it supports feminist viewpoints, and so forth. Ultimately, negatives must provide a way of thinking that is different from the status quo and from their opponents' way of thinking, a pattern of thought that leads to positive change.

Development K (1NC Shell)

1. **Economic engagement is a tool of neocolonialism. The plan furthers American interests under the guise of developing Latin America. This serves to entrench American exceptionalism under an imperial logic of eurocentrism.**
Veltmeyer 11 (Henry Veltmeyer, professor of Sociology and International Development Studies at Saint Mary's University, PhD in political science from McMaster University, "US Imperialism in Latin America: Then and Now, Here and There," *Critical Development Studies*, Vol. 1:1, 2011, pp. 92-94)

[Here, the negative reads the text providing the link to the kritik. Both the resolution and the affirmative plan call for increased economic engagement with Latin America. These types of policies are rooted in neocolonialist policies.]

2. **Until neocolonialism is eliminated, global war and massive poverty are inevitable.**
Nkrumah 65 (Kwame Nkrumah, first president and Prime Minister of Ghana through decolonization, advocate of Pan-Africanism, founding member of the Organization of African Unity, and winner of the Lenin Peace Prize in 1963, "Neo-Colonialism, the Last Stage of Imperialism," 1965, available online, //Evan)

[Here, the negative reads the text providing the impact of the kritik. Neocolonialism results in poverty and war.]

3. **Our alternative is a critical recentering of economic geopolitics. Voting negative recognizes the global south as an autonomous space, challenging the dominant narrative of economic eurocentrism and opening up a space in politics for counterhegemonic resistance.**
Werner 12 (Marion Werner, Department of Geography @ University of Buffalo, PhD in Geography from University of Minnesota, "Contesting power/knowledge in economic geography: Learning from Latin America and the Caribbean," http://www.acsu.buffalo.edu/~wernerm/Werner_CEG_Manuscript.pdf, pp. 21-22 //Evan)

[Here, the negative reads the text providing support of the alternative of the kritik. This alternative calls for a reorienting of economic geopolitics at the level of the U.S. federal government.]

Figure 8.1. Example of the kritik 1NC shell

The articulation of the alternative must include two parts. First, the negative should explain what the alternative is and how it works. It is insufficient to identify the "opposite" perspective of the affirmative, as if all patterns of thought are diametrically opposed ideas. Second, it should explore the implications of the alternative. The team must describe how the alternative thought process brings about positive change. In other words, it must provide a solvency story connecting the alternative itself to positive outcomes.

The Framework or the Role of the Ballot

On the face of it, kritiks really are simple. Identify a pattern of thought used. Indict that way of thinking as bad. Demonstrate an alternative perspective that is better.[2] In addition, different kritiks operate in unique ways within the debate round. Keep in mind that the earliest kritiks dealt with the language choices of debaters. To revisit the example I used earlier, an affirmative team may have been guilty of referring to doctors as "he" and nurses as "she," thereby reinforcing gender roles that are harmful to all individuals and women as a group. A problem would arise, however, if the affirmative speaker replied, "So I made a mistake . . . perhaps I even contributed to inequality, but I save thousands of lives . . . or millions . . . or billions." How does one reconcile this unquantifiable harm against that of the affirmative harms and solvency story?

Enter the framework debate, a debate over how the judge should evaluate the round.[3] In the previous example involving sexist language, debaters on the negative noted that when a judge votes affirmative in a debate round, nothing really happens. Fiat does not exist; the plan will not be implemented by the U.S. federal government. As such, the affirmative plan does not really save lives. Instead, they explained that debate is an academic activity, debaters are students, and judges are educators. Thus, the *role of the ballot* is to reward innovative thinking, promote positive educational outcomes, and so forth. In that scenario, the affirmative has created a harm in the real world by using sexist or discriminatory language. As such, the team should be punished. Furthermore, a ballot against it for this type of language encourages debaters to think through their errors and avoid repeating the mistake in the future. However, voting for the alternative invites discourse with inclusive language and promotes equality and fairness for both genders.

This part of the debate is paramount to understanding kritiks. The team running the kritik must explain to the judge exactly what the purpose of debate is and how the judge should best evaluate arguments within that context. It can offer any number of explanations as to why that framework is preferable, including academic discourse, educational development, ethical reasoning, and so forth.

However, critical frameworks get even more complex. Some kritiks are pre-fiat, meaning the impacts of the discourse should be examined before the substantive merits of the case, as in the example above. Some kritiks actually operate within a fiat-based examination of policies. In those instances, teams explain that the processes used by their opponents doom policies to failure or lead to harmful impacts. The alternative for those kritiks should require restructuring how the government makes decisions. Typically, these arguments have bigger, more quantifiable impacts, such as "Patriarchal decision-making in international relations inevitably leads to confrontation, conflict, and escalation."

This is where confusion in critical debates often arises. Many times, the impact of the kritik is nuclear war and the alternative involves reframing the decision-making process at the societal, national, or international level. Then, on the framework debate, teams say that the judge's ballot is a critical action and can change the system. Typically, each challenge to the system matters and must be made. Admittedly, we probably should challenge our leaders to use better systems for making decisions, but can a single ballot really be *the* key to change if fiat does not exist? What really matters on the framework debate is that teams explain how their kritik functions in the round—pre-fiat or fiat-based—and the impacts and alternatives should mesh with that interpretation of the role of the ballot.

Why Kritiks Win

Kritiks can win rounds in a number of ways. Most likely, one of five things happens in the round. First, the debaters offer a superior framework for evaluating the debate. In other words, the way we advocate for policies and the way we make decisions should be evaluated before the merits of the plan because this is an academic activity or because it would be unethical to vote for a harmful practice or thought process.

Similarly, negatives might argue that even in a fiat-based world, ethical policy makers should never support a policy that mistreats people, is unjust, or is immoral. In both of these scenarios, the negative should spend a significant amount of time discussing those ethical frameworks in the alternative of the kritik.

Third, the kritik's alternative could solve the affirmative's harms while showing that the method of thought used by the affirmative will make solvency impossible. Usually, there is something inherently destructive or counterproductive within the perspective used by the status quo in relation to the problem. The impact of the kritik, then, explains that continuing down this course will undermine solvency in the long-term. Conversely, the alternative offers a different paradigm that can solve the root of the problem. The interesting strategic benefit of this form of the kritik is that even if the negative loses the alternative or the framework debate, the impact of the kritik still functions as a solvency takeout, meaning that a disadvantage or case turn can still win the debate in a policy maker paradigm.

Fourth, the impact of the kritik may impact-turn the affirmative. In other words, the dominant way of thinking or that of the affirmative will actually make the problem worse in the long-term. As in the previous explanation, this also gives the negative debaters strategic options in the round, since they do not necessarily have to win the alternative or framework debate. Rather, they can collapse down to the link and impact of the kritik to win the round on a case turn.

Finally, the kritik may simply outweigh the affirmative. In this scenario, the negative proves that the impact of the kritik is simply larger than the advantages claimed by the affirmative. At a minimum, the negative debaters must win the alternative debate, showing that their frame of thought leads to superior impacts in the round. Then, they can show that reshaping the method of thought at the agent of action level will either lead to superior policy making or win the framework debate so that the benefits of the affirmative are null, because the only real impacts in the round are the direct result of what debaters say and do in the round.

Answering Kritiks

Beginning in Cross-Examination

When responding to kritiks, everything begins in cross-examination. If the kritik is confusing or the advocacy is unclear, ask direct questions at the earliest opportunity. First, make an effort to figure out what your opponents are talking about with their argument. Given the esoteric nature of much of the literature used for critical debates, you cannot blame yourself for being confused or lost when listening to your opponents read their evidence. The bottom line: you cannot debate what you do not understand. Ask questions about the link. Try to figure out what you did that is troublesome. Ask questions about the alternative. Try to figure out exactly what your opponents' advocacy is. Once you have done that, you can start to craft answers to the kritik proper: the link, the impact, and the alternative.

Second, ask questions regarding how the kritik should be evaluated in the round. Is it a pre-fiat kritik, or does it assume the role of fiat in the round? As noted in the previous section, some impacts do not mesh well with pre-fiat analysis. If you discover these inconsistencies, you can better question the ability of the alternative to solve the impacts.

Link Responses

As with a disadvantage, a kritik begins with the link. If it does not apply or connect to you, then it is irrelevant to the debate. The idea of replying to the link echoes what was discussed in chapter 6: no link, no specific link, no quantification of the link, and (arguably) no perception of the link. You may even identify missing or flawed internal links on the argument.

Keep in mind that if the negative's link was a generic one applied to a word or phrase in the resolution, you might be able to explain that your unique approach to the harms in the case avoids the link described in the negative's evidence. In addition, you may be able to turn the kritik, showing that you in fact move us further away from the way of thinking indicted by the argument.

Impact Responses

Similarly, responding to the impacts on a kritik mirrors responding to impacts on a disadvantage: mitigate the impact, deny the impact, demonstrate a lack of quantification of the impact, address the time frame of the impact, and impact-turn the kritik. In addition, remember to point out that the benefits of your case disprove the theory of the kritik at the practical level.

Alternative Responses

Next, you can answer the alternative of the kritik. As with counterplans, there are many ways to challenge the alternative. First, if the alternative truly competes with your perspective, then the case becomes a disadvantage to the kritik. If we adopt the negative's way of thinking, then we lose the opportunity to make the world a better place through actions like that of the affirmative.

Second, explore whether or not the alternative is actually a good idea. You can address the alternative's ability to solve the impacts of the argument.

Again, use the same process you would use to answer solvency on a counterplan or an affirmative case. Can the alternative actually bring positive change? Is it workable? Will it actually make matters worse?

Third, you may find that your opponent's kritik is actually using a flawed approach to decision-making. Thus, you could offer a counter-kritik by identifying his or her error in the round, demonstrating the harmful impact associated with it, and crafting an alternative perspective that meshes with the affirmative.

Fourth, attack whether the alternative is <u>competitive</u> with your own plan or way of thinking. Demonstrate how your way of thinking or forming your case conforms to the ideals of the kritik. Offer <u>perms</u> to show that your advocacy is not inherently at odds with the alternative viewpoint. If the alternative is not <u>mutually exclusive</u> with the affirmative plan, then it lacks justification for being a voting issue in the round.

Framework Responses

Finally, attack the framework of the kritik. Think of answering the framework offered by the opposing team in the same way you would think of a topicality argument on a first affirmative <u>constructive</u> (1AC) or a fiat abuse response on a counterplan. Has your opponents' introduction of the kritik or the framework they advocate had a negative impact on fairness or education? For example, if they assume they can completely overhaul how the federal government operates, have they accepted such sweeping fiat powers that it undermines the affirmative team's ability to compete?

You might also discuss whether the role of the ballot offered by your opponents will actually bring about change. Many high school debaters conflate the world of pre-fiat analysis and the substantive impacts of the mindsets. They claim the "bad" mindset will lead to policy failure, war, genocide, nuclear annihilation, extinction, and the like. This is problematic if they operate in the pre-fiat world in which only our words have impact on the people around us. In short, if the bad mindset really will cause extinction, how can our discussions in the round have any real-world impact on the course of history—at least, quickly enough to avoid annihilation?

Even if they claim the debaters' in-round discussions have a long-term impact that can shape the future, why would this one instance (one debate round) entrench the mindset or prevent us from challenging the system's mindset in the next round, at school, in the workplace, and so on? Furthermore, there is a time frame problem: either the alternative works too slowly to avoid the mega-impact or the impact is so far off that we do not need to act immediately if we have identified a real problem with a real solution that could be put to referendum, put to government leaders, or lobbied for to alleviate real suffering. In short, if the negative runs a kritik saying that only our in-round discourse matters but the impacts of the kritik are global or apocalyptic in nature, it is unlikely the ballot can bring meaningful change. As such, the argument is really a <u>non-unique</u> disadvantage masquerading as a kritik.

Finally, you can challenge the assumption that nothing really happens when we play the game of debate utilizing fiat. As a debater, you can discuss the educational merits of role-playing as though we are policy makers. Doing so helps us understand the real problems and solutions available in our society and how decisions are actually made. The game helps us develop the skills necessary to be informed voters, effective activists, savvy journalists, and responsible politicians.[4]

Again, although kritiks may seem complex, break them down into their fundamental parts: link, impact, alternative, and framework. Think about each of those pieces as they relate to you and your case. Find ways to diminish or deny those pieces. And offer a couple of responses on each level of the kritik. If you can beat any aspect of the kritik, you are *likely* to eliminate its relevance.

Critical Affirmatives

Up to now, we have explored the ways kritiks are run on the negative.[5] Kritiks are not the sole purview of the negative, however. Affirmative teams can also craft critical affirmatives. In these instances, they wish to challenge a pattern of thought or type of action. Thus, they construct their affirmative strategy around critical argumentation. Typically, this takes one of four critical affirmative forms: engaging the topic, policy making, using hybrid approaches, and refusing the topic.

Engaging the Topic Critical Affirmatives

Critical affirmatives that engage the topic develop their harms story around the flawed way of thinking found in the status quo. Typically, debaters offer a link to the status quo mindset with an observation on <u>inherency</u>. Then, they explain the harms associated with that thinking. Finally, they show how the alternative approach highlighted by the resolution is a superior perspective. The only thing missing is a traditional plan text because they subscribe to the notion that fiat does not exist. Rather, our educational discourse in the round is the only thing that matters.

As the negative, you have several options that have already been discussed. You can deny or diminish the link to the status quo. You can mitigate or deny the harm. You can criticize the alternative as a flawed approach or as an ineffective way to produce change. You can run a counter-kritik against the case.

In addition, you can distance yourself from the status quo by running a counterplan that challenges the status quo and the resolution while not linking to the kritik offered in the case. Ultimately, this would give you the superior advocacy in the round. Finally, you can challenge the framework of the affirmative by explaining why plans are necessary for fairness and/or education.[6]

Policy-Making Critical Affirmatives

Policy-making critical affirmatives use the exact same approach as above except that they provide a plan text. Thus, the affirmative advocates a specific course of action, which can overcome the harms of the existing way of thinking. This gives the judge something that can be visualized, which can be very useful in crafting a persuasive narrative in the closing <u>rebuttals</u> of the round. Ultimately, the affirmative uses a fiat-based framework showing how altering the perspective of government would lead to positive change.

Essentially, all of the techniques used to answer a kritik or a traditional policy case can be levied as responses to this type of critical affirmative. After all, this case still operates in the world of fiat, meaning that it is open to harms attacks, solvency attacks, case turns, disadvantages, counterplans, and counter-kritiks. Given that most judges at the high school level have an expectation of fiat-based debate, this approach allows critical debaters to speak persuasively to those critics.

Hybrid Approaches

The hybrid approach to a critical affirmative leaves the door open for advocating a pre-fiat or fiat-based perspective. The 1AC describes the pre-fiat implications of voting affirmative but also explores the benefits of implementing the plan. Thus, either the plan can be a case study for exploring the truth of the kritik in a pre-fiat world, or it can be the fiat-based advocacy of the affirmative, which solves the impacts of the kritik. Some debaters may choose to collapse to the pre-fiat case if their opponents are rooted heavily in the policy maker paradigm; conversely, they might opt for pushing the fiat-based framework if their opponents are critical debaters themselves. Personally, I think this approach is dodgy and opens the door for confusion in the round. I believe the debate gets much clearer, and easier to win, if the affirmative chooses to meet the negative debaters on their own terms. In other words, if the negative team focuses its efforts on pre-fiat kritiks, then go for the pre-fiat aspect of the 1AC. If the negative focuses on developing disadvantages or counterplans, then go for the policy-making impacts of the plan.

As the negative going up against a hybrid affirmative, your answers flow from the same places as they would if your opponents ran an engage-the-topic or a policy-making critical affirmative. In other words, anything you can say to one or the other applies to this round. However, you need to pin the affirmative debaters down early—in the first cross-examination—as to which world they advocate: the pre-fiat implications of voting affirmative or the policy-making impacts of the plan text.[7]

Refusing the Topic

The final form of a critical affirmative refuses to engage the resolution at all. In this scenario, the affirmative either believes the resolution requires immoral advocacy or finds it completely irrelevant to more important discussions. Thus, it runs whatever criticism it wants to inject into the round. Typically, these kritiks advance the understanding of systemic racism or inequality inherent in our society or even in academic debate. Thus, the team runs its kritik in every round, whether it is affirmative or negative.

As the negative, teams have their standard kritik answers, refuting the link, the impact, the alternative, and the framework. In addition, they can inject a heavy dose of their own framework theory, discussing the benefits of limiting affirmatives to a predictable topic area. Be careful, though, as much of the analysis supporting those parameters could be claimed as additional links to the kritik.

Kritiks offer a number of advantages for debaters. First, they provide an alternative to the strict utilitarian calculus of traditional policy debate. They give us an opportunity to investigate the underpinnings of our thought processes and approaches to problem solving and offer the chance to explore more illuminating ways of seeing things. Second, they give teams a potential strategic option generic enough to apply to almost any debate round. This can be a great equalizer for smaller teams without the capabilities to invest heavily in topic-specific research. That said, it is imperative that debaters think through their link, impact, and alternative carefully so they can correctly apply the framework that best complements the story of the kritik proper. Doing so will aid their ability to persuasively defend the argument, facilitate a clear and engaging debate with their opponents, and help the judge understand the role of the kritik in the debate.

9. Performance Debate

One of the most divisive issues in this century has been the rise of performance debate. Minority debaters and those using performance have risen to the highest levels of success, advancing to elimination rounds at the high-school-level Tournament of Champions, winning the National Debate Tournament and Cross Examination Debate Association national tournaments, and earning top speaker awards at the National Debate Tournament. Many of those who practice performance debate (but not all) also challenge the norms and conventions of the activity. This has drawn criticism from within the debate community and from outsiders commenting on the value of the activity itself.

The hostile reaction to performance stems from a lack of understanding of what it really is, why it developed, and how it functions. It stems from a fear of losing what "we" define as debate, an activity that "we" love. It may even stem from blatant racism, in some cases. Underneath it all, the debaters, judges, and coaches who participate in academic debate can be extremely passionate about it. People fell in love with it for a reason, as I did. Those reasons are different for different people, and they fear losing what made debate relevant and important to them. Their apprehensiveness has led some to mischaracterize what performance is and retaliate against it and the teams that look like they might practice it by dismissing its validity, expressing anger towards its practice, and rejecting the concept in its entirety. Some write off the success of performance by saying people are "afraid to vote against black teams" or that "minority debaters only win because of the tactic, not because of the skills of the debaters."

I find this perspective troubling on many levels. There is excellent justification for incorporating the ideals of performance into policy debate. There is ample room for it to exist within this academic discipline without destroying or diminishing traditional notions. Performance and the debaters who practice it can inject life into traditionalists and invigorate the activity. Debate is built on the idea of exploring different viewpoints, of seeing the world through other perspectives. It is an empowering activity. We should not exclude and fear what is new and different. We should welcome it with open minds. We should use it to more fully understand ourselves, make the activity even better, and create a springboard for better decision-making and social interaction in our everyday lives.

I do not intend to fully explore performance debate in all its forms and methods, as that would require an entire book in its own right. Performance is a catchall term with roots in the world of communication studies. It is incredibly broad in its practice. As such, a complete examination in this space is impossible. Nevertheless, I will examine what it is, why it exists, how it is used, and some of the ways in which debaters can respond to or engage with it.

Origins of Performance

Performative debate is a relatively new phenomenon with origins in the mid-1990s. Although not referred to or thought of as performance debate at the time, some competitors started incorporating third person *narratives* to develop their harms or impact stories. Many of those debaters were disenchanted with policy debate's trend toward discussing large impacts in a very clinical way. In other words, debaters regularly spoke of death and suffering without much or any thought to the very real pain associated with those harms stories and impact scenarios. Thus, those frustrated by this trend began reading narratives or personal accounts of the people who were suffering. This relied on an element of performance to make the judge *feel* the impact and to make him or her more inclined to vote for that team. For instance, in the fall of 1994, the Cross Examination Debate Association was debating issues of violent crime. A team running a case on drunk driving at that time might not have relied on public safety arguments steeped in statistics or the staggering economic consequences of accidents related to drunk driving. Rather, the team would perhaps have read the testimonials of family members who had lost a loved one or even the testimonial of a drunk driver whose life was destroyed after his actions killed another human being.

After several years, some debaters began to question why policy debate relied so heavily on jargon, speed, confrontational language, and the like.

They concluded and/or argued that debate had become elitist—a white man's game. It catered to the dominant culture's primary perspectives on communication while ignoring and marginalizing the ways in which people from other cultures communicate.

This is not to say that the activity is inherently racist. Rather, the perspective holds that the activity favors native English speakers who have grown up with the communication norms of the dominant culture; hence, those debaters experience privilege in the activity. This does not mean that the activity or the people who participate in it are nefarious; it simply suggests that members of the dominant culture benefit from the inherent privilege of growing up as part of that system.

Furthermore, debaters noted that different forms of communication offer unique insights into the world. Ask any foreign language instructor to tell you about the benefits of being multilingual. Thus, incorporating different cultural contexts into the debate actually fosters greater understanding of the world around us.

Take, for example, the insights offered by intercultural communications professors Pamela Cooper, Carolyn Calloway-Thomas, and Cheri Simonds. In their work, *Intercultural Communication: A Text with Readings*, they explain that

> *traditional standards of rationality* ask questions such as:
> 1. Are the claims supported by the facts?
> 2. Have all relevant facts been considered?
> 3. Are the arguments internally consistent?
> 4. Does the reasoning used conform to the tests of formal and informal logic?[1]

This is precisely what transpires in a traditional policy debate round. Debaters offer claims, read supporting quotations, and use their own analysis. They examine the evidence presented by themselves and their opponents for omissions, errors, and the like. Eventually the activity developed specific structures—stock issues, disadvantages, counterplans, and so on—for analyzing those arguments.

The authors, however, go on to explain that human beings are natural storytellers. Everything we do—the way we make sense of the world—is understood through narratives. This is true whether we use traditional Western patterns of thought in math and science or not. Thus, they explain that when communication occurs between people with different cultural backgrounds, it makes more sense to examine thoughts through narrative rationality, which is concerned with both coherence and fidelity, the idea being that there is internal consistency within the narrative and that the story itself "'rings true' to the listener." In terms of narrative rationality, they further explain that coherence asks such questions as these:

1. Do the elements of the story flow smoothly?
2. Is the story congruent with the stories that seem related to it?
3. Are the characters in the story believable?[2]

It is important to recognize that both methods of examining arguments and logic—traditional debate and performance—are legitimate. Both provide insight into the world. With performance debate, we simply acknowledge this fact. There are multiple ways of approaching the debate to determine the validity of the analysis provided. The different methods offer unique insight into the issues explored. Opening space for those methods also allows individuals from diverse backgrounds to access the benefits of the activity equally.

Once performance entered the world of competitive debate, teams took one of two directions. One group began indicting the system as elitist, claiming that the power structures of the activity are rooted in racism, sexism, classism, and so forth. They called upon judges to punish teams for playing the traditional game of policy debate. Then, they engaged in their own performative communication style—rapping, reciting poetry, singing, dancing, reciting personal testimonials, and so forth.

The other group sought to expand the scope of acceptable communication within the policy debate world. They chose to communicate in a more natural and oftentimes more culturally relevant way, using those same forms of communication. They asked judges to listen to their way of approaching the debate and not punish them for failing to play the game of their opponents. For example, they asked judges not to vote against them simply because they did not speak as quickly as their opponents or were not as familiar with the jargon used by traditional teams. Rather, they said judges should look at the holistic contributions to the debate to evaluate who made the most positive contributions to the content being debated. They reserved the punitive approach (used by the first group of performance teams) for opponents who refused to allow them space to engage in the debate using their own nontraditional communication style.

Unpacking Performance

Performance debate does not refer to a type of argument run by debaters. Rather, it refers to the way they present their arguments. The term "performance" stems from the world of communication studies in which any speech act can be considered a performance. Thus, even traditional policy debate using the linear approach of <u>line-by-line</u> debating is technically a performance or performative. For ease of communication, however, the term "performative" in the debate space refers to any style of debating that is not traditional. The differentiation in delivery matters for two primary reasons.

First, the language we use to express our ideas shapes the understanding of those thoughts when we communicate with others. While this is obviously true when comparing languages such as German, English, Chinese, Gwich'in, and Ahtna, it can be just as important when speaking from a place of cultural identity. The culture of the sender and the receiver(s) affects the understanding of our words. Exploring an issue in one's own cultural language makes it more personal and more understandable (to the student) than examining it purely through the expressions of language found in a foreign culture.

A cautionary word for debaters and judges from different sides of the performance issue: speaking in different cultural languages can hinder our ability to communicate effectively. A blatant disregard for the cultural identity of others in the room can make it nearly impossible to have a productive conversation. Thus, if debaters and judges are not using a common language, it may be difficult for the debate to progress in a positive, meaningful way. As such, the best debates occur when all participants make a concerted effort to work with one another in a productive way.

Second, the rhetorical delivery of our ideas also shapes the meaning and impact of the words we use. In short, how we speak matters; it creates meaning and shapes understanding. Take Martin Luther King Jr.'s address from the steps of the Lincoln Memorial. His speech is regarded as one of the most influential in American history. Throughout his speech he used historical examples, biblical allusions, references to commonly accepted political theory, and metaphors such as "a bad check" written to black people following the Civil War, all of which allowed the content to ring true with listeners. These elements alone probably would not have made it one of the most powerful speeches ever given, however. Reading the transcript of the speech is insightful, but listening to an audio recording or watching a video of the event is an entirely different experience.

Throughout his address, he used a cyclical organization pattern that emphasized key points over and over again. This ensured that the critical elements stuck with the audience. He also began the speech with a soft, deliberate speaking style. Over the span of roughly fifteen minutes, he gradually raised the volume and increased the cadence of his delivery, building in intensity. The overall effect of that delivery made it so powerful that it has stuck in the American conscience. It highlighted the injustice in society while also promising a brighter future. Truly, the delivery used in that address was just as important for conveying a meaningful message as the words themselves. Ultimately, performance debate is also about using various methods of delivery to create and shape meaning.

Performance in Practice

By now, it should be crystal clear that performance or a performative is not—in itself—necessarily a strategic act used to win the debate. The team running a performative usually attempts to win in one of three ways. First, it may try to win on the line-by-line that policy debate as it is traditionally practiced (or the <u>resolution</u> itself) is elitist, racist, or the like. As such, a team that plays by the rules of that game or advances the norms of that game should be punished with a losing ballot. Ironically, in order to win on this argument, the team often engages in some pretty heavy <u>theory</u> debate on the line-by-line, which is the very system it says is elitist, exclusionary, and/or racist.[3] Another way of looking at this is that they are doing a performance while winning on a <u>kritik</u> that indicts policy debate as harmful.

Second, a team may attempt to win by showing that its chosen performance is empowering, enlightening, or educational. Something about its chosen communication style has a distinct benefit to the individuals in the round or society as a whole, and the team using it in the round should be rewarded for bringing it into the debate space. For example, I once saw members of a performance team use music to tell the story of their case. They noted that music holds a unique place in society and is a source of power but argued that it is especially true within the black community, dating back from the days of slavery all the way to the present. They contended that music has two special roles. On the one hand, it provides a form of catharsis and escape. It helps those who are suffering to cope with their pain. It also highlights that they are not alone, that someone else understands their plight.

On the other hand, it is also a form of activism or a call to be activist. It generates purpose, will, and support throughout society. To see music at work, one need look no further than musical icons like Bob Dylan, Bob Marley, and Joan Baez. Even bands not generally considered activists often use songs to make a point: Black Sabbath warning of the dangers of nuclear holocaust, Green Day fearing the blind faith of going along with the system without asking questions, pop icons coming together in the 1980s to raise awareness and money to fight African hunger by singing "We Are the World." Ultimately, the team claimed the judge should vote for the medium of song as an agent of change. Thus, the speech act or performance of the team is actually a form of real-world, in-round activism. As such, the medium and message of the performance function as the alternative for a kritik.

With these first two strategies, students engaging in performance-based approaches are learning how to use their own cultural modes of communication to engage in constructive discourse and to highlight injustice present in our world. In the debate space, they are, themselves, activists. In a sense, they are educating the participants in the debate about the inherent imbalance of power within society's institutions. Furthermore, they are raising awareness by making those in the dominant cultural group feel uncomfortable, out of place, or marginalized. In a bit of role reversal, they help others to see the world through their eyes. As an educational activity, the goal of these approaches is to open minds in an effort to promote equality and empowerment.

Third, a team may attempt to win through standard cost-benefit analysis and usual forms of debate arguments, but members use a different mode of communication (or code) to advance their ideas. Thus, they use song, metaphors, irony, images, and so on to make arguments related to the topic. In this approach, they still advance a standard affirmative case through the stock issues or a disadvantage through link, brink, and impact, but they simply communicate those ideas differently.

Engaging Performance Teams

As noted earlier, many traditionalists question the validity of performance. They claim it is devoid of merit and wins only because people are afraid to vote against it. I find this claim suspect. Perhaps the real issue is that debaters have not figured out how to effectively engage performance teams. When kritiks were first introduced, some teams won with them not because they were skilled at using the strategy but because others had not yet figured out how to respond to them. At the time, there was a vehemently verbal group of people who said kritiks were killing debate, devoid of educational merit, and so forth. When counterplans were introduced as a new strategy, affirmative teams were plagued by a similar phenomenon. I suspect the same was true when generic disadvantages were first introduced. Why would the use of performance be any different? Rather than dismiss performance and levy ad hominem attacks against what might be performance teams, debaters should develop strategies for interacting in constructive ways with the debaters who practice it.

If you go up against a performance team, there are a plethora of ways to engage it. As with any argument that confounds you at first, <u>cross-examination</u> is critical for moving forward. You must ensure that you understand your opponents' point of view and what they hope to achieve. Thus, ask questions to get at the heart of their strategy:

How should the judge evaluate this round?
- Is he or she voting to challenge a corrupt system?
- Is he or she evaluating the merits of the substantive issues?
- Is the <u>framework</u> more important than the substantive issues related to the topic?

Why should the judge vote against us in this round?
- Is your contention that I am evil and should be punished?
- Is the judge making a statement about racism, classism, or something similar in the debate community?
- Are you attempting to prove that your side of the resolution is superior to my side?
- What if I agree with you? Why should I lose if we agree?

What was the purpose of the chosen performance?
- Was it an act of persuasion?
- Was it uniquely situated to earn a ballot simply because the code of communication deserves the ballot? If so, why? What makes it superior to all other forms of communication?

How can opponents assigned the opposite side of the resolution and paired against you win a ballot?

Second, remember that most performance teams still run arguments discussed in the previous chapters: a standard affirmative case, disadvantages, counterplans, or kritiks. Everything in the chapters on those types of arguments can be applied to the specific strategy of the teams being debated. Simply respond to their arguments as you would in any other round. If they advance a standard affirmative case, diminish the harms and <u>solvency</u> while running your own offensive arguments against them.[4] If they run disadvantages, answer the link, internal link(s), brink, <u>uniqueness</u>, and impacts. If they present a counterplan, respond by addressing its <u>competiveness</u>, ability to solve the <u>net benefit</u>, and so forth. If they develop a kritik, respond to the link, the impact, and the <u>alternative</u>.

Third, even if teams choose to disengage from the topic and the activity itself, they often use the fundamental elements of an affirmative case or the concepts of kritiks to develop their ideas. Thus, you can address whether or not the link applies to you and your strategy in the round; whether the impact of the rules, norms, and conventions of policy debate are harmful; and whether their alternative is beneficial or counterproductive.

At the impact level, if your opponents critique policy debate as evil, defend its merits. Highlight the educational benefits of interrogating a topic in this way. Explain that the system—for better or worse—is here to stay. There are systemic, institutional structures that cannot magically be whisked away. However, traditional policy debate is empowering. It helps us develop the tools necessary to navigate the political process, the legal process, corporate America, and the bureaucracies that surround us. If we want to effect real change in society, we must know how to navigate the system and beat those in power at their own game. For example, many in the Alaska Native community have begun to realize this firsthand. If they want to defend themselves against corporations wanting to set up shop in their lands, then they need to understand how to communicate effectively with those visiting their communities. If they want the power to control their own communities, they need to successfully navigate the legal and political systems of the state and federal governments.

This sets up a comparison with the alternative of disengagement from the system or the structures of policy debate. In the language of communication theorists, this ability to communicate in multiple cultural contexts involves code switching. Similarly, professors of communication Judith Martin and Thomas Nakayama explain that "knowledge about how other people think and behave will help you be a more effective communicator."[5] Knowing how to speak various codes and languages grants the speaker the ability to adapt effectively to the audience. Immersing oneself in the language of another group gives one the ability to understand that group and communicate better across cultural boundaries.

Asking the dominant players for a fair shake is insufficient and unlikely to yield favorable results. Likewise, disengaging from them actually allows them to ride roughshod over the disenfranchised group. However, knowing how to speak to that audience and how to use their systems for their own good grants the disenfranchised the ability to gain a foothold and to claw for acceptance, legitimacy, and influence.

Fourth, debaters could choose to indict the chosen communication code or performance as harmful. It is within the realm of possibility to argue that some communication styles are actually bad. Personally, I would steer clear of those types of arguments for multiple reasons. I do not believe that any communication style is inherently bad. Rather, people can choose to communicate in harmful ways. In addition, arguing that your opponents' method of communication should be rejected will most likely fuel their link that you are part of an elitist system that excludes minority voices. Finally, I believe that debate is communal in nature; we should seek to include others in the discourse, not drive a wedge between us. Ultimately, that is incongruous with the end goal of the activity.

Fifth, offer a counterperformance. Demonstrate that you are willing to communicate in other ways to help garner a more complete understanding of the issues. If they have indicted policy debate as evil, I would love to see a team offer a counternarrative of how policy debate has been beneficial to them and their peers.

Finally, and above all, I recommend debaters and judges make room for cultural differences in the debate space. Cooper, Calloway-Thomas, and Simonds note, "If we hope to be effective communicators in the educational environment we need to understand that cultural differences may result in differences in learning and/or cognitive style and affect the student-teacher relationship as well as the relationships among students."[6] No real benefit comes from silencing the cultural expression or voice of any debater in the round. Rather, give all participants the opportunity to speak, learn, and grow according their cultural identity. Make an honest effort to engage the other speakers in a meaningful way. Ultimately, this approach benefits all participants. All are welcomed into the debate space. All are given the opportunity to learn. We may even find that we learn something new through our exposure to different ways of learning and knowing.

There are many ways to answer performances. My advice: do not get caught up in the fact that your opponents are "running" a performance. Rather, think about what they are saying. Take a deep breath. Chances are, they are running a form of argumentation you are already familiar with from previous experience. Think critically about that argument and answer it.

10. The Evolution

I love debate in all its forms. I especially love policy debate. The reasons are numerous but include the length of speeches and the fact that all four debaters are given two of them. This gives competitors ample opportunity to interrogate the issues with an evidentiary foundation, analytic development and refutation, and comparative framing of what is most important. It also allows for creativity and experimentation. The debaters can inject themselves and their own ideas into the debate. As a result, the activity grows and evolves over time. But, unlike a true evolutionary process, nothing really goes away. Rather, participants build upon previous ideas, and the options available to them become more numerous.

Debaters, coaches, and judges around the country regularly find themselves confused by new types of arguments or are confounded by how they are supposed to evaluate them. Generally, the new arguments—be they generic <u>disadvantages</u>, <u>counterplans</u>, or <u>kritiks</u>—fail to make sense to them because they do not see the change that occurred within the activity.[1] This chapter explores this evolution of policy debate. It sheds light on the arguments or trends that participants may encounter when they venture outside their local circuit. Understanding why and how the arguments developed should help debaters craft answers to them, allow debaters to speak to the judge at the back of the room, and help coaches improve their ability to prepare students for the unknown.

Stage 1: The Judicial Model of Debate

In the beginning, all policy debate used the judicial model of analysis. This meant all debate centered on the <u>stock issues</u> in an effort to prove the resolution true or false. The affirmative team was tasked with proving it true, demonstrating the guilt of the status quo, so to speak. The affirmative, like the prosecution in a court of law, was given the first and last word in the debate. However, the status quo was given the benefit of the doubt. It was "presumed innocent until proven guilty."

The affirmative was tasked with demonstrating different elements of a case in order to prove that guilt. Just like in a criminal court of law where the prosecution has to prove means, motive, and opportunity, the affirmative had to prove five stock issues. First it established a harm happening in the status quo. Then it had to show that the harm was significant, rising to a level of severity or affecting enough people to justify our attention. Further, it had to demonstrate an inherent barrier, meaning it had to show that something actually prevented a solution from being put into effect. In addition, it had to identify a proposed course of action or plan that fell within the boundaries established by the resolution. Finally, it had to prove the plan could actually overcome the inherent barrier and solve the harm. The negative, on the other hand, only had to cast doubt on one of those five stock issues. If it did that, then the affirmative had failed to prove its case. Conversely, the negative succeeded in defending the presumed innocence of the status quo, and a negative ballot would be awarded by the judge.

Stage 2: The Legislative Model of Debate

Eventually, debaters recognized a disconnect between the topics debated and the judicial model of interrogation. The phrasing of the resolutions and the plans people advocated were similar to the questions debated in Congress, not in the courts. In short, it did not really make sense to use this judicial blueprint. When we debate policies that can go into effect, we do not decide whether or not the status quo is "innocent until proven guilty." Rather, when a decision is being made at a school board, on a city council, or in the halls of Congress, we examine whether the proposal will lead to more good than bad. Given the topics in the resolution and the plans offered by affirmatives, it only made sense to evaluate the consequence of the policy. Does it leave us better off with it than without it? If we would be better off with the plan, then the ballot should go to the affirmative.

This shift in the way of thinking had a number of effects on the stock issues. First, they lost their primacy in the debate. Nothing revolved entirely around the stock issues any longer. That is not to say they became unimportant. After all, they are still a useful storytelling device for showing why we need to change something or why we need the affirmative plan. With this perspective, though, the negative can cast a lot of doubt upon those stock issues but fail to win a negative ballot because we can still determine that some good can come from implementing the plan.

Second, significance and harms collapsed into a single idea. We were no longer concerned with both the quantitative and qualitative <u>impacts</u> of the status quo. Debaters simply examined whether there was some sort of benefit achieved by voting for the affirmative. Third, debaters no longer had to show an inherent barrier. They merely had to demonstrate that the plan was not being done now or to identify the reasons why the harm was occurring. In addition, debaters in the legislative model no longer saw the status quo as "innocent until proven guilty." That is, the negative no longer benefited from presumption because we were looking purely at the outcomes of the policy.

This explains some of the confusion that judges or debaters who were born into the judicial model have when they encounter cases run on the national circuit, for example. They look at those cases and say, "But they haven't shown a barrier . . . they haven't shown what is preventing the policy from going into effect." They are entering the debate from the judicial model of analysis, whereas the national circuit debater is grounded in the legislative model.

Something else happened that actually led to the growth of the legislative model. Debaters noted that whenever we pass a bill into law, decision makers evaluate a lot more than whether or not that law fixes a problem. They examine many possible effects of the policy. Affirmative teams thus began running additional advantages that were not directly <u>linked</u> to the topic area identified in the resolution. The resolution might be about the environment, but they included economics advantages, for example. Negative debaters began running disadvantages to show there were negative consequences of passing a policy—for instance, you pass this environmental legislation, and it has a negative effect on business confidence or economic development. Simply, the legislative model allowed debaters to have discussions that extended beyond the resolution and the affirmative case as presented in the first affirmative <u>constructive</u> (1AC).

After a number of years, debaters recognized that politicians often disagree with a piece of legislation not because of the unintended consequences but because it would prevent us from doing something else that would be even better for society. Thus, the idea of opportunity costs or counterplans came into play. Debaters began running counterplans as alternative policy options that would be lost if we voted for the affirmative.

Once again, debaters born in different eras have different conceptions of these arguments. Many coaches from traditional circuits who were trained in the judicial model of debate have a difficult time understanding the applicability of generic disadvantages, which apply to the whole resolution but do not clearly answer the case laid out in the 1AC. On the surface, these coaches do not see how those arguments necessarily indict the case presented by the affirmative. In the case of counterplans, they indicate that a superior option might be available, but such an option does not necessarily disprove the resolution. Of course, debaters growing up in the legislative model are wondering what on earth they are supposed to do to win the round when confronted with a judge who does not see the value in a disadvantage or counterplan. They are coming at the debate from two different perspectives. Those traditional judges give the negative team a great deal of latitude on the case debate to simply cast doubt on one of the stock issues, whereas the debater is thinking, "I have to prove that something bad happens when you vote affirmative, but you are telling me those arguments are not appropriate."

Debaters need to understand where their judges are coming from so that they can be more persuasive for that particular judge and can figure out how to craft their response. Likewise, if you are a debater trained in the judicial model who is confronted with an opponent using the legislative model, you can start to think about how you can answer those arguments given the perspective used by your opponents.

Stage 3: Beyond Utilitarian Consequentialism

In the 1970s, the landscape of academic debate began to change drastically in the United States. At the collegiate level, the Cross Examination Debate Association was formed as an alternative to the National Debate Tournament. At the high school level, Lincoln-Douglas debate was introduced as an alternative to the policy format. The founders of these alternatives sought to move away from the complexity of policy debate. As teams transitioned to the legislative model, arguments became more complex. This had a ripple effect on speeches: they became more technical, the amount of jargon or shorthand increased, and the rate of delivery skyrocketed as time constraints made it difficult to truly explore these complex ideas. Simply, as debate became more complex and more in-depth, debaters found that they no longer had the time to fully develop their ideas. Thus, they started talking faster . . . and faster . . . and *faster*. Many coaches wanted an alternative to that highly technical, jargon-laced, and fast-paced delivery. Furthermore, they recognized that we already had a format dedicated to exploring the pragmatic impacts of policies. Thus, they focused the new events on the value model of debate, giving debaters the opportunity to explore the principles that guide our decision-making. They believed that by shifting away from the pragmatic to the principled, we would naturally encourage debaters to slow down.

However, policy debaters recognized that those principles affect the way we think about specific policies, too. Thus, they began incorporating the ideas of the value model into policy debates. The first step witnessed the introduction of the goals-criteria case (discussed in chapter 5). In reality, a goals-criteria case is not that different from the value-criterion structure of a Lincoln-Douglas debate case. A goals-criteria case provides an opportunity to identify a goal or principle worth pursuing and demonstrates that the plan and resolution support that goal. The 1AC speaker establishes a goal or value that we should try to uphold. Then that speaker describes the criterion used to evaluate whether the value had been upheld. Finally, he or she presents a relatively traditional affirmative case that meets the criterion and upholds the value.

At the same time, debaters discovered they did not necessarily have to get into detailed analysis of how to incorporate principled decision-making into the policy maker process. Sometimes we can identify principles that we think are simply paramount in our society. Justice, equality, and the avoidance of genocide are generally accepted as good. Debaters labeled those impacts as decision rules or moral imperatives. It was another way of incorporating value principles, but it allowed them to bring those ideals into a specific round, whether they were affirmative or negative. When labeled a moral imperative or decision rule, it operated as an a priori impact in the round.[2]

A few years later, as collegiate policy began to look similar in both the Cross Examination Debate Association and the National Debate Tournament, the concepts trickled into high school rounds. However, the creation of nonpolicy formats of debate had another effect on how debaters thought about arguments. They began to realize that they could question the assumptions of the other team, the way they approach decision-making, and the nature of ethical speech. They concluded that there were principled ideas or patterns of thought that are destructive and should be avoided. This is where kritiks came from, addressing the language of the opponents, the way they carried themselves in the round, and the way they constructed their ideas.

Nothing really new was happening, of course. Debaters borrowed the structures of earlier arguments to construct new ways of criticizing the opposition on a deeper level than substantive impacts. They took the link and impact chains of disadvantages to identify a flawed way of thinking or acting. They developed an internal link chain to arrive at a negative consequence or impact. Likewise, they used the concept of a competing policy option to develop the notion of an <u>alternative</u> mindset or behavioral system. Finally, they made the issues more relevant to the decision in the round by borrowing the <u>theory</u> argumentation that developed around <u>topicality</u> and <u>fiat</u> abuse to create discussions of pre-fiat implications arising from in-round discourse.

Now, why do kritiks not make sense to so many judges? As a debater, why are you confronted with judges from local circuits who dislike or do not buy the story you are selling with the kritik? If they grew up in the legislative era, they do not start from a point that considers pre-fiat implications. They are concerned with evaluating the substantive impacts of the plan. They are sold on the educational merits of engaging in some degree of role-playing in the policy maker process. They see the academic benefits flowing from learning how to navigate an understanding of what happens when a policy option is implemented. Thus, the kritik does not naturally fit into their frame of reference. For those who began in the judicial model, the kritik really fails to prove anything. They do not naturally see how the kritik proves or disproves the resolution.

However, if you as a debater recognize the judges are coming from either the judicial or legislative model, you can tailor or focus your efforts on the parts of the argument that resonate with them. If they are from the judicial model or traditional debate mindset, you can point out at the very beginning that the affirmative team has to justify where it comes from in the round. If those debaters cannot justify their decisions and the way they approach the round and you identify the flaw in their thinking and why that is bad, perhaps they have failed to develop their case because the entire foundation of their argumentative approach is corrupt. For the policy maker of the legislative model, your efforts should focus on the pre-fiat implications of unethical speech or the practical effects of building a policy on a flawed way of thinking. Obviously, clash can still flow from all these points, but this should help everyone understand how to make arguments relevant to different judges.

Stage 4: Presentation Matters

As debaters questioned the ways they thought about arguments through the use of the kritik, they began to think about how we were actually interrogating the topics. We regularly discussed pain and suffering in our harms stories or impact scenarios. In some cases, we even discussed nuclear war and annihilation. However, it was done in a very sterile way. Debaters were disassociated from the impacts. It was like doing a math problem. Whoever could tally the most dead bodies on the <u>flow</u> won the round. But these issues are about real people who suffer real harms and experience real pain. Debaters began to say, "Wait a minute, let's make the judge feel the pain."

So, they introduced third-person narratives as a way of exploring the real effects on people. This allowed judges to identify with the victims, the people suffering in the status quo. However, mainstream debaters pushed back against this persuasive device by pointing out that their opponents showed suffering of a few but did not quantify how many people suffered. Thus, they argued that their large impacts outweighed the pain of a handful of individuals.

Many debaters responded by using what they learned about kritiks to challenge the practices of mainstream debaters. They ran speed and apocalyptic kritiks to try to ground the debate. They claimed that other debaters were going about the activity in the wrong way. They argued that those practices separate us from real people who experience real harm. Those strategies cater to people who can talk really fast and have the resources to do extensive research. They disenfranchise or exclude nonnative English speakers or debaters from outside the white cultural power structures, not to mention those who compete on small <u>lay judge</u> circuits. This served as a springboard for the next step within the debate community.

The majority of debaters pushed back against these kritiks by saying, "Hey, this is how the game is played. If you don't like it or can't do it, then you don't deserve to win." Then students and coaches responded by noting that there are many different ways to communicate effectively. There are different ways of knowing and of making sense of the world. Why should the methods of the dominant majority or privileged debaters set the tone for everyone? Thus, a minority of students and coaches decided to abandon the entire system. They created their own rules by running arguments criticizing the dominant structures, speaking of the importance of minority empowerment, and presenting their material in culturally relevant ways.

Thus, performance-based approaches to debate took hold. Today, we have competitors singing, rapping, reciting poetry, using imagery, and giving personal testimonials. Sometimes they advance traditional arguments that include an affirmative case complete with the stock issues, disadvantages, counterplans, and kritiks. Sometimes they present their own performance as the alternative for a kritik on the activity—a kritik that argues the activity is devoid of benefits, has become elitist, and is no longer useful in a democratic society, which should be responsible to all students rather than to a chosen few.

Stage 5: What's Next?

Everything in debate is ever-changing. Nothing really goes away. We still have judges and debaters operating within the judicial model of debate who are rooted heavily in the stock issues. We have debaters, judges, and coaches firmly planted in the legislative model of debate, evaluating the plan through cost-benefit analysis with the use of advantages, disadvantages, and counterplans. We have debaters who grew up questioning the utilitarian consequentialist perspective through the use of kritiks and pre-fiat analysis. Finally, we have debaters challenging the norms and conventions of the activity itself, arguing that there are other ways to present ourselves that are more relevant, culturally appropriate, educationally sound, and empowering for the individual. What comes next? Who knows? I am sure that based on decades of changes as my proof, someday debaters and coaches will develop something new. Furthermore, what is divisive today—the performance—will no longer be seen in that light tomorrow. It will be viewed as just another way of presenting an idea, equally as valuable as the forms and structures that came before it.

11. Establishing Credibility

Up to this point, I have discussed the nature of policy debate: what it looks like, how it developed, its argumentative structures, and how those arguments are evaluated. The remaining chapters examine tangential issues that have a profound impact on the outcome of decisions but are distinct from the systems used to develop and evaluate arguments.

Aristotle, the father of rhetoric, identified three sources of persuasion: logos, pathos, and _ethos_. He explained that all three are necessary to be convincing. Per his definitions, logos refers to sound logical structures. Pathos refers to the speaker's concern for the well-being of the audience. And ethos refers to the speaker's credibility. The first two have been discussed in great detail earlier in this work.

Within the context of policy debate, logos refers to your arguments.[1] Do they contain the critical elements that tell a (mostly) complete story? Are they constructed well? Are they adequately researched? While policy debate places a high degree of emphasis on this concept in theory, pathos and ethos play critical roles in the outcome of decisions in practice. Pathos in policy debate refers to the debaters' ability to adapt to the judging paradigm of the critic at the back of the room. By figuring out the initial mindset of judges, debaters can adapt to them. Do they follow a policy maker paradigm, a stock issues paradigm, or a tabula rasa paradigm? Do they enter the debate from the mindset of the judicial model, the legislative model, or the later eras of debate? Do they have pet peeves, likes, dislikes? Debaters who determine the answers to those questions can adapt as needed.

Finally, debaters have a much higher likelihood of winning a ballot if they are credible and believable speakers. As much as we like to believe "professionally trained" judges focus exclusively on the objective evaluation of arguments made by the debaters, a degree of subjectivity creeps into almost any decision. Any number of subjective elements will come into play in a given debate round. What constitutes a new argument in <u>rebuttals</u> and is therefore not allowed? Do judges allow cross-applications from one argument to another in rebuttals that were not made in earlier speeches? Will they allow a holistic response to an argument or require a high degree of articulation on the <u>line-by-line</u>? Will they allow a following speaker to explain in detail what was confusing, unclear, or not enunciated well by a debater's partner? What arguments truly beat another? These are all questions without clear answers. Furthermore, perceptions can dictate a judge's feelings on these questions when they evaluate any particular debate round.

Holding a high degree of credibility in the mind of the judge can go a long way in your favor. Debaters' ethos is developed through presentation, personality, and the attitude in the way they approach the round, present their arguments, interact with their partners, and engage their opponents. In fact, the judge—consciously or unconsciously—begins judging debaters before the round even begins.

Before the Round

Looking as though you care about the round has a profound impact on judges' perceptions of you. I once had a student who could not figure out why his winning percentage dropped off significantly during his second year of debate, despite competing against most of the same people he had encountered the previous season. Obviously, there were likely several factors in play. However, one thing he did not understand was why several judges were making comments about him not caring or not appearing to care. So, I decided to watch one of his rounds unannounced. I arrived a little more than five minutes before the start time, and his opponent and the community member assigned to judge the round were already there. Ten minutes later, after the round was supposed to have started, he walked into the room nonchalantly. He looked at his opponent and said, "Oops, I forgot a pen." Ten minutes after that he returned to the room and sat down. He looked around at the desk, stood up, and said, "I forgot paper." As he started to walk out of the room, the judge said, with more than a little irritation in his voice, "Here, take some of mine." My student looked a bit like a deer in the headlights and returned to his seat. The round had not even begun, yet my debater was already losing the ballot.

There are any number of factors related to debaters' behavior before the round starts that dictate how they are perceived by the judge. Be on time. Dress appropriately for the circuit on which you compete.[2] Look engaged and ready to debate. Be friendly and chat with your opponents and judge as you wait to get started. If you look frantic, standoffish, or too wrapped up in the upcoming debate, you can create a negative impact with many judges. Ultimately, you want to appear interested in the debate and the other participants. Demonstrating to the judge that you respect the activity and everyone's time will go a long way toward setting you up for success in the round.

During the Round

Once the round begins, there are a number of ways you can ensure the judge sees you as a student prepared for the activity at hand. First, your delivery should sound confident and relaxed. This means different things on different circuits. On local <u>lay judge</u> circuits, debaters should be able to recite much of the first affirmative constructive and first negative constructive from memory. They should have significant eye contact, even though they are reciting <u>cards</u> written by various authors. On the national circuit, debaters should be able to calmly deliver those speeches without appearing rushed or forced. A debater who is aware of his or her surroundings and can look up from time to time to see if the judge is <u>flowing</u> or lost has a greater ability to adapt to the judge, as well.

This is especially true during the delivery of the first affirmative constructive and first negative constructive since debaters have ample opportunity to prepare and practice the materials that are read during those speeches. Stumbling over words, mispronouncing them, and being disorganized are all surefire ways to send a message to the judge that debaters are unprepared to debate.

In later speeches and during <u>cross-examination</u>, debaters should demonstrate they understand their terms. If it becomes apparent that they did not really grasp a concept or did not know how the central aspect of the case functioned, it will be difficult to convince the judge that their arguments are valid in response to those made by their opponents. If the negative runs a Federalism <u>Disadvantage</u>, those on that team should know what federalism means. If the affirmative runs an ocean thermal energy conversion affirmative, teammates should be able to explain what that is and how it works. If the <u>impact</u> on an affirmative case or disadvantage is U.S. hegemony, debaters should know how to say it, what it means, and why it is important.

Throughout the round, debaters should demonstrate to the judge that they are a team. If it appears that one person is doing all the work or that the only material that matters is that presented by the second speaker, the judge may start subconsciously dismissing the efforts of one or the other member of the team. In short, they should build off each other. They ought to demonstrate how the analysis in each other's speeches ties in with the other. Finally, they should use the words "we" and "our" any chance they can.

After the Round

In addition to judging debaters before and during the round, critics also watch competitors after the round. Many judges show up to multiple events throughout the year or simply judge multiple rounds at the same tournament. They are always watching competitors. The things that transpire throughout tournaments influence their view of debaters moving into the future. Your actions immediately after the round are most important. That is, be gracious in winning and in defeat. Show the judge that you are interested in learning from your mistakes, that you appreciate any feedback he or she gave you, and that you are interested in your opponents, as well. I have heard more than a few judges express irritation with a team—or even cut post-round feedback short—because debaters began packing up during their opponents' final speech or while the judge was trying to give an oral critique after the round. Listen to your opponents, look at the judge, and take notes.

Unfortunately (or fortunately), *your* behavior is not the only thing affecting your ethos; the people you associate with also influence how you are perceived by judges. Your past success and the success of your teammates can have an undeniable impact on your future success. In close rounds, whether we like to admit it or not, judges may feel swayed to vote for those who have demonstrated success over the long haul. Simply, it is easier for them to justify that decision to themselves and to anyone who asks.

In addition, I can speak from experience that many community members have expressed their irritation toward various debaters they witnessed engaging in excessive horseplay or disrespecting the school in which an event took place. Some even told me they felt bad after voting against some of these contestants because they were not sure how much they let those students' behavior influence them when deciding the outcome of the round.

Watch what you say about competitors and judges. Everyone who participates in a competitive activity will get upset from time to time. However, you need to learn how to cope with those feelings in a professional manner. Furthermore, talking badly about someone behind that person's back may *actually* be talking about that person behind his or her back. A colleague of mine once relayed a story from his days as a college debater. He and his partner felt that a particular judge might not have liked them all that much. After one particular round in which they really thought they should have won the ballot, they were criticizing, complaining, and talking negatively about the judge while waiting for the awards ceremony to begin. After several minutes of this, they heard someone clear his throat loudly. They looked and saw the judge sitting a few rows in front of them. He looked at them and said, "And you thought it was hard to win by ballot before." Be cognizant of your surroundings. More important, think critically about what people have said and not said. You will find that every judge has valuable insight to offer you. Take the time to figure out why you were ineffective in your communicative efforts and make yourself better in the process.

Finally, represent yourself and your team positively during the awards ceremony. Competitors should remain in competition attire. So many students change into pajamas or sweats before the ceremony because they are thinking ahead to the long bus ride home. At local tournaments, community members often stay for awards, and some of them have expressed their dismay at the lack of professionalism among some teams. If you are at an awards ceremony and did not do as well as you hoped, buckle down and be respectful of those who did earn the awards. If you are still frustrated on the bus ride home, discuss it with your friends in that confined and safe space. Perhaps most critically, if you experience success at awards, act like you have been there before. No one likes to see you gloat. Excessive celebration tells others that you do not care about them. Furthermore, the judges watching awards ceremonies start forming assumptions about those who react inappropriately, perceiving those individuals as jerks or as one-hit wonders. Neither reaction helps the competitor gain success at the next event.

This is by no means an exhaustive discussion of ethos, how it is enhanced, or why it is critical for debaters who want to win ballots. Nevertheless, it should have introduced you to the idea that presence matters. How you conduct yourself affects the perceptions that judges have of you. If they see you in a positive light, you are more likely to pick up their ballot in a close round. So, take the time to ensure that you have a polished delivery, that you dress appropriately, and that you show respect for the other participants in the activity.

12. Cross-Examination

Like ethos, the role of cross-examination (or CX or cross-x) is under-valued by debaters throughout the country. As debaters, we are practically fanatical with the line-by-line debate, responding point-for-point and tit-for-tat along various lines of argumentation. As critics, we are borderline obsessive-compulsive when it comes to following the linear path of thought on each piece of argumentation and evaluating the debaters' efforts to compare argumentation with other arguments in the round. Admittedly, CX is not flowed in policy debate, meaning that most experienced judges evaluate only the argumentative efforts of debaters in their speeches.[1] Nevertheless, CX plays a vital role in clarifying the debate, setting up arguments and answers, and establishing ethos.

Major Reasons for Cross-Examination

Different judges place different levels of importance on CX. Many lay judges and traditional coaches listen intently to every word exchanged between the debaters. Some community lay judges may even base their decision upon something that happened in cross-x. Conversely, many national circuit judges may not listen to CX at all.[2] Nevertheless, an effective CX can be critical to winning a ballot even when you have that judge who decides to take a nap while you ask questions of your opponent. How can that be? CX serves five main purposes in policy debate.

    1. *It clarifies misunderstood/missed points.* This is probably the most important purpose of CX. As my former boss at the University of Alaska Anchorage, Steve Johnson, used to say, the paradox of debate is that it is

about agreement as much as it is about disagreement. One aspect of that statement pertains to the idea that you cannot engage your opponents unless you understand what they said. Quite simply, things will be missed during a speech. Use cross-x to figure out what you missed. In addition, things will be said that you may find confusing. Use cross-x to clarify what your opponents' meant. Making certain you have a solid grasp on what they said ensures you can mount a defense against it.

2. *It makes your opponents take a stand.* There is nothing worse for a judge than having a debater refuse to take a stand in his or her speech. At the end of the round, the critic must understand what the debaters stood for. Likewise, you cannot engage an opponent who refuses to present a clear advocacy. Thus, you should use CX to pin your opponents down on anything that seemed vague or unclear. If they refuse to take a stand when confronted with a direct question, their ethos will suffer.[3]

3. *It sets up arguments.* One routine function of CX is simply to set up arguments you and your partner intend to make in the next speech. In some instances, you may zero in on a vague statement found in the previous speech that you wish to capitalize on to create a disadvantage link or turn story. Thus, you can ask for clarifying statements or more detailed analysis from your opponents, effectively creating an analytic link for your argument that stems directly from your opponent's mouth. In other situations, you may identify logical flaws or inconsistencies in your opponents' arguments. You may also ascertain that your opponents do not truly understand the arguments they ran. Then, you can ask questions that highlight for the judge those flaws, inconsistencies, or misunderstandings. In the next speech, you can exploit them by crafting damaging attacks on the arguments themselves.

4. *It creates prep time for your partner.* Perhaps one of the most under-rated functions of cross-x is that it serves as prep time for your partner. Every second of CX is time he or she can spend prepping responses to an argument or wrapping his or her mind around the argument you were just blindsided by in the first negative constructive. Never yield your CX time to history. Dig, grasp at straws, and ask clarifying questions you already know the answer to. Whatever you do, do not rob your partner of prep time.

5. *It establishes ethos.* Finally, CX provides a perfect opportunity for showing the judge that you are prepared for the debate. Display confidence at all times. Demonstrate understanding, even when you do not really have it.

Rules for the Road

An effective CX is easier said than done, however. I, for example, never truly conquered the task of being the questioner. I approached almost every cross-x as an opportunity to move through the motions. Sure, I clarified points and made my opponent take a stand. However, I never really stood out at setting up arguments for the future. Two of my debaters from South Anchorage High School, Austin Heyroth and Jesse Lehmann, excelled at this endeavor. They were masters at digging deeper until they either reached the point at which their opponents no longer understood their own point or could no longer justify a claim or trapped them in a logical loop without an exit. Regardless, it made it difficult for their opponents to win rounds when they controlled CX so effectively. How can you learn from them? Keep five things in mind.

1. *Have a purpose.* Enter the CX period with a clear goal in mind. Know what you want to accomplish. Set a priority for the things you want to ask. Have you identified a major flaw in your opponents' case? If so, ask questions that get at the heart of that flaw. Above all, know where you want CX to end.

2. *Follow up.* Too many debaters ask insightful questions and highlight flaws in their opponents' arguments but fail to follow up on them during the next speech. If you do not bring it up in the next speech, all of your effort is probably for naught.

3. *Phrasing matters.* Unlike a criminal court lawyer, debaters are allowed to ask leading questions. It is okay to guide your opponent where you want him or her to go. Ask questions that are likely to get the responses you want. That said, never force your opponents into a *yes* or *no* response. Many questions require more than a simple yes/no answer. Judges find it annoying and detrimental to a high-quality debate to hear questioners demanding such responses.

4. *Know when to stop.* Occasionally, debaters find they cannot get an answer to the question they want addressed. There is typically one of two explanations for this scenario. First, a communication breakdown is taking place because the question is unclear or the opponent simply does not understand it. Second, the opponent is purposefully dodging the question. It's time to give up and press on to the next question when (a) you have repeated the question once and rephrased it once to no avail, (b) your opponent begins to ramble, or (c) he or she begins rephrasing your questions. In those instances, you have hit a wall, and it is time to move on to the next series of questions.

5. *Style counts.* How debaters approach CX dictates the judge's perception of them. Having a strong, friendly presence gives debaters an ethos bump that could pay off later in the round. Here are several stylistic suggestions:

GENERAL TIPS
- Be bold and aggressive without moving into jerk and arrogance territory.
- Be controlled, yet relaxed.
- Be cooperative, not provocative.
- Do not ask if everyone is ready. Look around the room for nonverbal cues.
- Stand next to your opponent.
- Look at your opponent when a question is being asked.
- Look at the judge when the question is being answered.
- Smile. Be friendly.

TIPS WHEN ASKING QUESTIONS
- Do not be overly theatrical.
- Do not make editorials or arguments. Ask questions.
- Do not demand unreasonable responses.
- Do not badger.
- Maintain control of the CX period.
- Avoid statements like "This is my cross-x." Try "Thanks, let's move on."
- With the rambler, smile and politely interrupt with "Thanks, I'd like to move on."
- Highlight dropped arguments.
- Do not blindly use terms you do not understand. Ask for clarification.
- Smile. Be friendly.

TIPS WHEN ANSWERING QUESTIONS
- Be confident.
- Do not be afraid to say, "I don't know."
- It is okay to say, "I made a mistake."[4]
- Avoid saying, "My partner will read that in his next speech." Instead, offer to find the evidence and read it aloud or let your questioner see it.[5]
- Minimize tag-team cross-x.[6]
- Do not ramble.
- If given the opportunity to go into depth on a harms or solvency story, take it!
- Be honest.[7]
- Smile. Be friendly.

Dealing with Difficult Cross-Examination Situations

Every debater will eventually face a jerk who raises his or her voice, gets overly aggressive, or is downright mean-spirited. This individual may make you feel uncomfortable and even want to escape to someplace other than a debate tournament. The first thing you should do is take a deep breath, recognize that the person is being a jerk, and remind yourself that he or she is probably making the judge as uncomfortable as you feel. The absolute worst thing you could do is respond in kind, leading to an escalation that ends in a shouting match. Here is my three-step method for dealing with this type of individual:

- Have a shocked or surprised look on your face.
- When the judge is not looking, take a half step backward to ensure your opponent is closer to the judge than you are. Also, lower your volume just a notch.[8]
- If your opponent persists, arch an eyebrow, and connect with your judge.

The bottom line is that you should always remain calm and poised. Be pleasant and innocent. Be the person whom your judge wants to vote for at the end of the round.

13. Flowing

Newcomers and onlookers are often confounded by the terms thrown around by debaters in everyday conversation. Within the debate community, we have developed a system of verbal shorthand to ease communication with one another, hence the prevalence of words like topicality, link, brink, paradigm, and mutually exclusive. While all these terms represent basic concepts, casual observers are often left scratching their heads, wondering what language they are hearing. Take flowing, for example. Reflecting back on rounds, competitors and coaches refer to their flows. Experienced judges discuss their decisions according to what was on the flow as opposed to what was not on the flow.

Flowing simply means taking notes in a debate round. The flow refers to the notes or the record of the round. However, debates have distinct characteristics setting them apart from a lecture or a staff meeting. Typically, those latter settings have a single narrative progressing in a relatively straightforward and natural manner. In a debate, however, multiple stories are told by the debaters. Furthermore, each speech presents an aspect of almost every story. Taking notes straight down the page as one would in a class or meeting would fail to illuminate what transpired at the end of the round. That method fails to make natural connections between the portions of the story told by different debaters. Thus, participants in academic debates created a specialized way of taking notes that allows us to see the narrative of each argument as it progresses or flows from the first speech to the last.[1] This chapter offers a brief introduction to why the flow is important and some helpful suggestions for maintaining an effective flow.

1NC	2AC	Neg Block	1AR	2NR	2AR
Sample Flow DA					
1) Link evidence	1) No Specific link response	1) Extend link evidence from 1NC	1) First response 2) Second response	1) First response	1) First response 2) Second response 3) Third response 4) Fourth response 5) Fifth response
		2) New link evidence		2) Second response	1) First response 2) Second response 3) Third response 4) Fourth response
2) Uniqueness evidence			1) This is not a specific link either	1) Cross-apply the two responses above	
			2) Second response	2) Second response 3) Third response	1) One response
3) Brink evidence			3) Third response	1) One response	
4) Impact evidence	2) No link response	1) One response	1) First response 2) Second response	1) One response	
	3) Turn response	1) First response 2) Second response with evidence	1) First response 2) Second response	1) First response 2) Second response	
			3) Third response	1) One response	
	4) Non-unique response with evidence	1) First response with evidence 2) Second response	1) One response		
	5) No threshold response	1) One response	1) First response 2) Second response 3) Third response	1) First response 2) Second response	1) First response 2) Second response 3) Third response
	6) Turn response with evidence	1) One response			
	7) Turn response with evidence	1) One response			
	8) No impact response	1) First response 2) Second response 3) Third response	1) Extend		

Figure 13.1. The anatomy of a flow

Why We Flow (Well)

There are several reasons for maintaining an accurate flow of the round. Over the years, several of my students have insisted that they did not need to flow the round because they could keep track of arguments in their head. In recent years, debaters have argued that they do not need to flow the round on paper because their opponents share their speech documents with them via a flash drive. However, when I questioned about what transpired in rounds or tried to ascertain why they lost a particular ballot, it became apparent that things were getting missed. Inaccurate or nonexistent record keeping hindered their competitive success and educational development.[2]

1. *It is a record of the round.* An effective flow provides benefits for the future. Coaches rarely have the opportunity to watch their debaters on a regular basis. Having a complete flow allows them to have meaningful discussions with their debaters after the round or tournament. It enables them to dissect what transpired and consider better ways of approaching similar situations in the future. In fact, debaters with stellar flows can provide enough detail that they can redo speeches with their coach to facilitate development for the future. Furthermore, flows are critically important to judges, who use their flows when the debate ends to determine the winner. A solid flow allows them to see which arguments were answered, which were not, which were extended to the end of the debate, how they were evaluated, and so forth.

2. *It is a record of opponents' arguments.* Maintaining a detailed flow of opponents' arguments has two very specific benefits for debaters. After a tournament, they can evaluate effective strategies used by other teams and emulate them in the future. Furthermore, it allows them to conduct focused research against opponents they are likely to debate at other tournaments.

3. *It serves as speaking notes.* The volume of data and quantity of information arising in any given debate round is difficult to process for a listener. As a speaker tasked not only with listening and analyzing what was said but also with generating responses, that burden would be impossible without something to serve as a speaking guide. The flow becomes that speaking aid. A good flow enables the debater to track what was said previously. In addition, debaters often write their responses down on the flow during prep time. Thus, the flow becomes a speaking outline.

4. *It provides organization.* Closely related to the previous concept, judges would get lost if debaters jumped back and forth between different stories or arguments in the round. Likewise, jumping from the middle to the beginning to the end of a story can also make processing what was

said difficult. Debaters who stick to the flow, however, are unlikely to jump around in a disorganized fashion.

5. *It helps win in* _rebuttals_. Finally, a good flow provides a big-picture snapshot of an argument. Seeing the big picture enables the final rebuttalist from each team to craft a compelling narrative that hopefully translates to a win. Likewise, a good flow helps the judge see the big picture so that the proper decision is rendered on the ballot.

Tips for Generating Effective Flows

1. *Use legal-size paper.* To take effective notes in a debate round, we need space. It is difficult to predict which arguments will grow or which parts of arguments will grow as the debate progresses. Thus, larger paper is better. Most debaters and judges find legal-size paper to be adequate in this regard.[3]

2. *Use columns to flow each speech.* Just as you would take notes straight down the page in class, you still travel down the page when taking notes in debate. However, you need to leave room on the page for subsequent speeches to address the points being made. Thus, debaters divide the page into columns for each speech.[4]

3. *Decide between vertical or horizontal flows.* Novice debaters can usually get away with using a landscape or horizontal orientation. Typically, there is less information presented in novice rounds, and beginning debaters have not developed a system of shorthand or minuscule handwriting. As such, they need wider columns. As they gain more experience flowing and the rounds they participate in become more complex, they will find they need more space for arguments to develop. Thus, a portrait or vertical orientation becomes the preferred way of flowing rounds, with one argument per page (see the next point).

4. *Flow one argument per page.* Every new argument or position run in the round—harms story, solvency story, disadvantage, counterplan, kritik, and so on—should be placed on a separate sheet of paper. In part, a separate sheet for separate arguments is important because of the need for space as the argument develops. In addition, it allows debaters to put their flow sheets in the order the arguments will be treated during each speech.

5. *Use space.* Leave space on the sheet of paper between responses. This allows room for development of the ideas to occur on the paper. Your opponent may put three or four responses on everything you say in your speech. It is important that you leave enough room on the flow so that you can see where those responses line up with one another.

6. *Number responses.* Every response made in a debate should be numbered or lettered. This allows subsequent debaters to refer to ideas with very clear <u>signposts</u>—or markers—indicating where they are on the flow. This serves the same function as signposts along the road. They help us navigate; they help us know where we are at any given time.

7. *Write down only key words.* You do not need to write down everything your opponents say in a speech. Rather, you need to capture the key idea they present in the <u>tagline</u>. Often, you can shorten what they said down to two to four words. If there is something within the body of the <u>card</u> or

---

Generic debate
Aff – affirmative
Neg – negative
Rez – resolution
USFG – U.S. federal
    government

Affirmative Case
Ⓗ – harm
Inh – inherency
Ⓢ – solvency
Adv – advantage

Topicality Ⓣ
CI – competing
    interpretations; also
    counterinterpretation
R2P – reason to prefer
BL – bright line
Ⓛ – limits
Ⓟ – precision
F – fairness
E – education
Ed – education
V – voter
AP – a priori

Disadvantages DA
Ⓛ – link
IL – internal link
Ⓑ – brink
Ⓤ – uniqueness
TF – time frame
TH – threshold
! – impact

Counterplans CP
P – perm
NB – net benefit
ME – mutually exclusive

Kritiks Ⓚ
Alt – alternative
FW – framework
RoB – role of the ballot

Miscellaneous
↑ – increase; more; grow
↓ – decrease; less; shrink
= – equals; same
≠ – does not equal;
    different
→ – leads to; results in
Δ – change
Ø – no; none; not; zero
> – greater; more
< – less than
o/w – outweigh
ev – evidence

Topic specific
Cap – capitalism
Dev – development;
    develop
Econ – economy
GW – global warming
Ⓙ – justice

Figure 13.2. Examples of common shorthand used by debaters

analytic that you want to use against them, immediately jot that down as a response in your column of the flow.

8. *Develop a system of shorthand.* Debate is full of its own unique abbreviations and acronyms. In addition, draw upon math, science, and old-fashioned texting language for more ideas on useful shorthand.

9. *Use two (or three) colors.* Use a different color of pen for each team. This creates a clear visual delineation between the affirmative and the negative, which will help you identify who said what and when. When I was a competitor, I used a third color to circle things I wanted to follow up on in cross-examination or to write questions I wanted asked in CX.

10. *Carry extra pens and paper.* Always have backups at the ready. You never know when you will run out of ink or paper in the middle of a round, so always keep a stock of extra supplies on hand. As a judge, I always pull a stack of legal paper out before every round to ensure I do not run out. Likewise, I place two blue pens and two red pens in front of me. If a pen runs out of ink, I drop it on the floor and pick up the next one. That way, I do not miss critical information while I look for a replacement.[5]

An effective flow is critical to good decision-making as both a judge and a competitor. Take the time to work on your flowing skills. Take advantage of these tips to help you become better at flowing debates. I promise, working to develop a good flow will pay dividends in your future success as you move up the ranks of competitiveness, as you take better notes in class, and as you translate those skills to meetings in the workplace later in life.

14. Sample Debate

This chapter presents a mock debate round, bringing together the various concepts discussed in this work. It is a truncated (and lightly edited) version of an actual debate on the 2012–13 national policy debate topic: *Resolved: The United States federal government should substantially increase its transportation infrastructure in the United States.* This shortened debate is typical of what you might find on a local circuit in front of a traditional coach or a community judge with little or no experience. Figures 14.1 through 14.4 illustrate a judge's flow of the debate round.

Sample First Affirmative Constructive Script

Oh, we love our cars. This love ignites the thirst—the thirst for oil. A thirst so great, we are dependent on an oil-based economy. We think we should change that.

OBSERVATION 1: Inherency

1. Oil industry receives $250 billion per year in subsidies.[1]
    ECONOMIST '08   (*Economist.* "The Power and the Glory."
                                                21 June 2008, 4–6)

Look beneath, though, and **the** whole **energy sector is riddled with subsidies, both explicit and hidden**, and costs that are not properly accounted for. Drawing on the work of people like Boyden Gray, a former White House counsel, Mr. Woolsey estimates that

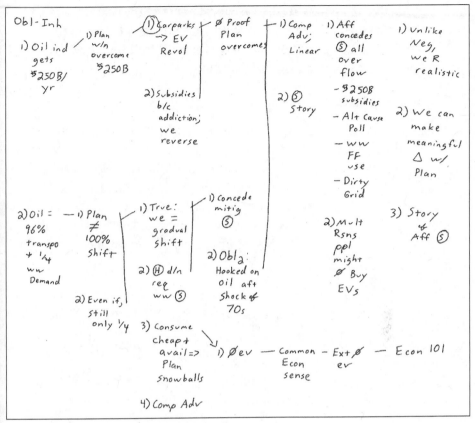

Figure 14.1. Inherency flow of the sample debate

American oil companies receive preferential treatment from their government worth more than $250 billion a year.

2. Oil accounts for 96% of our transportation energy—¼ of global demand and growing.

    DOGGETT '07   (Doggett, Tom. "Leading the Drive to End Dependence on Oil." *Boston Globe*, 14 October 2007, F2)

We're still hooked on oil more than **three decades after the** first **supply shocks caused long lines at the pump** and the only real cure can be found in alternative fuels.

That's the premise of author David Sandalow in his new book, "Freedom from Oil: How the Next President Can End the United States' Oil Addiction" [*sic*] (McGraw-Hill, $26.95).

Energy challenges are dire, as Sandalow notes. **The** **U**nited **S**tates still **relies on oil for 96 percent of its transportation fuels and the daily oil fix is growing—averaging almost 21 million barrels** of crude **a day, a fourth of global demand**.

OBSERVATION 2: *[Pause]* Harms

1. Oil production destroys farmlands, biodiversity, drinking water, and people's lives.

    KARL '04   (Karl, Terry Lynn. "Oil-Led Development:
                      Social, Political and Economic Consequences,"
                  prepared for *Encyclopedia of Energy*, 2004, 26–28,
                      iis-db.stanford.edu/pubs/21537/No_80_Terry
                      Karl-_Effects_of_Oil_Development.pdf)

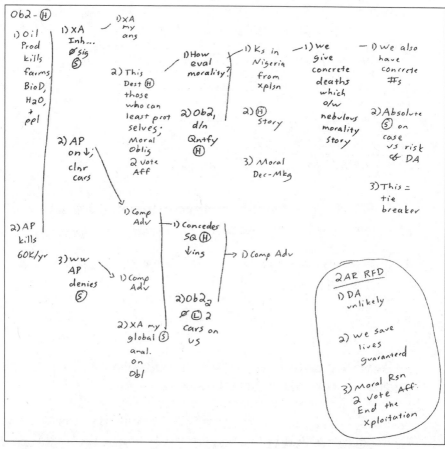

Figure 14.2. Harms flow of the sample debate

The environmental dimension of **oil exploration is a chief cause of social dislocation. Hazardous wastes, site contamination, and the lack of sufficient protection of surface and subsurface waters, biodiversity and air quality** (both **in the** immediate **vicinity of the** oil **project** and in relation to global concerns such as ozone depleting substances and greenhouse gases) **have endangered the health of local populations** near oil installations and pipelines **and destroyed** local **livelihoods** such as farming and fishing. Local communities, for example, report a sharp rise in infantile leukemia near oil facilities.

This disruption is most profound among ethnic minorities and indigenous peoples who live off the land and whose customs and traditions may also be threatened. In Ecuador, the Cofan Indian Tribe reports the contamination of its drinking supply, In Colombia, where at least 2.1 million barrels of petroleum have been spilled since 1987 (approximately eleven times as much oil as was spilled in the Exxon Valdez disaster of 1989), **severe damage** to this tropical ecosystem **includes air pollution, land clearings, water contamination, soil erosion, sedimentation, and the disturbance of wildlife habitats. Petroleum wastes wash directly into local waterways,** and Colombia's Institute of Natural Resources (INDERENA) has repeatedly condemned the presence of high concentrations of heavy metals and toxic polycyclic aromatic hydrocarbons, which are 300 times higher than drinking water standards in the North and 50 percent higher than international standards for oil discharges to surface waters.

But the fate of **the Niger Delta region**, where exploration began in 1958, **is the best known example** of the local impact of oil exploration. **Although two million barrels per day are pumped out of the Niger Delta**'s mangrove swamps every day, providing Nigeria with a large share of its GDP, over 90 percent of its export earnings, and almost all its tax revenues, **the people** in the region **have barely benefited**. Despite producing energy for the country and the world, many of them do not even have electricity. While compensation paid for land acquisition and oil spillages have aided some individuals from the Ogoni minority whose land is affected, **the local economy and the environment have been devastated. Gas flaring has permanently scorched the earth, destroying** food **crops and** rendering **farmlands** barren. **Some scientists believe that the incomplete combustion of** the **flares has resulted in acid rain** that, in turn, has damaged crops and drinking water. **Oil spillages (an average of three per**

month) and ruptured pipelines (either from improper maintenance or sabotage) **have destroyed streams, farmlands and aquatic life. Thousands of villagers have been killed in pipeline explosions** resulting from leaks, including over 700 people in one leak alone in October 1998.

2. Air pollution kills 60,000 every year in the U.S.
    EILPERIN '06   (Eilperin, Juliet. "EPA Cuts Soot Level Allowable Daily." *Washington Post*, 22 September 2006, A3)

Vince Morris, a spokesman for D.C. Mayor Anthony A. Williams (D), said the city is disappointed with the decision to leave the annual fine-particulate standard unchanged. "It's discouraging to see the EPA take this approach, but it's not really surprising," Morris said. **"We're trying to make the air cleaner** for District residents **against an avalanche of suburban sprawl and upwind factories**, and this decision isn't going to help us at all. It's really a shame."
Public health activists, who **noted that 60,000 Americans are estimated to die prematurely each year because of air pollution**, were harsher in their assessment.

[Pause]
We may love our cars, but we don't love what our addiction is doing to us. Let's keep our cars, while promoting developments that breaks the cycle of addiction with the following plan:
[Pause]

I. The United States federal government will substantially increase its transportation infrastructure investment in the United States by installing car parks in the parking lots of all government buildings. Car parks are parking stations with electrical sockets for drivers to use to recharge their vehicles. Usually, these structures are self-sufficient, generating electricity from renewable sources. Where this is not feasible, the car parks draw *some* of their energy from these sources.

II. In addition to federal installations, we appropriate funds to build car parks for other actors—state agencies, shopping malls, grocery stores, and so forth—who want them. We appropriate funds for filling stations to convert fuel pumps to rapid charging stations. All terms are defined operationally. We reserve the right to clarify plan.

III. Funding and enforcement are guaranteed through normal means, including legislative intent and fiat. Oversight for the project will come from the Department of Transportation, including consultation with the Department of Energy.

OBSERVATION 3: *[Pause]* Solvency

1. Infrastructure key to boosting market demand for electric vehicles.

    MCCURDY '10   (McCurdy, Dave. "Electric Ready." *National Journal*, 21 June 2010, http://transportation .nationaljournal.com/2010/06/what-should -transportation-dep.php)

While the majority of charging is likely to occur at the home or workplace, **public**ly available **charging access will** be important to **ensure the successful adoption of** battery **electric vehicles** and plug-in hybrid electric vehicles. **To gain widespread usage** of battery electric vehicles, the issue of consumer **"range anxiety" must be addressed**. In the near term, **access to public stations will provide the necessary reassurances to drivers of** battery electric vehicles and plug-in

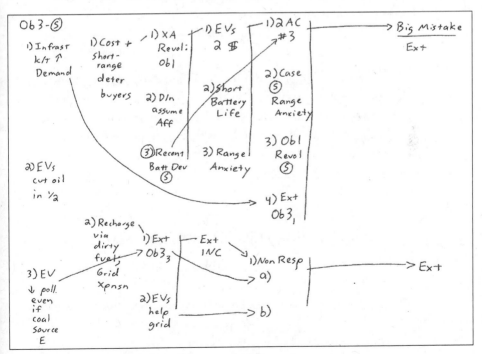

Figure 14.3. Solvency flow of the sample debate

hybrid **electric vehicles** that **they will have the ability to recharge at locations other than home and work. Publicly available sites also serve to increase consumer awareness of electrification as a viable alternative to traditional energy technologies**.

2. Plug-ins cut our oil consumption in half.
    ECONOMIST '08   (*Economist*. "The End of the Petrolhead."
                                              21 June 2008, 21)

   In a plug-in, the electricity comes from the mains, via **an ordinary electrical socket**. Some intermediate designs retain the idea of two sorts of engine, but the goal is that the car should be powered by electric motors alone. **If the batteries run down, a petrol-powered generator will take over.** (Existing batteries are too expensive to give such a car the range of a standard petrol-driven machine.) **But most cars, most of the time, are used for short journeys.** Gerbrand Ceder, a battery scientist at MIT, reckons that **if the first 50km of an average car's daily range were provided by batteries rather than petrol, annual petrol consumption would be halved**.

3. Plug-ins dramatically decrease air pollution, even if the car park links into coal utilities.
    ECONOMIST '08   (*Economist*. "The End of the Petrolhead."
                                              21 June 2008, 21)

   The **widespread adoption of plug-ins** might also **reduce** carbon-dioxide **emissions**, depending on what sort of power station made the electricity in the first place. **Even energy from a coal-fired station is less polluting than the serial explosions that drive an internal-combustion engine. If the energy comes from a source such as wind or nuclear, the gain is enormous.**

Sample First Negative Constructive Script

Before I begin my speech, a quick roadmap. I will have one off-case position followed by the case in order.[2]

[Brief pause as the first negative speaker looks around to ensure everyone is ready.]

First, the Saudi Oil DA.

1. High prices preserve Saudi stability, reducing civil unrest.
    MAUGERI '03   (Maugeri, Leonardo. "Time to Debunk
                        Mythical Links between Oil and Politics." *Oil
                        and Gas Journal*, 15 December 2003, n.p.)

__Countries such as Saudi Arabia have doubled their population__
in 12 years. __Sixty percent__ of the gulf countries' population __is less than
21 years old. This__ demographic explosion __has created expectations
and frustrations to which stagnant and monocultural economies
cannot give a credible answer. Only sustained oil revenues allow
these countries to temper social unrest by preserving huge social
assistance programs__. Gulf countries' oil revenues are already much
lower today than 20 years ago, and __cheap oil prices mean a dramatic
dip in per capita oil income__. Therefore, frustration and __violent revolt
may erupt whenever the minimum needs__ for living __are endangered
by decreasing oil prices, particularly among people who already
live in poverty__ and cannot permit themselves the luxury of hoping
for a different future.

2. U.S. energy restrictions drive oil prices through the floor, ensuring
    Saudi collapse.
    ROBERTS '04   (Roberts, Paul. *The End of Oil: On the Edge
                            of a Perilous New World*. Boston:
                            Houghton Mifflin, 2004, 323)

__Because the__ United __S__tates __is so large a market for world energy__
products, __a U.S. energy revolution would function as a catalyst__ in
the transformation of the global energy economy, initiating a "domino effect" in energy that could ultimately change everything from
emissions and energy use in the developing world to our oil-dominated geopolitical order. __The last time the United States got__ really
__serious about__ energy __efficiency__—after the 1974 oil price shocks—
__U.S. oil use fell so low that OPEC was nearly wiped out. A more
permanent reduction—even if__ partly __offset by rising demand in__
the fast-growing __Asian economies—would completely change the
global oil order. As oil prices fell__—to as low as fifteen dollars a barrel,
some analysts say—__many big oil states would see their geopolitical
status tumble__. Some, like Russia, Venezuela, Iran, and Qatar, which
have enormous gas reserves, could compensate by stepping up efforts

to sell gas, especially to gas-hungry markets like China, India, and the United States. Other petrostates—like Mexico and Algeria, for instance—might be pushed into bankruptcy and would then require a massive, and inevitably United States–led, bailout. **Falling oil prices would** also **splinter OPEC. As Saudi Arabia, Kuwait, the United Arab Emirates, and Nigeria** all **tried to compensate for lower prices by boosting oil production**, analysts say **the** inevitable **glut would drive prices down** further. Oil **revenues would fall so sharply that many OPEC countries would suffer profound civil unrest**. Some analysts believe **unstable countries like Saudi Arabia would collapse**.

3. Decline in oil revenue threatens strife, civil war, and ethnic conflict.
   MCKILLOP '04   (McKillop, Andrew. "A Counterintuitive
                               Notion: Economic Growth Bolstered
                               by High Oil Prices, Strong Oil Demand."
                               Oil and Gas Journal, 19 April 2004, n.p.)

   Higher revenues for many low-income oil exporter countries— notably for the special cases of Nigeria, Saudi Arabia, and especially Iraq—**may be the only short-term way to stop these countries from falling into civil strife, insurrection, or ethnic war, let alone making vast investments to maintain or expand their current export capacity**.

   Now, to Ob[servation] 1—inherency. *[Pause]*
   Off the Ob 1-1. Plan cannot overcome $250 billion in yearly oil subsidies. No way plan overcomes that type of incentive to maintain the oil-based economy.
   Off the Ob 1-2, I have two responses.

1. Plan does not achieve 100% shift to electric vehicles. Don't let them claim total solvency for the 96% of transportation based on oil.
2. Even if plan achieved a total shift to EVs [electric vehicles], that's only a decrease in ¼ of global oil consumption. The harms in Ob 2 still exist post-plan.

   [Pause] To Ob 2—harms. *[Pause]*
   Group Ob 2. I have three responses to their harms.

1. Cross-apply my answers on inherency. They won't achieve significant solvency of the harms.

2. Air pollution has been declining for more than two decades.

POLLUTION ENGINEERING '10   (*Pollution Engineering*,
10 May 2010, 12)

A number of reports released in early 2010 speak to tremendous successes in controlling air pollution in the United States over the last few decades. According to Consumer's Report [*sic*], a car today produces an average of 95 percent fewer harmful air emissions. According to the EPA, national air quality since 1990 has significantly improved for the six common air pollutants that are tracked. That would be ground-level ozone, particulates, lead, NO_2, CO, and SO_2. Toxic air pollutants such as benzene also have been reduced by about 40 percent during that time.

3. Global air pollution is inevitable and denies solvency.

WATSON '05   (Watson, Traci. "Air Pollution from Other
Countries Drifts into USA." *USA Today*,
13 March 2005, http://www.usatoday
.com/weather/resources/climate
/2005-03-13-pollution-_x.htm)

Mercury from China, dust from Africa, smog from Mexico—all of it drifts freely across U.S. borders and contaminates the air millions of Americans breathe, according to recent research from Harvard University, the University of Washington and many other institutions where scientists are studying air pollution. There are no boundaries in the sky to stop such pollution, no Border Patrol agents to capture it. Pollution wafting into the USA accounts for 30 percent of the nation's ozone, an important component of smog, says researcher David Parrish of the National Oceanic and Atmospheric Administration. By the year 2020, Harvard University's Daniel Jacob says, imported pollution will be the primary factor degrading visibility in our national parks. While the United States is cutting its own emissions, some nations, especially China, are belching out more and more dirty air. As a result, overseas pollution could partly cancel out improvements in U.S. air quality that have cost billions of dollars.

[*Pause*] Ob 3—solvency. [*Pause*]
I have two responses to the solvency story.

1. Cost and short range of EVs deters consumers.

   MILO '11   (Milo, Paul. "It's the Battery." *EE-Evaluation*
                               Engineering, September 2011, 6)

   Electric vehicles, not hybrids, **are having a hard time being
   accepted and** subsequently **purchased by the** driving **public. The
   reluctance to buy an EV boils down to just a couple of reasons:
   price** of the vehicle **and driving distance. Once you get over the
   sticker shock**—the cheapest one I could find was from Coda Auto-
   motive which debuts this year at just under $40,000 with the federal
   tax credit—**the concern is how far can you drive the vehicle until
   it has to be recharged**. As stated in an article in *SiliconValley.com*,
   "**Future of electric cars hinges on better batteries**" by Dana Hull,
   "**Experts agree consumers will never fully embrace electric vehicles
   until they can travel as far as a gas-powered car on a single charge**."

   [Pause] Simply put, this card tells us consumers will not buy EVs
   even after the affirmative plan.

2. Recharging still provided by dirty fuel. Grid expansion has negative
   impacts.

   SANDERS '11   (Sanders, Sol. "Obama's energy disaster: One
                               part black magic, two parts propaganda."
                               WorldTribune.com, 4 July 2011, http:
                               //worldtribune.com/worldtribune
                               /WTARC/2011/s0817_07_04.asp)

   **Politically correct spokesmen and the mainstream media prom-
   ise black-magic energy solutions such as electric cars, ignoring
   both the fact that almost three-quarters of our electricity for recharging batteries is produced with coal and gas and the enormous costs and problems of grid expansion required for a massive
   changeover.**

   [Pause] This card tells us there are multiple environmental harms
   associated with the plan. Because EVs get their "fuel" from the power
   grid, they are still fossil fuel–based vehicles, meaning that pollution
   still occurs. Furthermore, the existing power grid can't handle all
   these charging stations. Places like Phoenix and southern California
   already suffer brownouts and rolling blackouts. The grid will have
   to be expanded to accommodate the plan, and that could have environmental side effects.

Sample Second Affirmative Constructive Script

A quick roadmap before I begin: Oil DA, then case in order—inherency, harms, and solvency.

[Brief pause as the second affirmative speaker looks around to ensure everyone is ready.]

On Oil, I have five responses.

1. *No threshold.* How much do oil revenues have to decrease to trigger the impacts? They assume a collapse of the Saudi government's ability to provide social services. Unlikely my plan triggers that type of downturn overnight.

2. *No quantification of the link.* Cross-apply the 1NC answer on Ob 1-2: U.S. transpo[rtation] is only one-quarter of global oil demand. Also, we are a gradual shift away from oil.

3. *No internal link.* Saudi Arabia prepared for the end of oil.

SAGIA 2007   (Saudi Arabian General Investment Authority. "Heading Strongly into the Future." *The Kingdom of Saudi Arabia: Strategic Powerhouse, Global Strength, Part II*, http://www.sagia.gov.sa/Documents /Download%20center/International %20Media%20%20Publications /saudi_arabia_2.pdf)

But **what is to happen with Saudi Arabia when its oil era finally ends? The House of Saud has contemplated this inevitable reality and created** the above-mentioned **projects as a motor for diversification, part of a National Industrial Strategy known as "Vision 2020." Already over the past three decades the non-oil sector has grown from 35 percent to more than 60 percent of the total GDP. Saudi financial institutions forecast that by year's end the non-oil private sector will grow 8.9 percent in real terms,** the highest growth in 25 years.

4. *No link.* Saudi Arabia will be its own largest consumer and will thrive off other exports.

KING '07   (King, Neil. "Saudi Industrial Drive Strains Oil-Export Rule." *Wall Street Journal*, 12 December 2007, 36)

Long the biggest spigot for crude oil, Saudi Arabia now has broader ambitions. It wants to become a big exporter of chemicals, aluminum and plastic, and in the process to create jobs. So **Saudi Arabia is on a building binge**. In the works are new seaports, an extended railroad system, a series of new industrial cities and a score of refineries, power stations and smelters. **Over the next dozen years, such Saudi government investments are expected to consume $600 billion. But they will also consume something else: large quantities of Saudi oil—oil that otherwise could help slake other countries' growing thirst.** Much as China leveraged its asset of low-cost labor to make an industrial leap, **the Saudis and their oil-rich neighbors are tapping their own prime asset to fuel development**.

5. *Case outweighs.* The DA has a terminal impact of "civil strife" versus the 60,000 people who die every year from low-level air pollution and the destruction of lesser developed nations and the people who live there.

[Pause] To Ob 1. *[Pause]*
Off the Ob 1-1 oil subsidies, they say we cannot overcome a $250 billion incentive. Two responses:

1. Construction of car parks in public places drives a plug-in revolution.
   ECONOMIST '08   (*Economist.* "The End of the Petrolhead."
                                                            21 June 2008, 21)

Google is already **experimenting with photovoltaic car parks. These have awnings covered in solar cells which** will **shade** its **employees' cars and simultaneously recharge them. That** is an **idea** which **could spread. Supermarkets**, for example, **might find that car parks with plugs would attract customers who wanted to top up their cars. And the more opportunities there are for stationary cars to be recharged, the more likely they are to be bought.**

2. Subsidies exist because of our addiction to oil. We reverse the cause of subsidies. Government is compelled to subsidize oil because there aren't other options. Plan changes that.

On Ob 1-2, they have two responses. Group them.

1. These points are true. We are a gradual shift away from oil.
2. Our harms do not require global solvency. Low-level air pollution is U.S.-specific. We create a linear reduction in oil exploitation harms. As oil profits decline, less drilling occurs.
3. Countries and people consume what is cheap and available. That's human nature. Plan has a snowball effect. As we make EVs more affordable, people around the globe will be incentivized to buy them.
4. We are a comparative advantage over the status quo.

[Pause] Ob 2—harms. *[Pause]*
First, they cross-apply inherency attacks to mitigate solvency.

1. Cross-apply my answers from that flow.
2. The destruction described in our first card hurts those who can least protect themselves. The indigenous people in these countries—and in the U.S.—lack resources to defend themselves against exploitation by Big Oil and industrialized nations. Further, they lack the resources to protect themselves physically from the pollution and damage done during the exploitive process. Last, their governments often lack the health care infrastructure to help people after the damage is done. You have a moral obligation to vote Aff.

Second, they say global air pollution is declining. So what? People are dying and the environment is suffering. We are a comparative advantage.

Third, they say global air pollution denies solvency.

1. Again, we are a comparative advantage. They may mitigate solvency, but we still save lives.
2. Cross-apply my global solvency analysis on Ob 1. As EVs become affordable, global oil consumption declines.

[Pause] To solvency. *[Pause]*
First, the 1NC says multiple factors deter consumers from buying EVs. I have three responses:

1. Cross-apply the 2AC card on Ob 1, which says we lead to an EV revolution. They become more affordable as the auto industry sees there is a viable market. Thus, we solve consumer concerns.
2. This card is descriptive of the status quo. It does not assume the affirmative plan.

3. Recent battery developments make plug-ins acceptable for noncommuter traffic.

   ECONOMIST '08   (*Economist.* "The End of the Petrolhead."
                                                    21 June 2008, 22)

   <u>GM is collaborating with A123Systems</u>, a firm started by Dr. Ceder's colleague Yet-Ming Chiang, <u>to develop batteries with iron-phosphate cathodes for the Volt</u>. A123's particular trick is that <u>the iron phosphate in its cathodes comes in the form of precisely engineered nanoparticles. This increases the surface area available for the lithium ions to react with when the current is flowing, so</u> such <u>batteries can be charged and discharged rapidly</u>.

   <u>The Lightning</u>, too, <u>is making use of nanotechnology. Its batteries</u>, developed by Altairnano of Reno, Nevada, <u>replace the graphite anode with one made of lithium titanate nanoparticles</u>. The firm claims that <u>its batteries are not only safer</u> (graphite can burn; lithium titanate cannot), <u>but can</u> also <u>be recharged more rapidly. Using a 480-volt outlet, such as might be found in a roadside service station, the job should be done in ten minutes.</u>

   <u>Dr. Ceder reckons he may be able to do even better</u> than this. <u>His version of an iron-phosphate battery can charge or discharge in ten seconds. It, too, could be recharged rapidly at a roadside filling station.</u> He reckons <u>the process</u> would have to be controlled to stop overheating, but a safe refill <u>would take only five minutes. And</u> he thinks <u>batteries might get better still</u>.

   Next, they say electricity uses dirty fuel and plan requires grid expansion.

1. Extend Ob 3-3—EVs decrease pollution even if powered off coal-fired electric plants. Plus, they do not assume renewable energy sources as well as self-sufficient renewable car parks.
2. EVs help the grid, not overwhelm it.
   MUELLER '10   (Mueller, Jan. "Plan for Electric Drive Communities."
                          National Journal, 21 June 2010, http://transportation
                                   .nationaljournal.com/2010/06/what-should
                                                        -transportation-dep.php)

   <u>Electric vehicles can</u> also <u>have significant value for managing the electricity grid. Electric cars will typically be parked for most hours of the day. When they are plugged in and connected to the</u>

grid, they can provide important storage, frequency regulation, and load management services.

Sample Second Negative Constructive Script

For a roadmap before my speech: case in order, Ob 1, 2, 3—that's inherency, harms, solvency.[3]

[Brief pause to ensure everyone is ready.]

On Ob 1-1, the subsidies. Group the 2AC responses. She never offers proof the plan overcomes a quarter trillion dollars in annual subsidies. That's a huge incentive to maintain the oil economy.

On Ob 1-2. Group the first two responses.

1. Aff concedes they don't get total solvency and the transition won't be immediate. This means the DA outweighs the benefits of plan.
2. 1AC #2 evidence says decades after the oil shocks of the '70s, we are still hooked on oil. Oil prices spiked and habits didn't change. This implies the cost of refueling vehicles is not a significant factor in our driving habits.

The 2AC #3 on Ob 1-2 tells us we will see a global transition. She reads no ev[idence] supporting a global shift.

[Pause] Move to harms. *[Pause]*

Go to the 2AC's second response on the flow, the moral obligation.

1. How do you evaluate a moral impact in this round? She gives no standard for morality, why this is a moral imperative, or why it should be the a priori impact in the round.
2. The 1AC's Ob 2 #1 does not quantify how much harm is done. It describes horrible impacts in Nigeria but does not give us a tangible way of evaluating the degree of impact occurring from oil exploitation.

Next, group the Aff's answers to the 1NC #2 and 3:

1. She concedes the harms are on the decline. This reduces the need for the plan as well as the amount of benefit she can claim.
2. The 1AC #2 card citing 60,000 deaths is not limited to automobiles or U.S. causes. There are many sources of low-level air pollution. Cars are not the only cause. This severely mitigates the number of lives the Aff can claim to save. In addition, the global pollution card in

the 1NC still applies. Pollution knows no boundaries. How often do we see smog from China or dust blowing from the Gobi desert over Anchorage? Pollution can travel vast distances. Plan cannot solve that impact.

[Pause] Solvency. *[Pause]*
Off the 1NC #1—consumer anxiety. Group the 2AC responses.

1. Cost of electric vehicles deters consumers.
   MILO '11   (Milo, Paul. "It's the Battery." *EE-Evaluation Engineering*, September 2011, 6)

   <u>Although Coda and Tesla will soon have EVs that extend driving distances to further levels, the battery essentially remains the big factor in gaining meaningful acceptance by the</u> driving public. <u>How many people will shell out about $60,000 for the experience to own an EV? Until the cost of the battery is reduced substantially, only a select few drivers will avail themselves of these cars.</u>

2. Short battery life makes EVs unappealing to consumers.
   ZEHNER '12   (Zehner, Ozzie. "Tesla SUV with Wings or Not, We Should Kill the Electric Car." *Christian Science Monitor*, 13 February 2012, http://www.csmonitor.com /Commentary/Opinion/2012/0213 /Tesla-SUV-with-wings-or-not- we-should-kill-the-electric-car)

   But <u>if buyers</u> intend to <u>drive their electric car beyond the length of the extension cord from their garage, they won't be able to take advantage of</u> that <u>cheap electricity. They'll have to rely on a battery—a battery they can only recharge a finite number of times before it must be replaced, at considerable expense. The battery-construction step, not the "fuel" step, is the expensive part</u> of driving an electric vehicle.

3. Range anxiety deters purchase.
   PLUMER '12   (Plumer, Brad. "Automakers still see electricity as their future." *Washington Post*, 9 January 2012, A11)

Pure **electric vehicles** like the Nissan Leaf **still face hurdles. There's the phenomenon of "range anxiety," in which would-be buyers of plug-in electric cars fret that their batteries will run out of juice and leave them stranded.**

[Pause] These cards provide three independent reasons why consumers are unlikely to buy electric vehicles. Taken together, they cast significant doubt on the plan's ability to solve.

Finally, extend the 1NC #2. Plan will not solve because EVs recharge their batteries off dirty power stations and the power grid is inadequate to support new charging stations.

Sample First Negative Rebuttal Script

For a roadmap, just the Oil DA.

[Pause to ensure everyone is ready.]

The 2AC #1 says no threshold.

1. The relationship is linear. Decreased consumption decreases oil revenue, which decreases the quantity and quality of social services the Saudi Arabian government can provide, which increases discontent and unrest among the poor.
2. Saudi Arabia is highly dependent on oil revenues. It's vulnerable.

NORENG '02   (Noreng, Oystein. *Crude Power: Politics and the Oil Market*. New York: St Martin's Press, 2002, 130)

Even after a remarkable consolidation of its economy in the mid-1990s, leading to a virtual elimination of the current account deficit by 1997, **the 1998 oil price collapse** once more **demonstrated Saudi Arabia's economic monoculture, the dependence on oil revenues and the sensitivity to oil price changes**. With oil prices in real terms at the low levels of the early 1970s, **Saudi Arabia's economy suddenly faced one of its greatest challenges in years, putting heavy pressure on the Saudi government** to reach the OPEC deal that in 1999 significantly raised oil prices and revenues. **Oil revenues still make up around 85 percent of total Saudi export earnings, and 40 percent of the country's gross domestic product, indicating a persistent vulnerability.**

2AC #2 says no quantification of the link.

1. Again, it's linear.
2. U.S. is the linchpin of Saudi Arabia's oil economy.

    MORSE AND RICHARD '02   (Morse, Edward, and James Richard. "The Battle for Energy Dominance." *Foreign Affairs*, March/April 2002, http://www.foreignaffairs.com/articles /57803/edward-1-morse-and-james-richard /the-battle-for-energy-dominance)

One of the hidden aspects of the relationship is the Saudi dependence on the United States **for providing an expanding market. Although Asian demand for oil is expected to grow dramatically** in coming decades, **no other economy rivals that of the** United States **for the growth of its oil imports**. Over the past decade, the increase in the U.S. share of the oil market, in terms of trade, was higher than the total oil consumption in any other country, save Japan and China. The U.S. increase in imports accounts for more than a third of the total increase in oil trade and more than half of the total increase in OPEC's production during the 1990s. This fact, together with the fall in U.S. oil production, means that **the United States will remain the single most important force in the oil market. The hope of Saudi Arabia** and OPEC **for an increased market and for greater market share is uniquely dependent on growth in U.S. demand. Hence it is not for security alone that Riyadh depends on the United States but for the very economic basis of the Saudi regime, which relies almost entirely on oil for revenue.**

Group the 2AC #3 and 4—no internal link and no link.

1. These cards assume a gradual transition away from oil in the status quo, not the accelerated world of plan. They speed the transition, making Saudi Arabia vulnerable to price fluctuations.
2. Every dollar drop in the price of oil costs the Saudis 3 billion.

    BAER '03   (Baer, Robert. *Sleeping with Devil*. New York: Three Rivers Press, 2003, 162–63)

Because roughly **85 percent of Saudi Arabia's total revenues are oil-based, every dollar decline in the price of a barrel of oil translates to** about **a $3 billion loss to the Saudi treasury**. From there, the math is easy.

3. Saudi Arabia's domestic consumption doesn't offset the decline in revenue described by the 2AC. We consume 25% of the world's oil. U.S. action has a tremendous impact that cannot be offset by domestic use alone.

The 2AC #5 says case outweighs.

1. That assumes 100% solvency, which they don't get.
2. Poor economic conditions make Saudi a breeding ground for terrorists.

LOONEY '04   (Looney, Robert. "Can Saudi Arabia Reform Its Economy in Time to Head Off Disaster?" *Strategic Insights*, vol. 3, issue 1, January 2004, http://calhoun.nps.edu/bitstream/handle /10945/11277/looneyJan04.pdf?sequence=1)

Population growth (about 3.3 percent per year) **has exceeded** Gross Domestic Product **(GDP) growth for several decades**. The result has been a decline in per capita GDP from more than U.S. $15,000 in 1980 to about U.S. $9,000 in 2003 (adjusted for inflation). **There is high unemployment** (20 to 30 percent by some measures), while up to 20–30 percent of the population falls below the poverty line. **Translating these figures into more tangible signs of trouble for the Saudi Government**, Kim **Murphy has observed: The dozen years since the Persian Gulf War have seen slums grow** up on the outskirts of Jeddah and Riyadh, the capital. Beggars hawk bottles of water at intersections. Penniless women huddle in strips of shade outside their crumbling mud-brick houses, begging for money. Many families in the capital are so poor they can't afford electricity. Raw sewage runs through parts of Jeddah. **The increasingly perilous economic situation that all in Saudi Arabia** but the royalty **face** today **may be a big factor in recruiting young Saudis to terrorist groups such as Al Qaeda**. Chronic joblessness, **diminished incomes and difficulty in collecting enough money to marry and start families are all issues that can evoke anger**.

3. Another terrorist attack could lead to a downward spiral of destruction.

LIFTON '05   (Lifton, Robert Jay. "In the Lord's Hands." In *Annual Editions: Violence and Terrorism 05/06*, edited by Thomas J. Badey. Dubuque, IA: McGraw-Hill Higher Education, 2004, 151)

<u>Woodward ends his book</u> on Bush <u>on a mystical note</u>. He describes a scene in which twenty-five men from different Special Forces and CIA teams gather at a desolate site in Afghanistan, where they have arranged a pile of rocks as a tombstone over a buried piece of the demolished World Trade Center. One of the men leads a prayer as others kneel, consecrating the spot as a memorial to the dead of September 11, and then declares: <u>"We will export death and violence to the four corners of the earth in defense of our great nation."</u> <u>Woodward presents the scene as depicting the determination of an aggrieved nation to strike back. But it also suggests a sequence leading from memorialization to self-defense to apocalyptic militarism.</u>

<u>Such fundamentalist and apocalyptic tendencies by no means determine all of American policy, which can alternate with inclinations toward pragmatic restraint. But impulses toward regeneration through apocalyptic violence are an ever-present danger.</u>

The Bush administration should by no means be seen as a mirror image of bin Laden or Islamism. Rather it is part of <u>an ongoing dynamic in which the American apocalyptic interacts</u>, almost to the point of collusion, <u>with the Islamist apocalyptic, each intensifying the other in an escalating process that has in it the potential seeds of world destruction</u>.

The apocalyptic risk of this DA outweighs the unquantifiable advantage of the Aff. At the end of the day, you vote Neg to avoid this risk.

Sample First Affirmative Rebuttal Script

Case in order, then the DA.

[Pause to ensure everyone is ready.]

On Ob 1, group the first three responses from the block.

1. We give you a comparative advantage over the status quo. If nothing else, we have a linear improvement over the way things are.
2. In the status quo, politicians subsidize oil because we are hooked on oil and lack alternatives. We provide a means of escape. Car parks reduce the fears of consumers and embolden auto manufactures. That incentivizes EVs and reduces the need for subsidies of oil.

Drop to the global transition analysis in the 2AC. That's my partner's #3 to their attack on our second card in case. They say we offer no evidence. It's common sense. People buy what is cheap or available. We drive costs down. We make tech more available. What more support do we need?

[Pause] To harms. *[Pause]*
Go to the moral obligation debate off the 1NC #1.

1. The last line in the card says thousands have died in Nigeria from pipeline explosions. This is only one type of harm in one country. That alone is significant. We can assume similar impacts globally.
2. Look, the card details a laundry list of harms from oil extraction and production. People are dislocated by projects, hazardous wastes are deposited in the environment and drinking water, farmlands are destroyed, air pollution is rampant, wildlife habitat is destroyed, people die in explosions. Tack on to that the people do not benefit from the industry because it is a resource extraction industry benefitting companies in foreign lands, and you have a pretty clear impact story worth voting on.
3. As a moral being, you have an obligation to consider injustice and vote on principle when warranted. We give you a clear scenario of the wealthy benefitting at the expense of local populations. We give you an alternative, which reduces that harm. You should vote here.

[Pause] Solvency. *[Pause]*
Group the cards on anxiety.

1. 2AC #3 already answered the battery life concern. That's being solved now; we reduce it further.
2. Case solves range anxiety by putting charging stations everywhere. You can plug in while getting groceries, while working, while doing just about anything.
3. The Ob 1 plug-in revolution card solves anxiety.
4. Ext Ob 3-1. That card indicates we address the anxiety problem.

On dirty fuel sources and grid expansion, the 1NR is nonresponsive. He merely says, "Extend the 1NC." My partner gave you two clear answers. Ob 3-3 says we reduce pollution even if electricity comes from fossil fuels. Plus, we have renewable energy sources. Also, the 2AC reads ev that says we improve the grid with car parks.

[Pause] The DA. *[Pause]*

Go to the 2AC #1—no threshold. They say Saudi is highly dependent on oil revenue.

1. Not true: 2AC #3 says only 35% of its GDP is oil-based.
2. 2AC #3 indicates the government is planning ahead. They know oil revenues are drying up and are making changes to insulate the economy.
3. 2AC #4 says domestic consumption dwarfs U.S. imports. We are 25% of global demand, but they are still their number one buyer.

Go to the 2AC #3—no internal link. They say our card assumes a gradual transition, which is okay, but not the accelerated rate of plan. Plan is not instantaneous, and we never claimed it was. It allows time for domestic planning in Saudi Arabia. Don't confuse our revolution of the EV industry with an instantaneous transition from the internal combustion engine to an all-electric fleet of cars.

Go to the 2AC #5 where they add the terrorism impacts.

1. Turn—U.S. oil policy fuels terrorism. Most of our hard power engagement in Southwest Asia stems from the need to protect oil. This has real consequences; see Osama bin Laden's outrage with the U.S. and Saudi. Not only did it give him a platform against the U.S., but it also made the Saudi government a target and Saudi citizens potential recruits. Our involvement in the region over oil is one of the primary causes of anti-Americanism and terrorism.
2. Best case, we turn this impact into an affirmative advantage. Worst case, it's a wash; both sides fuel terrorism in different ways.

Sample Second Negative Rebuttal Script

A quick roadmap: I will go Ob 2, Ob 1, Oil DA.

[Pause to ensure everyone is ready.]

Affirmative harms are unquantifiable. It is unclear how much they solve. The risk of terror and civil war in Saudi Arabia outweighs case.

Let's look at Ob 2. The only thing I care about is the moral imperative argument. We give you concrete deaths, which outweigh the nebulous morality story of the 2AC. You still don't know why it's a moral imperative, how to evaluate these moral impacts, or how much good you can do by voting Aff. Don't let them make this a trump impact in the round. They haven't done enough work to justify it.

[Pause] Go to Ob 1. *[Pause]*

1AR leads off with the statement that they are a comparative advantage over the status quo and can somehow magically overcome one quarter of a trillion dollars incentivizing oil consumption.

1. The affirmative concedes solvency mitigators all over the flow.
   - $250 billion in subsidies make it unrealistic we will see a drastic shift away from the oil.
   - Multiple alternate causes to air pollution—electricity generation is just one example that they cannot solve with plan.
   - Global fossil fuel use for electricity, manufacturing, and automobiles means their air pollution solvency is suspect, not to mention the oil extraction harm.
   - Plug-ins still get their power from dirty electricity.

Taken together, there is significant doubt regarding the Aff's ability to solve the harms.

2. There are multiple reasons people might not buy EVs. Electric vehicles are expensive, their battery life is short, and people fear running out of a charge in the middle of nowhere. This brings into question whether people will even buy EVs after plan. This further reduces affirmative solvency.

Skip to the 2AC #3 on our answers to Ob 1-2. This is the global transition story. They still don't read you any evidence indicating people will buy EVs globally as a result of plan. They read no evidence that foreign governments will follow the U.S. lead and install car parks.

[Pause] To the DA. *[Pause]*

On the threshold debate. Group the three 1AR answers.

1. The linear risk is great. Every shift away from oil ripples through the economy, disrupting the government's ability to provide social services. Any decrease in services translates to increased unrest.
2. On Ob 1, the 2AC says plan leads to an electric vehicle revolution. If that's true, we have a massive shift away from oil, triggering the disadvantage.

Go to the 2AC #3—no internal link. The 1AR claims plan doesn't lead to an instantaneous transition. Cross-apply my answer above;

they read you a card in the 2AC saying this leads to a revolution. That gives us the propensity for a shift significant enough to disrupt Saudi Arabia's ability to provide the support needed to maintain stability.

Go to the 1NR's terrorism impact scenario.

1. The threat of terrorism is real. Terrorism is on the rise globally. We've seen airplanes used as weapons of mass destruction. There have been countless attacks around the world.

2. Our story is plausible. Organizations like al Qaeda recruit by targeting individuals suffering in poverty and those who feel ignored by society. When the government defaults on its ability to provide a social safety net, the number of potential recruits increases dramatically. Thus, plan creates a very real threat because it strengthens terrorist organizations.

3. Worse still, the American public is primed for retaliation post-9/11. If a terrorist organization hits America at home again, we can only imagine the public outcry. The masses will want blood, and there will be no stopping the military-industrial machine as people demand revenge.

[Pause]

This round is simple. Case is severely mitigated. There are too many questions surrounding solvency. How much of the harm is actually caused by American automobiles? Can the plan actually overcome $250 billion in subsidies and consumer anxiety? We have shown that it is incredibly unlikely. They won't achieve much movement in solving low-level air pollution or the dangers of oil extraction. Don't let them fool you into voting on the moral obligation argument; they didn't do enough work on it.

On the other hand, it is clear they increase the risk of a terrorist attack. The Saudi government is tied to oil revenue. If plan reduces oil demand, it loses the ability to provide services for its people. If that happens, civil unrest follows and the entire country will be a plucking ground for terrorist organizations. Not only is there a very real risk of a terrorist attack, but the even more deadly response of the U.S. must be considered. In short, the risk of voting affirmative is simply too great. Vote negative and preserve stability.

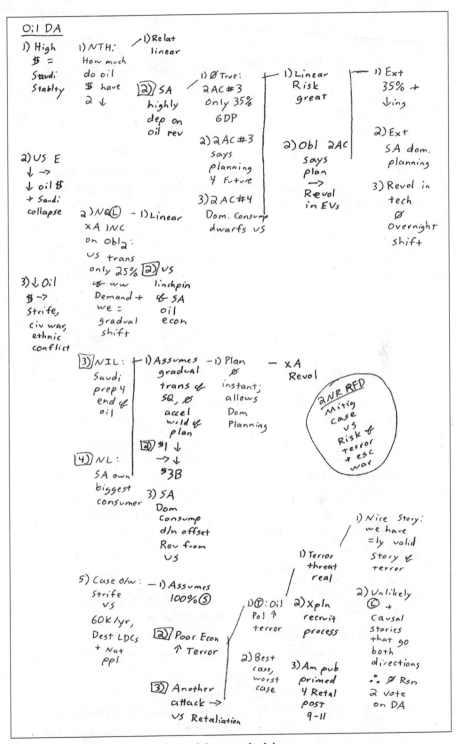

Figure 14.4. Disadvantage flow of the sample debate

Sample Second Affirmative Rebuttal Script

For a brief roadmap: Ob 3—solvency, Ob 1—inherency, the Oil DA, and Ob 2—harms.

[Pause to ensure everyone is ready.]

The Saudi Oil DA is not a game winner for the negative. There are too many questions on whether the link is strong enough to trigger the impacts. Furthermore, we have an equally—if not more—compelling turn story. A vote for the Aff ensures lives are saved.

[Pause]

On solvency. The 2NR makes a big mistake dropping solvency. She tries to make cross-applications from this flow to inherency, but she drops my partner's specific answers in the 1AR. This specificity beats the block analysis and ensures their solvency attacks do not stand.

First, they give us three cards in the block, indicating electric vehicles are too costly, have battery life issues, and range issues that scare consumers. My partner gives you specific answers to each of these.

1. The battery life argument was answered by the 2AC #3, which explained recent technological developments solved the battery issue. Furthermore, case accelerates EV development, meaning we get better batteries post-plan.
2. The range anxiety problem is specifically addressed by plan by installing charging stations across communities nationwide.
3. We answered the "costly argument" on Ob 1 when I read the card about sparking an EV revolution in the auto industry.
4. The original Ob 3-1 card answers all of these attacks by indicating that car parks infrastructure is key to boosting consumer demand.

Second, they never answer the arguments found in the 1AC Ob 3-3 card, which tells us we significantly reduce pollution even when you account for dirty fuel power stations. Not only that, we use renewable energy as part of the car park design when feasible. The 2AC extension card also says we improve the power grid with our plan.

[Pause] Go to the inherency flow. *[Pause]*

The 2NR tries to kill our solvency by making cross-applications from other parts of the flow, most of which I just answered—and the 2NR ignored. I have three specific responses to the 2NR claim that we "concede solvency mitigators around the flow" and that there are multiple reasons people might not buy EVs.

1. Unlike the negative, we are being realistic. We know we can't solve 100%. But, we don't have to. We only have to make the world better, which we do.
2. We can bring meaningful change with our plan. Our plan improves air quality, saving lives. We start to wean our auto industry off oil, which reduces the harms associated with oil extraction.
3. Look, here's what happens. In the status quo, politicians are compelled to provide $250 billion in subsidies to the oil industry because our entire economy is built on oil. There are no viable options within that system. Without those subsidies, the economy would falter. We inject the system with a means of escape. By promoting car parks, we let manufacturers see that EVs are viable options for the road. An awareness is growing within the U.S. of the need for ending the addiction. But, the cost in the status quo is prohibitive. Likewise, people fear running out of a charge on their way to work or wherever. Car parks give us a way out. They reduce anxiety. Automakers will capitalize on this opportunity—that's the revolution card I read in the 2AC. When the plan gives us a way out, politicians can reduce and end those subsidies.

The 2NR also continues to pester us for evidence about the global transition. It's Econ 101; it's common sense. If EVs get cheaper and are more available, people will buy them.

[Pause] To Oil. [Pause]

Go to the 2AC #1—the threshold debate.

She says the linear risk is high and our plan is clearly big enough to trigger the DA because we spark an EV revolution. Three responses:

1. Extend the 1AR #1; oil only accounts for 35% of Saudi Arabia's GDP and declining.
2. Extend the 2AC #3 card, which says the Saudi government is planning for the future by decreasing its reliance on oil and establishing itself as its own largest oil consumer. This minimizes the harm plan could have on their economy.
3. The revolution they try to capitalize on is referring to technological advances, not an overnight shift to electric vehicles. They have yet to answer any of these points head-on.

Drop to the terrorism impact debate at the bottom of the flow.

1. Nice story in the 2NR. We give you an equally valid story of terrorism and how status quo oil policy is one of the primary causes of terrorism. We solve that cause.

2. Between the unlikely link debate and the fact that things could be good or bad either way, there is no justifiable reason to vote negative on the DA.

[Pause] Go to harms. *[Pause]*

The only argument remaining on this flow is that our morality argument is nebulous and not developed.

1. Remember, we give you concrete lives saved, too. Domestically, we reduce low-level air pollution and save lives. Globally, we reduce the need to extract oil, which translates to lives saved as we decrease environmental and agricultural destruction, not to mention the lives lost in explosions.

2. We have absolute lives saved on case, whereas the DA is only a risk.

3. Use the morality argument as a tiebreaker and vote Aff.

[Pause]

The round is clear.

The DA is incredibly unlikely, and we have a viable turn on it. At the link level, they cannot prove our plan will drain Saudi Arabia's oil revenue enough to trigger the impact. We give you multiple reasons for that. Furthermore, our turn story—which she drops—indicates that it is our need to protect our oil supply that actually promotes terrorism. A vote for the plan ends that cause of terror.

On case, we save lives guaranteed. Even if you can't pinpoint an exact number, you know we save lives. Even if they won the DA (which they didn't), they don't tell you how many people would die in a possible terrorist attack, either. Conversely, we know we can improve air quality and save lives. We know we can reduce the thirst for oil and mitigate the harms of oil extraction worldwide.

Finally, you have a moral reason to vote Aff: end the exploitation of indigenous people who are ignored by the capitalist industrial system.

Notes

Introduction: Debate Is Life

1. I remember the first time an opponent used speed (in other words, talking fast) as a tactic to defeat me. I was at a high school tournament in Springfield, Missouri, during my junior year. Robert Copple and I were up against Eric Slusher and Eddie Bull from Rockhurst High School, Missouri. As things would have it, our judge was a college debater named Ken Delaughder. Slusher and Bull talked so fast that I had no idea what was going on. I could have gotten discouraged and decided I wanted no part of this "speed." Instead, I was intrigued by the thought of sharpening my mind so that it could keep pace with and even think faster than this rapid-fire delivery. Eventually, I was able to think and debate intelligently while speaking in excess of four hundred words per minute.

2. Glossary terms are underlined at their first appearance in each chapter.

3. Referred to as flowing in debate.

1. The Playing Field

1. Do not confuse the rule of "no new arguments" in rebuttals with "no new responses." Rebuttal speakers are not relegated to merely reiterating the arguments made in the constructives. Rather, rebuttalists are allowed to make new responses to new arguments made in the constructives and are also allowed to further develop the arguments made in those speeches. The line between what is considered an extrapolation of a previous idea versus a new argument is often blurry. These types of distinctions are left for the debaters to hash out in the rounds. In addition, most debaters and experienced judges can tell when an argument is new or not.

2. Traditionally, a team takes prep time only before its own speeches. For example, the negative team usually takes prep time before the first negative constructive, second negative constructive, and/or second negative rebuttal. Although

unorthodox, the negative team might choose to take prep time before cross-examining the first affirmative constructive or second affirmative constructive.

3. This section of the text specifically examines the foundations of policy analysis or substantive arguments. Policy debate, as an activity, also has arguments related to the rules of the game. For example, the negative team could win the debate round by proving that the affirmative team failed to offer a plan supporting the resolution or debate topic. Procedural arguments such as these will be discussed later in the work. The most common example is that of topicality, which is discussed in chapter 2.

4. For example, the title "China DA" might refer to a disadvantage explaining how, by voting affirmative, the judge would cause a war between China and Taiwan. The title "Topicality—Increase" might refer to a topicality argument indicating the affirmative plan does not fall within the realm of the resolution because it does not increase policy. The title "Fossil Fuels Lead to Global Warming" might refer to a harm cited by the affirmative team indicting the status quo for poor environmental policy.

5. You may notice that a great deal of my writing style and format comes from my debate experiences. Hence, I have an overall goal, which is to teach the reader more about debate (the affirmation of my own resolution, so to speak); I have multiple chapters or "arguments" supporting my case; I provide several tags or subpoints within each of those chapters; and then I provide my analysis of those points.

6. I use the term "expert" loosely because not all printed material is created equal. Some writers are more qualified than others. However, do not fall into the trap of thinking that because a particular author is more qualified than another, his or her work is automatically the most credible. Sometimes lesser-qualified writers (or the debaters themselves) can provide better logic to support their side of the argument.

7. A procedural argument refers to any number of theory arguments a debater might run (or make). The most common procedural argument is topicality. The bottom line: anytime debaters discusses the rules of debate, they are creating a procedural or theory argument.

8. Substantive arguments are those that discuss a visible impact such as environmental harm, violating a person's human rights, or death. Commonly, these arguments take the form of significance, harms, solvency, disadvantages, counterplans, and so on and form the basis of the section "Two Basic Questions of Policy."

9. In 2015, two of my debaters from South Anchorage High School found themselves in the octafinal round of the National Catholic Forensic League Grand National Tournament. At the conclusion of the first affirmative rebuttal, Skyler realized that he misplaced his flow of the counterplan, failing to offer a single response to that argument. Undaunted, he laughed at his mistake. Terek could

have been angry. Instead, he smiled and rolled with the punches. In the second affirmative rebuttal, he explained why Skyler didn't need to answer the counterplan to win the round. Ultimately, they advanced to quarterfinals on a 2-1 decision.

10. A break round simply refers to a preliminary round in which the outcome will determine whether or not you make it into out rounds (or the final brackets). In baseball, a break round would be that win at the end of the season that determines whether or not a team makes it into the playoffs. Out rounds would be the playoffs.

11. I once attended a seminar at which Mark David Jones (business programs facilitator, Professional and Group Programs, Disney Institute) was the guest speaker. He warned against this trap by explaining that "a strength overdone becomes a weakness." Strengths are wonderful, but devoting all your time and energy to them breeds overreliance and stagnation. In fact, my overreliance on rapid-fire delivery during my freshman year in college initially gave me a chance to win rounds but eventually became a crutch that hindered my development. Thanks to excellent mentors and a handful of highly respected college coaches who called me on that empty tactic, I adjusted course. They taught me that speed was a tool to add depth to complex ideas and discussions, not the be-all and end-all of debate.

2. Stock Issues

1. I say here how *people* are hurt, but a harm can refer to any number of things, ranging from environmental damage to the defacing of important landmarks.

2. Sometimes debaters refer to an "inherent barrier" rather than use the term "inherency." This stems from a difference between the judicial and legislative models of debate.

3. However, most judges would still vote affirmative because it offers an improvement. Thus, the negative would have to prove why the minor repair inhibits fair or educational discourse. Alternatively, most contemporary debaters run the same argument as a topicality violation on the word "substantially" in the resolution.

4. In my opinion, negative teams are better off running a pretty good disadvantage than a strong inherency card if for no other reason than disadvantages are offensive weapons (whereas inherency attacks are defensive) and because most judges are not inclined to vote on inherency.

5. Topicality arguments stem from the plan and only the plan. Observations within the affirmative case may have absolutely no relevance to the resolution and the affirmative would still be topical, as long as the action described in the plan falls within the bounds of the resolution. Again, case-side arguments (advantages and harms) are not constrained by the resolution; only plan action must fall within the resolution's parameters.

6. Figure 2.2 identifies the pieces of a topicality shell. There are two schools of thought on how topicality shells should be constructed. This one uses the standards-violation-voters format. Alternatively, many coaches prefer the violation-standards-voters format.

7. If the counterstandards you have chosen are the same ones the negative used in its topicality shell, there is no need to waste your time providing them. Instead, use your speech time to show how your interpretation meets the negative team's standards.

8. Counterplans will be discussed at length in a later chapter. However, traditional counterplan theory holds that a negative counterplan must both be nontopical and solve the affirmative's harms. Therefore, a plan that is effects-topical destroys negative counterplan ground because it is a counterplan to begin with. Alternatively, you could contend that the affirmative plan is actually a warrant against the resolution. In other words, the affirmative team has proven the resolution is not needed since a plan falling outside the realm of the resolution would do a terrific job of solving the harms cited by the affirmative.

9. Spiking a disadvantage occurs when the affirmative team knows its plan will cause a specific disadvantage to occur. Thus, the team adds an action to the plan that solves for that disadvantage or prevents the disadvantage from occurring. If that addition to the plan can occur through topical action, it is legitimate. If the addition falls outside the resolutional boundary, it would not be allowed.

10. A perfect example of this occurred during my freshman year in college. While attending a tournament at the University of Kansas, our squad broke a new disadvantage, meaning that we ran it for the first time that season. The disadvantage argued that if a new policy was enacted, the government would slash money going to some other vital program rather than generate new spending in the budget. Late in the tournament, my partner and I debated a team that had already lost to another Air Force Academy team. Therefore, those team members decided to spike out of our disadvantage by adding a nontopical funding mechanism to the plan, specifying that the money would not be taken from the program identified in our disadvantage. In this way, they diverted money from a program of lesser significance than the one we identified. In response, we ran an extra-topicality violation on the funding mechanism. We impacted the argument by giving the affirmative an option: admit to exceeding the mandate of the resolution and debate us on whether topicality was a voting issue, or sever the funding mechanism and debate us on the merits of the disadvantage. (In the 1NC, we ran both an extra-topicality argument and the Spending Tradeoff Disadvantage.)

11. If you did not have a piece of evidence listing these other factors, you could list them from your own knowledge. Obviously, a piece of evidence with statistical factors would hold more weight in the judge's mind, but even the mention of these other factors casts some doubt upon the affirmative's claims of

solvency and shows the judge that you are thinking on your feet and making an effort to clash with the affirmative's case.

12. The example I used in the section on inherency to demonstrate how the affirmative fails to overcome the barrier (regarding speed limits) is also an example of a circumvention argument.

13. For example, in the mid-1990s, West Point debaters ran a dolphins/tuna case. They claimed the implementation of their plan would lead to ratification of the Global Agreement on Tariffs and Trade (GATT), the Nuclear Non-proliferation Treaty (NNPT), and several other international agreements. However, the cards in their case said the U.S. action on dolphins/tuna was *one* of the necessary steps in the achievement of those larger international treaties because it showed a commitment to cooperation. Their solvency story depended upon GATT and NNPT ratification. The cards in their case did not, however, say the action related to tuna fishing alone would be enough to propel us toward GATT and the NNPT. Thus, while being a necessary step in the right direction, there was no indication the affirmative policy would be enough to elicit the advantages they claimed in solvency.

3. Speaker Duties

1. In this chapter, assume that the affirmative team is made up of two females, the negative team is made up of two males, and the judge is female.

2. Such a critic is a <u>lay judge</u>.

3. Utilize speed (talking very quickly) to your advantage.

4. You should also ensure that the pages of your speech/case are in order before you begin speaking. There is nothing more damaging to the 1AC than messing up your delivery because you did not take the time to make certain you were organized before speaking. However, if you do make this mistake and you are familiar with the case structure before the tournament, you should be able to ad lib until you can get the pages back in proper order.

5. "Hitting" refers to the team you have been paired against for that particular round. For instance, the Chiefs hit or played the Broncos in week four of the season.

6. "Pulling" all of your arguments before the round means to take them out, have them ready to go, put them in front of you, pull them out of your binder or file box, or consolidate them into a new speech document if you are using laptops.

7. The affirmative should also generate pre-flows of the 1AC before attending the tournament or between rounds.

8. The 1NC may need to take up one and a half minutes of prep time, if the first negative speaker has been stumped by the 1AC and isn't quite sure what to do. Anything over two minutes and the negative team is probably hosed, as it will not have enough prep time left to adequately prepare for the 2NC and 2NR.

9. Many younger teams make the mistake of saving "add-on" advantages for the 2AC. The problem with this is twofold. First, you lose the opportunity to provide depth to your story. Second, you run the risk of getting spread out of the round by the negative. In other words, you make it highly likely that the negative will have too many arguments for you to answer effectively while still maintaining your own justification for an affirmative ballot. By enhancing the reasons to vote affirmative, I mean give depth to your arguments, give specificity to the harms stories, show how your case necessarily solves or prevents the scenario in your opponent's disadvantages, and so on.

10. Put a star next to (or boldface or bracket) your best responses. This makes it easier for you to skip to the most important ones if you are in a time crunch. It also helps your first affirmative rebuttalist identify the strongest responses to extend in rebuttals.

11. Power-wording refers to the idea of marking the portions of a text that will be read during the speech. Three rules of power-wording: (1) do not leave out important information or make it incomprehensible, (2) do not alter the meaning of the evidence, and (3) highlight the parts you want read but do not mark out the parts to be skipped.

12. Analysis within a piece of evidence (or card) or during an analytic are often referred to as internals, as in, "The internals of the card explained . . ."

13. Like the 1NC speaker, you should take more than thirty seconds of prep time only if you were completely blindsided by the negative's strategy.

14. My junior year in college I used the filler phrase "Next, you will be seeing that." This was a pointless phrase that wasted my own speech time and distracted the audience. I would have been better off simply saying "Next."

15. If responding to an a priori (procedural) argument like topicality, a reverse voting issue serves the same purpose.

16. This can be an effective tactic in any debate. My freshman year in college, Brent Baldwin and I ran an iron seeding case. In this case, we advocated seeding the ocean with iron in order to boost plankton growth. The advantages were twofold. First, plankton trap CO_2 and help solve global warming. Second, many studies indicate that plankton are the base of the food chain. Every team had a plethora of global warming takeouts and would dump arguments all down the global warming advantage. When it came time for my 1AR, I granted one of the negative team's cards that indicated that the global warming theory was untrue. Then I extended the second advantage, which indicated that plankton were the basis of all life (which most teams failed to address). My job in the 1AR became very easy. First, the second advantage outweighed most disadvantages. Second, it eliminated a major portion of the debate. Thus, I had ample time to more than adequately address the remainder of the negative's arguments.

17. This process is not unique to the 2AC.

18. A number of debaters make the mistake of explaining their opponent's argument. You should do this only when you think your opponent was relatively incoherent. In that event, do your best to ascertain what he or she was trying to argue. State that; then respond. Never deliberately attempt to mislead the judge.

19. When I was competing, I immediately handed my flows to my partner after the 2AC so he could compare my flow to his while the negative was engaging me in cross-examination. He would then annotate his (or my) flow appropriately if there were changes/additions during my speech.

20. In fast rounds, keep your summary simple and direct in about ten to fifteen seconds. In slow rounds, particularly with lay judges, your summary should last thirty seconds or so.

21. Pre-flow refers to flowing arguments before the round starts. I used to pre-flow my major positions (to include the 1AC, 2AC front lines, and 1NC off-case shells) on strips of sticky paper or Post-it strips. This allowed me to reuse my pre-flows throughout the entire tournament and season.

22. Do not simply ignore the arguments you no longer want to discuss. Extend the "no link," "no internal link," and/or "no impact" arguments the affirmative made in the 2AC. Make it clear to the judge you are no longer going for this argument. In addition, you need to kick out of the argument cleanly to ensure that the affirmative has not turned the disadvantage into an affirmative advantage. Extending the types of arguments I just mentioned is the best way of making certain that does not happen.

23. But remain flexible.

24. I cannot tell you how many times my partner used to scare me with this. Aaron Rhodes, my debate partner my sophomore year in college, was not the fastest debater, but he was one of the smartest. Many times I would be listening to his 1AR and start getting concerned. I remember one such round where the time clicked thirty seconds and he still had two disadvantages that he had not even mentioned. He turned to the first disadvantage and casually made two responses in fifteen seconds. Then he turned to the second disadvantage and did the same. I do not need to tell you how excited the other team was. The second negative speaker stood up and talked about how my partner had really messed up and how he undercovered the arguments. During my speech, I stood up and said something to the effect of "Aaron may have made only two responses on each of these arguments, but they were the right two answers." I then proceeded to explain to the judge why those two sets of responses completely took out the disadvantages. The short story is we won.

25. Many coaches recommend the reverse time allocation. That approach ensures that the debaters get the opportunity to tell their story during the rebuttal. After all, many rebuttalists get caught up in the line-by-line and fail to leave enough time for the wrap-up. However, you benefit most if you can be disciplined

at getting through the line-by-line and spend the final forty-five seconds on the wrap-up so that the very last thing the judge hears is an explanation of how the arguments fit together in the big picture and why you win the round.

26. If you go for topicality (or any other procedural argument), your strategy changes slightly in that you need to focus only on the first and last portions of the line-by-line debate. First, you should kick the extraneous negative arguments. This can be done in one breath: "I am going for topicality. All substantive arguments are irrelevant since topicality is an a priori issue. If the affirmative violates the rules of the game, the debate is over . . . regardless of the merits of the plan."

27. See figure 13.1 for a sample flow that will help you visualize the progression of arguments throughout a debate round.

4. Judging Paradigms

1. For instance, if a case attempts to solve global warming and you can show, through a disadvantage, that the plan will cause other environmental destruction, you could contend that the plan fails to solve environmental destruction. Likewise, if the disadvantage shows that the plan leads to a war, you could contend that by addressing one harm, the affirmative actually causes another more significant harm.

2. Keep in mind that not all judges match this mold exactly. Even some modern policy makers expect teams to meet the stock issues out of the 1AC. They may even listen to other procedural arguments over the rules of the game.

3. I once had debaters close out the final round of a regional tournament in Alaska. They were not looking forward to debating each other in the final round, but they also wanted to have a productive debate for the community judges who had donated their time and for the thirty or more people who came to watch and learn from them. So, they agreed to incorporate as many Sarah Palin-isms as possible into their speeches. The trick was that they had to engage in a meaningful debate. They couldn't randomly start spouting quotations. The lines had to actually make sense in context.

4. *The American Heritage Dictionary of the English Language*, 4th ed.

5. While I assert that the negative debaters should not focus on the stock issues burdens of the 1AC, I am assuming the debaters on the affirmative team did their job crafting a compelling affirmative case. If they blatantly ignored or violated one of the stock issues, then the negative ought to develop an argument around a prima facie voter; however, the debaters should approach the argument like a coach walking a novice debater through the material.

6. Some tournaments such as the National Speech & Debate Association's national championship tournament and the National Association of Urban Debate League's urban debate championship will compile judging philosophies for competitors as well.

7. Find the JudgePhilosophies wiki at http://judgephilosophies.wikispaces. com/; see Tabroom.com at https://www.tabroom.com/index/paradigm.mhtml; and go to http://www.planetdebate.com/philosophies for Planet Debate.

5. The Affirmative Case

1. Alternatively, you may modify one that you can find in any number of paid resource guides or free materials (such as those found through the National Debate Coaches' Association with the Open Evidence Project). Some debaters try to simply download and use these cases as is. My recommendation is that you use them as a starting point. Combine resources from multiple research guides and rearrange them to suit your interests, debate circuit, and judging pool. As the season goes on, do your own research to update and improve upon the initial case.

2. This strategy should also foster team discussions on the strengths and weaknesses of the case. Following each tournament, you should sit down and discuss the aspects of the case that various teams had difficulty explaining. In some instances, you will be able to come up with answers as a team. In others, you may need to develop your research further.

3. The negative team could contend that when the affirmative agrees to uphold the resolution, it agrees to uphold *all* aspects of the resolution. This viewpoint has several flaws. First, it minimizes the negative's research burdens because it allows the team to perform negative research on one case and avoid learning about all the other ideas that are out there. Second, it places an unfair burden on the affirmative team, because the debaters would have to perform research supporting and defending all affirmative cases. Some may ask, "Wouldn't that be fair since the negative is supposed to be prepared to argue against any number of affirmative cases?" You might have a point; however, even the affirmative must debate on the negative side eventually. Therefore, it would be nearly impossible for every team to research every case from both the affirmative and negative points of view. Put simply, parameterizing the resolution makes it easier for both teams to focus their research and learning. It also makes each debate round more educational in that it focuses the discussion on a single policy option, which has the added benefit of increasing direct clash in the round.

4. The affirmative team does not have the burden of proof to find every answer to its case or defend every aspect of it. The debaters need only to minimally demonstrate that the case meets its prima facie burdens. In other words, they structure the case logically and support it with enough evidence on key points to reasonably tell a compelling story. If the answer is yes, they met their burden of proof. Asking the affirmative to prove things that pave the way for the negative team's offensive arguments goes beyond this burden. When the negative seeks to run offensive arguments, it has its own burden to prove that case.

5. Fiat also gives the negative team the power to implement a <u>counterplan</u>.

6. This layout mirrors that taught in introductory speech classes using the problem-solution format of a persuasive speech.

7. Remember that <u>topicality</u> stems from the plan text, not from the advantages gained through implementation of the plan. This aspect of the comparative advantage case often confuses many novice debaters. For example, the resolution may require governmental regulation of private industry to decrease environmental degradation. As long as the plan text falls within that realm, the affirmative case can still discuss additional economic or social advantages that may result from the implementation of plan.

8. Negative teams defending against the criteria case should not blindly accept the affirmative criteria. They may be able to prove the criteria do not adequately address the problem and/or that an alternate set of criteria would actually be more useful.

9. Anyone familiar with the Lincoln-Douglas debate format should find this case structure familiar.

10. Critical affirmatives will be discussed in chapter 8.

11. Many newer debaters want the 1AC to answer every question about implementation that pops into their heads. This is incredibly unrealistic. Even my analogy to congressional legislation breaks down. Federal legislation can span hundreds of pages. There is no way an affirmative could detail everything in an eight-minute speech.

12. If your judges tend to vote on the stock issues (as many traditional high school coaches do), you may want to use a need-plan structure. On the national circuit and the college circuit, most judges are predisposed to consider a policy maker's approach, so a comparative advantage case may make the most sense. In high school, I tended to opt for the comparative advantage structure because most critics in Missouri were <u>lay judges</u>. Simply, I found it relatively easy to mold community members into policy makers rather than try to teach them the stock issues paradigm that most coaches in the area subscribed to when evaluating debates.

6. Disadvantages

1. These four types of disadvantages are the primary ways of conceptualizing them. Every disadvantage has a primary focus for the <u>link</u> story: a straightforward X causes Y, a perception-based reaction, or an effect on some movement that is galvanizing support in the <u>status quo</u>. This is the story that will likely be told in the first negative constructive. In reality, the complex stories found in a disadvantage almost always incorporate elements of all three. Thus, by the <u>negative block</u> (and in your research), all DAs probably will be told using the complex classification.

2. Spending money in and of itself is not necessarily bad. I spend money almost every day to buy food at the grocery store. The affirmative team's case has demonstrated on the surface that spending money is good because it solves some harm found in the status quo. The negative must show why spending is bad. More accurately, with a spending disadvantage the negative team must show why the harms of spending this particular amount of money is *on balance* bad. For example, the team may prove that funding the affirmative plan will trade off with another (more beneficial) program or that deficit spending will occur, thereby triggering a depression and any number of negative impacts associated with a depression.

3. This impact may sound far-fetched. On lay judge and local circuits, the disad should probably end in a recession. Then, the team can impact the argument by discussing the various harms on society during a recession.

4. Resolved: That the U.S. federal government should substantially change its foreign policy toward Mexico.

5. In the 1990s, China was developing an international relations strategy called the south-south strategy. It was based in the rhetoric of the global north and global south (similar to the first world and the third world, the developed world and lesser developed countries). The idea was that China, as a nation undergoing rapid transition from the economic south/developing world to the economic north/developed world, had much in common with the global south/developing countries.

6. Ideally, the negative has conducted research in order to read a specific link. Even without that research, the negative should use the affirmative evidence or logic/analytics to make the specific link.

7. This should not be taken to mean the negative must read every single internal link to what can be extremely complex disadvantage stories. On the surface, the negative must tell enough of the story to make it plausible and to allow the judge to understand and picture the argument. The affirmative, not the judge, is tasked with identifying the broken or missing pieces of the link chain. The negative simply needs to be prepared to defend against those affirmative attacks.

8. Many beginning debaters are confused by the meaning of uniqueness or by what it means to be unique to the affirmative. They erroneously come to the conclusion that the affirmative plan must be the only way to trigger the disadvantage and that it is unacceptable if it can apply to any affirmative case or similar type of action. This is incorrect. Uniqueness simply argues that the disad will not occur in the status quo. As such, the plan uniquely triggers the link chain and impacts. Let me illustrate with an example of personal finances. Let us suppose that my budget is planned out so that I can just manage to pay all of my monthly bills and purchase the needed clothing and food to ensure my personal well-being. Any significant increases in spending or obligations would mean that a tradeoff must occur: the electricity bill will not get paid, I will have to skip meals, or similar harm. In the status quo, I have uniqueness because

my budget is balanced. If the affirmative plan is to purchase a Honda Civic, the disad is triggered. It does not matter that purchasing a Saturn Ion or even a home entertainment system would also trigger the disadvantage because, *in the status quo*, I have no plans to purchase a new vehicle or an entertainment system.

9. The story told on the Environmental Movements DA earlier in this chapter would most likely be a linear disadvantage. In other words, the higher profile the issue addressed by the affirmative or the more sweeping the change, the greater the disruption to the movement.

10. Quick affirmatives may try to use this disguise to make the same argument twice in hopes of stumping the negative team or causing it to undercover the argument in the negative block. Smart negatives, however, will simply cross-apply their responses from one answer to the other. In a round, they might say, "On the 2AC #4—no quantification of the link, cross-apply my answers above on no threshold. The affirmative uses the same analysis on both arguments."

11. This does not mean I think nuclear war impacts are without merit. It simply means you should not allow your opponents to overstate the analysis in their evidence. This is known as overtagging, and you should point out that fact to the judge as your first line of impact mitigation.

12. Most judges are loath to intervene in the round. It isn't so much that their uncertainty over the argument leads them to not weigh it heavily in the round. Rather, you should make the argument that the uncertainty with the scenario offered by your opponents, compared with the specificity and certainty of your own, means that an affirmative ballot should be rendered.

13. Obviously, the negative team will also have to spend time answering any internal link takeouts, threshold takeouts, and so on, or the affirmative will still be able to get out of the double turn by breaking the links in the chain that get us from the initial link turn to the impact turn.

7. Counterplans

1. *Opportunity cost* is an economics term referring to something you give up when you purchase something else. When you choose to spend money, you give up money that could be used to buy something else. The thing or activity you had to give up is the opportunity cost.

2. As with the types of disadvantages discussed in the previous chapter, these characterizations are not steadfast, nor do they stand in isolation. First, debaters may come up with new types of counterplans; these are simply the most common. Second, many counterplans serve multiple functions and may incorporate ideas or elements from several of the characterizations identified here. These classifications are articulations of ideas to help you conceptualize how and why you may choose to run a counterplan. They are not meant to serve as rigid classifications.

3. Recall from chapter 6 that uniqueness refers to whether or not the disadvantage is likely to occur in the status quo. If the DA is unique, then we are safe from the impacts of the DA. If it is non-unique, then we believe the disad will be triggered by or has already been triggered by something in the status quo.

4. This counterplan would also act as a link magnifier for a Federalism Disadvantage. This could be useful if the affirmative plan is relatively small, which would bring into question whether or not it is large enough to trigger the link or to linearly decrease federalism enough to matter. Since the counterplan uniquely moves us toward state power and away from national power, we are better off under the negative's counterplan since we would prevent any erosion of federalism.

5. The agent of action is the actor found in a plan text. In its most general form, the agent of action is the U.S. federal government, as identified in most policy debate resolutions. However, the actor can be more narrowly defined as the president, the Department of Energy, the Supreme Court, and so forth.

6. Personally, I dislike this counterplan. I think it is abusive in that it steals the entire affirmative case, eliminating the need for the negative to conduct any real research on the topic. I think it leads to bad debates because we do not really have clash in the round. With this strategy, the negative provides an additional warrant for the resolution and shares almost total advocacy with the affirmative, and debate has difficulty progressing. The list goes on, but suffice it to say, I am not a fan of this strategy.

7. The way this argument is presented by the negative team largely determines whether I think it is a strategic argument. The negative team might argue that it should be rewarded for crafting the superior policy option, but I cannot say that I am a fan of this CP as it has a lot of similarities to the Executive Order Counterplan I addressed earlier: it steals the affirmative case, it provides a warrant for the resolution, and so on. If, however, the team uses the counterplan to show that the affirmative, despite having *unlimited prep time*, chose poorly when writing its case, there can be some interesting clash in the debate.

8. With the Anarchism CP, my debaters usually run the version that is actually bottom-up governance advocated by authors such as Murray Bookchin. This form of governance is quite similar to the notions of direct democracy found in ancient Greece and is quite different from the lawlessness and absence of government pursued by those who call themselves anarchists while supporting extreme forms of individual liberty. In fact, one of my teams from South Anchorage High School, Terek Rutherford and Skyler Hektner, ran the Anarchism CP at the Catholic Forensic League Grand National Tournament in 2014. Although that tournament has a decidedly conservative judging pool, Terek and Skyler picked up all six ballots when running the CP. They even convinced one coach who had never voted for a CP to vote on it. Why? To paraphrase her, "Because they used it to truly test the advocacy of the affirmative."

9. Keep in mind the one rule of debate: *there are no rules*. These stock issues or requirements of the counterplan can be debated in any given round. Nevertheless, they provide a starting point for understanding the nature of the counterplan.

10. As with topicality and plan text, only the counterplan text matters when determining whether it is topical or non-topical. With the counterplan, at least some portion of the text must fall outside the boundary established by the resolution.

11. This standard of competition, in its truest form, could pass for <u>mutual exclusivity</u> because you would not physically have the resources to implement both plans simultaneously.

12. For experienced debaters scratching their heads, I have not addressed net benefits as a standard of competition. That is intentional, as it was never a standard of competition in the traditional view of counterplans. I will address this idea in the next section on the contemporary view of CPs.

13. Admittedly, this resembles the philosophical standard. With that standard, the approaches crafted by the affirmative and negative are based on distinct philosophical perspectives. With the resolutional integrity standard, the affirmative and negative implement solutions working from opposite directions. Thus, these standards do go hand in hand but deal with different aspects of the two teams' strategies: thinking versus implementation.

14. Although debaters holding this view say the only requirement of the counterplan is that it be competitive, they are actually falling back on the traditional stock issue of net benefit.

15. The obvious flaw with this view of unlimited fiat is that by extension the negative could fiat anything, including that all governments in the world will simultaneously engage in total disarmament of their military forces and will live in peace and harmony. Clearly, this makes it impossible for any affirmative to win.

16. By extension, the scope of the action should also be relatively equivalent.

17. Although I suggest writing a three-part argument against the counterplan (interpretation, violation, voters), the affirmative does not have to structure a fiat abuse argument in this way. It can simply make an analytic explaining why the counterplan is flawed.

18. You will need to explain those reasons by the first affirmative <u>rebuttal</u>, if not the second affirmative constructive. If you decide to go for competition in the second affirmative rebuttal to beat the counterplan, you must clearly explain why competition matters and why the plans are not competitive in that final speech.

19. This is different than banning the affirmative to test the effectiveness of the solvency mechanism. For example, if the affirmative used subsidies to promote transportation infrastructure development, a counterplan that banned subsidies to prove that private enterprise and local governments are superior actors would not be artificially competitive. Conversely, a counterplan that subsidizes other

forms of infrastructure development but bans the one found in the plan text would be artificially competitive.

20. Many negative teams respond to perms with voting issues, arguing that the perm is abusive because it represents a shift in advocacy. However, the affirmative shifts advocacy only if it, indeed, advocates the perm. I rarely recommend that the affirmative advocate the perm, but that is a decision for you to make.

21. Some teams simply say, "Perm—do both" and move on to the next response. That degree of brevity can often come back to haunt them later in the round. Conversely, the second affirmative constructive could develop the perm by actually reciting what the permutation of the plan looks like, as I do in the sentence connected with this footnote. Furthermore, you may find <u>cards</u> that could be read indicating that the plans could be done together.

22. Or incorporates the counterplan and part of the plan, or part of the plan and part of the counterplan.

23. Some judges assert that you must have a counterplan in order to win on the negative. That statement is absurd and most likely stems from imprecise language or even strategically lazy thinking. If the disads that a negative runs are tenuous at the link and internal link level or have small impacts, then a well thought out counterplan can be the difference between a win and a loss. However, strong disadvantages and case debate can still win a round quite easily.

24. Ryan Davis, my debate partner for the better part of a semester at the Air Force Academy, was a master at creating in-round counterplans. He listened closely to the affirmative <u>inherency</u>, harms, and solvency evidence. Often, he found cards in the 1AC that indicated that another actor could implement the plan. At times, there were gaps in the analysis that allowed him to cross-apply the analysis to another actor or similar solvency mechanism. Occasionally, he reviewed the cards and found in the parts not <u>power-worded</u> (or not read by the 1AC) that authors mentioned alternative solutions. Thus, he was able to quickly craft counterplans, using the affirmative's own evidence as support, which took me twenty to forty-five seconds to read in the first negative constructive.

8. Critical Argumentation

1. Some affirmative teams use rhetorical links and assumptions-based links to run kritiks in the second affirmative constructive against the negative, as well. If the negative used flawed language or built disadvantages using dangerous assumptions, the affirmative could very easily run kritiks as a new argument against the negative.

2. For those with a background in Lincoln-Douglas debate, this is not that much different from identifying your opponent's value (the link), explaining why that value is bad (the impact), and presenting your own value and justification for it (the alternative).

3. Framework debates also occur when you have a tabula rasa judge. You must explain to the judge how he or she should evaluate the round—as a policy maker, a games player, or a stock issues judge. If the two teams disagree, then you engage in a debate over why one perspective is preferable to the other. That is also a framework debate.

4. One note of caution: the team running the kritik could grant this analysis. Then, it could claim that reshaping the way we approach decision-making (as described in the alternative) yields more benefits than you achieve under your approach.

5. The second affirmative constructive speaker could run kritiks against his or her opponent's language, a counterplan, or even the way the negative constructed its disadvantages.

6. Some debaters refer to this as a vagueness position. They explain that without a specific plan endorsed by the 1AC, we do not truly know what the affirmative supports. As such, affirmative teams can evade just about any attack thrown at them by claiming, "Well, that's not us."

7. For those critical affirmatives taking my advice about meeting your opponents on their ground, let your opponents know right away in cross-examination that that is what you intend to do. If they ask in cross-examination which worldview you will go for in the second affirmative rebuttal, just say it depends on their strategy. If they go for pre-fiat kritiks, so will you. If they want this to be a traditional policy round, you will play along with that game.

9. Performance Debate

1. Pamela J. Cooper, Carolyn Calloway-Thomas, and Cheri J. Simonds, *Intercultural Communication: A Text with Readings* (Boston: Pearson Education, Inc., 2007), 9.

2. Ibid.

3. That irony should not undermine the legitimacy of the argument, however.

4. Do not get so caught up in the performance that you lose sight of what your opponents are actually doing. At the 2014 Urban Debate National Championship I witnessed a team from a traditional circuit go up against an affirmative performance team. The affirmative ran a fairly conventional (lift the) Cuban embargo case complete with significance, harms, inherency, a topical plan, and solvency. The team members merely recited poetry and rapped in between cards. Even when reading cards, they did not sound like the typical policy debate team. The negative became hyperfocused on the performance and ran eight minutes of theory in the first negative constructive about how the affirmative must run a topical plan, embrace the role of fiat in the round, and so forth. The debaters on the affirmative had an easy win because all they had to do was say, "That's exactly what we did."

5. Judith N. Martin and Thomas K. Nakayama, *Intercultural Communication in Contexts*, 3d ed. (Boston: McGraw-Hill, 2004), 410–11.

6. Cooper, Calloway-Thomas, and Simonds, *Intercultural Communication*, 201.

10. The Evolution

1. Generally speaking, debaters, coaches, and judges are grounded in the era in which they were "born" into the activity. Their understanding of what debate is and how we make sense of arguments is heavily influenced by the view of debate they originally learned. Different debate circuits predominantly prescribe to one of the stages described in this chapter. In addition, debaters learn from coaches and coaches learn from their mentors, all of whom had a different initial experience with the activity, coloring their perceptions and ideas about debate and argumentation.

2. Debaters could still have a very detailed and complex debate over what the principle means, how it should be evaluated, and whether it was actually the most important impact in the round. But, by identifying it as a moral imperative early, it allowed the debate to unfold as needed in the middle speeches of the round.

11. Establishing Credibility

1. For most judges trained in policy debate, logos maintains a place of primacy. The format itself was constructed to place a high degree of emphasis on building logical chains of thought, identifying flaws in those chains, and comparing those chains to other argumentative efforts in the round. This belief has been bought into so completely that we tend to hold ourselves to a very high standard of nonintervention as judges.

2. Debaters on local circuits tend to wear suits while debaters on the national circuit are far more casual. Nevertheless, looking professional can make a huge difference to many judges, while looking sloppy sends the message that the debater does not truly care about the activity.

12. Cross-Examination

1. This is also true in Lincoln-Douglas debate. To my knowledge, only the Public Forum Debate and British Parliamentary formats encourage judges to evaluate these exchanges between debaters.

2. When I was in college, it was not uncommon for a judge to put on headphones or take a bathroom break during cross-x.

3. One caveat: some debaters will offer an if-then response, which I usually find fair and compelling. In those instances, they answer the question with something along the lines of "If you argue X, we will respond Y. If you argue B, we will contend C." While this lacks a clear advocacy, it still provides stable footing from which the debate can progress.

4. During a round in college, I keyed in on a piece of evidence that I thought said our opponents' case would promote economic growth in developing countries. Due to a lack of options, I decided to read the De-Development DA in the first negative constructive. In cross-x, my opponent stood up and said, "You just spent over two minutes reading De-Dev. Where is your link? How do we promote growth?" I told him which <u>card</u> in the case indicated the affirmative plan spurred economic growth. He told me the card did not say that. So, I asked if I could see it. After spending a few seconds reading through the card and ensuring that I had the piece of evidence I was expecting, I said, "You're right. I'll drop De-Dev." He stood there in silence for a few seconds and asked, "What do you mean?" I told him we were dropping the argument, and he again asked me what I meant. After repeating this loop a few times, I managed to convince him that the second affirmative constructive did not need to answer the argument and that I was actually <u>kicking</u> the argument in CX. In the end, I think the judge appreciated the fact that I did not try to make a bad situation worse. Even better, I am pretty sure we still won the round on a different argument.

5. Saying you will read something in your next speech commits you to reading evidence that may not be relevant to the debate. If your opponents do not make an argument requiring it, you waste your speech time. However, some lay judges will wonder why you never read the evidence your opponents asked for in CX.

6. Tag-team cross-x refers to those instances when both debaters on either side are engaged in the exchange. Both partners are asking questions and/or both partners are answering questions. Tag-team cross-x is important if something in the round is unclear. In other words, the sitting partner should speak only if he or she believes it will help your opponents understand something that will lead to a higher quality debate round. So, before engaging in tag-team CX, ask yourself whether jumping in will add to a better debate round, not whether or not you believe your partner can handle things.

7. Being dishonest is a guaranteed way to turn a judge against you. Judges want to see that you are being sincere and engaging your opponents directly.

8. This highlights the aggressiveness of your opponent relative to you. It has the added benefit of making it appear that your opponent is yelling at the judge rather than at you.

13. Flowing

1. Figure 13.1 provides a snapshot of a debate flow (see figures 14.1–4 in the next chapter for more detailed flows). In the first negative <u>constructive</u>, the negative presented a <u>disadvantage</u> with four subpoints. All were supported with evidence. In the second affirmative constructive, the affirmative provided eight responses—five analytical and three with evidence. In the negative block, the

disad was developed by providing multiple, in-depth responses to each of those presented in the second affirmative constructive. In the first affirmative rebuttal, the affirmative narrowed the discussion to only those areas where she thought the disad was weakest, most poorly developed, or most vulnerable. Next, the second negative rebuttalist responded to the remaining arguments and tried to present the big picture. Finally, the second affirmative rebuttalist closed the issue by discussing only those areas the affirmative felt were most crucial.

2. The one notable exception was Michael Imeson, one of my collegiate debaters who participated in the worlds style or British Parliamentary debate format, which is a less linear debate format anyway.

3. I am a firm believer that debaters need to flow on paper. While the trend in the debate community is to go paperless, this is one area where I think old technology is the hands-down winner. I have yet to find a debater successfully flow on a laptop. I have heard numerous judges swear by it, but I remain skeptical. Even when given the opportunity to examine "e-flows" of other judges following the rounds, I have been unable to clearly follow the linear trains of thought embedded in each argument. I have also read studies that indicate that people who take notes on paper have greater recall of information than those who type notes on computers.

4. See figures 13.1 and 14.1–4 for visuals of what I mean by flowing each speech in a column.

5. Etiquette dictates that I clean up after myself, of course. I would not want to leave trash in the facility where the debate is held. After the round or during prep time, I take the time to throw away my waste.

14. Sample Debate

1. Two important remarks on reading <u>cards</u> in debate rounds: (1) Typically, debaters provide only the author's last name and year of publication orally. Occasionally, they provide the author's qualifications if the tournament requires it or the month and date if it is relevant for establishing a <u>brink</u>. (2) Only the <u>power-worded</u> portions of the card are read aloud. This is the portion highlighted or underlined or in boldface. It is imperative that the power wording not alter the meaning of the card. In addition, debaters should *never* delete or obscure the words they do not intend to read. They must always be visible for the other debaters and judges to review.

2. Most judges allow an untimed <u>roadmap</u>. In public speaking situations, presenters often provide handouts detailing the agenda or order of topics for the audience. In debate, this is not practical. Thus, many judges expect a quick outline of the topics to be covered so they can get their flows in order before the debater begins his or her speech.

3. Given the truncated first negative constructive, this is not entirely indicative of what a second negative constructive should look like. In a real round, in front of a <u>lay judge</u>, I recommend having two or three <u>off-case</u> positions in the first negative constructive. This sample round has only one, the Saudi Arabia Oil Disadvantage. If there had been two negative positions, the second negative constructive would take one of them and the affirmative case, leaving the Saudi Oil DA for the first negative rebuttal.

Glossary

Presented here is an alphabetical listing of key words and terms used in this book. If applicable, the chapter or chapters in which these terms are treated in depth are shown in parentheses.

alternative. *Also alt.* One of the key elements of a kritik. It provides an alternative way of thinking than the one offered by the opposing team. (8)

a priori. A phrase that designates an argument as the most important in the round. Typically, this arises when one team believes that the other has violated a rule of the game, such as topicality or fiat abuse. Some debaters will identify certain substantive issues, such as those related to morality, as a priori impacts.

brink. One of the key elements of a disadvantage. It demonstrates that we are on the verge of something bad happening. (6)

cards. Quoted evidence used by debaters. The word is a holdover from the days when debaters physically cut quotations and glued them to index cards.

case. Generally refers to the story told by the affirmative team during the first affirmative constructive.

competitive. *Also competition.* Debate is defined by competing alternatives. All advocacies presented by the negative team should be competitive with the affirmative, meaning that they cannot coexist. The debate is between the plan and the status quo, the plan and the counterplan, the affirmative mindset and the negative mindset, and the like. See also *mutually exclusive.* (7)

constructives. One of the first four speeches in the debate. Key features: they are longer than rebuttal speeches, new arguments are allowed, and the arguments are fully developed and explored. (3)

counterplan. *Also CP.* A course of action advocated by the negative team as an alternative to the affirmative plan. It is one of the main offensive arguments used by negative teams. (7)

cross-examination. *Also cross-x, CX.* The period of time following a constructive speech in which the opposing team may ask questions of the speaker. (12)

disadvantage. *Also DA, disad.* An unintended consequence of an action. It demonstrates that something bad will happen if a plan is passed. It is one of the main offensive arguments used by negative teams. (6)

effects topicality. *Also FX, FX-T.* A variation on topicality. The plan starts outside the boundaries established by the resolution but through the effects of solvency appears to be topical. (2)

ethos. The speaker's credibility in the mind of the judge or audience. (11)

extra-topicality. *Also extra-T, xtra-T.* A variation on topicality. A portion of the plan falls outside the boundaries established by the resolution, from which the affirmative gains additional advantages or benefits. (2)

fiat. Grants the affirmative team the power to implement a topical plan. The power of fiat allows participants to pretend as though the affirmative plan would truly go into effect if the judge votes affirmative at the end of the round. (5)

flow. *Also flowing, flows.* The notes of what transpired in a debate round or the act of taking those notes. It usually refers to a very specific method of taking notes that allows participants to track the arguments in a debate as they progress throughout the round. (13)

framework. Refers to how judges should evaluate the round. What types of arguments matter and what types do not matter? What roles ought debaters play? See also *theory.* (4, 8)

front line. The prewritten first line of responses to an opponent's arguments. Debaters often prep front lines to potential arguments that their opponents might run and place them on prewritten blocks.

games player paradigm. A judging paradigm in which debate is viewed as a game with rules that govern how it is played. Debaters may contest and establish the rules of the game. (4)

harms. One of the five stock issues of an affirmative case. It refers to the qualitative damages found in the status quo. It is what the affirmative team hopes to fix with its plan. (2)

hypothesis tester paradigm. *Also hypo-tester.* A judging paradigm in which the resolution is viewed as a hypothesis to be tested by the debaters. (4)

impact. One of the key elements of a disadvantage or kritik. It is the equivalent of a harm. It is often used to explain why an argument matters in the debate. (6, 8)

inherency. *Also inh, inherent barrier.* One of the five stock issues of an affirmative case. It demonstrates that the affirmative plan is not being done in the status quo. (2)

kick (a position or **out of a position).** *Also kicking, punt, punting.* The act of conceding that a major argument is no longer relevant in the round. Affirmative teams might kick an advantage or harms story. Negative teams might kick a topicality argument, disadvantage, counterplan, or kritik. (3)

kritik. *Also K.* An argument that challenges the assumptions, logic, or thought processes present in the round. It is one of the main offensive arguments used by negative teams. (8)

lay judge. A judge who lacks formal training in academic debate. (4)

line-by-line. The point-for-point discussion on an argument. When viewing the flow of a debate round, one can see the various lines of argument that occurred. The line-by-line refers to examining each line of argument in turn.

link. One of the key elements of a disadvantage or kritik. It explains why the argument applies to the affirmative case/team. (6, 8)

mutually exclusive. The notion that two perspectives or policies cannot coexist. Since policies and ideas advocated by debaters are thought of as *competing* policy options, interpretations, or perspectives, the two teams' advocacies ought to be mutually exclusive. See also *competitive.* (7)

negative block. *Also the block.* The point in the debate where the negative team has back-to-back speeches. Most members of the debate community conceptualize the second negative constructive and the first negative rebuttal as a single speech given by two debaters. (3)

net benefit. An additional advantage achieved with a competing advocacy. For example, a counterplan may accrue an additional advantage that the affirmative team's plan does not achieve. (7)

non-unique. An affirmative response to a disadvantage. The disadvantage is going to occur in the status quo. (6)

off case. The portion of debate not contained specifically in the first affirmative constructive. Off-case debate includes topicality arguments, disadvantages, counterplans, and kritiks.

on case. The portion of debate related to the ideas contained in the substantive aspects of the first affirmative constructive. On-case debate includes the affirmative harms, inherency, solvency, and advantages.

paradigm. The lens through which one views debate. Judges hold different views about what debate should look like, what is acceptable and not acceptable, the types of arguments that should be run in debate rounds, and how debates should be evaluated. (4)

perm. *Also permutation.* A test of competition between the affirmative and negative advocacies to determine if the plan and counterplan or the affirmative and the alternative can coexist. The affirmative may offer a perm to show how its advocacy can be combined with the negative's advocacy. (7)

policy maker paradigm. The most common judging paradigm. This judge evaluates the debate through the lens of two competing policy alternatives, using cost-benefit analysis to determine the superior policy option. (4)

power wording. The act of marking a piece of evidence in a way that designates which portions will be or were read by the speaker.

prima facie. A Latin phrase meaning "on its face." Within academic debate it refers to whether, at first glance, a debater has presented a coherent argument or case. (2)

rebuttals. The last four speeches in the debate. Key features: they are shorter than constructive speeches, new arguments are not allowed, and the arguments are summarized and compared. (3)

resolution. *Also rez.* The broad topic to be debated. It is usually set by a governing organization such as the National Speech & Debate Association or the Cross Examination Debate Association.

roadmap. The order in which arguments will be addressed, provided by the speaker to the other participants before his or her speech begins.

shell. The bare-bones version of an argument. It is developed enough to make sense when taken at face value but leaves significant room for development in later speeches.

significance. One of the five stock issues of an affirmative case. It refers to the quantitative or numerical harm in the status quo. (2)

signposting. *Also signpost.* The act of verbally identifying where the speaker is on the flow. Usually done with an alpha or numeric identification in conjunction with a tagline.

solvency. One of the five stock issues of an affirmative case. It refers to the affirmative plan's ability to reduce or eliminate the harms identified in the case. (2)

standards. One of the key elements of a procedural argument, such as topicality. Standards provide a framework for evaluating the acceptability of a procedural argument. (2)

status quo. *Also SQ, squo.* The present system. The way things are now.

stock issues. The five core elements of an affirmative case. (2)

stock issues paradigm. One of the most common judging paradigms. It evaluates the debate round by examining whether the affirmative team effectively upheld the five stock issues. (4)

tabula rasa paradigm. *Also tab.* One of the most common judging paradigms. Judges are a blank slate with no preconceived notions about what debate should look like, the acceptability of arguments, or how debates should be evaluated. (4)

tagline. *Also tag.* A one-sentence summary of a piece of evidence or analytical response.

theory. *Also theory debate.* The portion of the debate in which students discuss how the game should be played, how the judge should evaluate the round, and so on.

topicality. *Also T.* One of the five stock issues of an affirmative case. Affirmative plans must fall within the parameters established by the resolution. (2)

turn. *Also case turn, impact turn, link turn.* The act of taking an argument run by your opponents and turning it against them. (2, 6)

uniqueness. One of the key elements of a disadvantage. It explains that the disadvantage is not going to occur in the status quo but will occur if the affirmative plan is passed. (6)

violation. One of the key elements of a topicality argument. It explains why the affirmative plan falls outside the boundary established by the resolution. (2)

voters. The impacts of any procedural or rule of the game argument. They are the explanation for why an argument will win a debate round. Usually, voters reference the rules of the game, fair competition, or educational benefit. (2)

Index

disadvantages, demonstrating: overview, 69, 86; affirmative responses to, 83–85; case turn compared, 32; elements of, 72–76, 195nn6–8; for judging paradigms, 53–54, 55; during negative constructives, 38–39, 40, 43–44; shell construction for, 76–78; spiking tactic, 30, 188n8; types of, 69–72, 194n1; value of, 187n4. *See also* kick opportunities

disadvantages, in sample debate scripts: in affirmative constructive, 165–66; in affirmative rebuttals, 176, 182; flow from judge, 179; in negative constructives, 160–62; in negative rebuttals, 171–74, 177–78

dolphins/tuna example, solvency arguments, 189n13

double turns, 85, 196n13

dress styles, 140, 142, 201n2 (ch 11)

drunk driving examples, 103, 104, 121

Ecology Kritiks, 109

education model, topicality arguments, 24

effects topicality arguments, 29

efficiency, speaking, 41, 47, 191n24. *See also* preparation and organization; style and delivery

ethos, Aristotle's, 138

"even if" statements, 48–49

evidence: card reading guidelines, 203n1; cross-examination period, 146, 202n5; in first affirmative constructive, 36, 37; in first affirmative rebuttal, 47; for framing arguments, 9–10; role of personal knowledge, 12, 188n11; in second negative constructive, 44; in solvency arguments, 33–34. *See also* sample debate scripts

exclusionary counterplans, 92–93, 197n7

executive order counterplans, 89, 197n6

existential inherency, 19

experts, for evidence, 9–10, 12, 186n6

extra-topicality arguments, 30, 92–93, 132, 188n10

failure to overcome barrier method, attacking inherency, 21–22

fair burdens standard, topicality arguments, 25, 28

fairness model, topicality arguments, 23–24, 26, 28

Federalism examples, counterplans, 88–89, 90, 197n4

Feminism Kritiks, 109

fiat powers: in counterplans, 62, 100–101, 198nn15–17; critical affirmatives, 118–19; debate purposes, 62, 194n5; and kritiks, 112–13, 115, 116, 117, 135; in sample debate scripts, 159

first affirmative constructives (1AC), 36–37, 53–54, 62–68, 154–60

first affirmative rebuttals, 46–48, 78, 174–76

first negative constructives (1NC), 37–40, 45–46, 76–78, 160–64

first negative rebuttals (1NR), 43–46, 47, 171–74

flawed interpretation refutation, topicality arguments, 29

flows: effectiveness strategies, 151–53; partner comparisons, 43, 191n19; purposes, 148, 150–51; from sample debate scripts, 155, 156, 159, 179; structure overview, 149, 202n1

follow-up questions, cross-examination, 145

format for flows, 151–53

framework debates, kritiks, 112–13, 116–17, 200n3

functional mutual exclusivity standard, counterplan competitiveness, 96–97

games player paradigm, 55–56, 192n3

gap inherency, 19

GATT ratification debate, solvency arguments, 189n13

global warming debates: harms demonstrations, 17–18, 192n1; impact arguments, 75–76; kickout tactic, 190n16; solvency arguments, 33

Shawn F. Briscoe is the program director for the St. Louis Urban Debate League in Missouri. A former all-American of the Cross Examination Debate Association, he has coached high school and college speech and debate competitors to local, state, national, and international awards.